# 女性たちのヒロシマ

## 笑顔かがやく未来(あした)へ

創価学会広島女性平和委員会 編

第三文明社

広島平和記念公園の「SGI世界平和の樹」。このクスノキは1995年(平成7年)、世界青年平和文化祭で広島を訪れた55カ国・地域のSGI(創価学会インタナショナル)メンバーが植樹した

The SGI World Peace Tree in Hiroshima Peace Memorial Park. This camphor tree was planted in 1995 by Soka Gakkai International members who gathered in Hiroshima from 55 countries and regions for the World Youth Peace Culture Festival.

アメリカの現職大統領として初めて広島を訪れ「核兵器なき世界を追求する勇気を持たねばならない」と語るオバマ大統領
（2016年5月27日）

President Obama, the first sitting U.S. president to visit Hiroshima, spoke about needing the "courage to pursue a world without nuclear weapons." (May 27, 2016)

オバマ大統領が持参した自作の折り鶴

Paper cranes folded by President Obama

# 女性たちのヒロシマ──笑顔かがやく未来(あした)へ

## はじめに

「被爆者のファッションショーに出られませんか?」との声かけに、今回証言してくださった方から「まあ本当! 嬉しいですよ。私は白いウエディングドレスを着たいわ!」と弾んだ声が返ってきました。

その言葉に私は胸を突かれ、熱いものが込み上げました。

顔に大火傷を負い、結婚も断念。「人のために生きよう」と決意し、今日まで、世界を巡って核廃絶運動に奔走してこられた彼女は現在八十四歳。

"原爆さえなかったら"との思いが幾たび胸に去来したことでしょうか。

　もう一人の証言者は、被爆一年後、原爆で右目を失った母と一緒に住んでくれるという男性と結婚し、赤ちゃんも生まれました。原爆で何もかもなくした家族にとって、新しい生命の誕生は、大きな生きる希望でした。

　ところが、生後十八日目のこと。二時間前まで元気にお乳を飲んでいた赤ちゃんが急に苦しみ始め、あっけなく息を引きとったのです。赤ちゃんの胸からお腹にかけて、自分の腕にあったのと同じ、薄紫色の斑点がビッシリ出ていました。病名は「原爆症」でした。

　本書は、創価学会広島女性平和委員会が、女性ゆえに味わわなければならなかった偏見や差別、後遺症への不安や恐怖の体験を十四人の被爆女性から聞き取ったものです。

ある人は病院のベッドの上で補聴器と格闘しながら、またあるときは広島城跡に残る中国軍管区司令部があった半地下壕の中で、辛い過去と向き合い、涙しながら被爆時の状況を語ってくださいました。

タイトルを決めるにあたり、"もう二度とあの悲惨を繰り返さないで！"という証言者の強く深い思いを、どう表したらいいのか議論を重ねました。絶望の淵から這い上がり、強く生き抜いた彼女たちの願いは、母と子が安心して暮らせる平和な未来の実現なのではないかとの思いにいたり、『女性たちのヒロシマ──笑顔かがやく未来へ』となりました。

明年は私たち創価学会の平和運動の原点となる、戸田城聖第二代会長の「原水爆禁止宣言」から六十年を迎えます。戸田第二代会長は、原水爆は「悪魔の兵器であり、人間の生存を奪う、生命の奥に潜む魔性の働き」

と断じました。そして、その遺志を継いだ池田大作SGI（創価学会インタナショナル）会長によって、今、世界中に平和へのうねりが大きく広がっています。

原爆は、命を生み、守り、育む女性たちから結婚の夢を奪い、出産さえも恐怖に陥れる、まさに悪魔の仕業という以外にありません。核兵器がひとたび使用されれば、いかに非人道的、壊滅的な結果をもたらすか、ヒロシマの女性たちの証言から知っていただきたいのです。

私たちは「他人の不幸の上に、自己の幸福を築くことはしない」との信条を大切にし、平和のバトンを受け継ぎ、母なる地球を核兵器のない笑顔輝く未来にするために、まず「目の前の一人」を大切に、友情と信頼を築いてまいります。

本書に収録された貴重な被爆証言が世界に発信されるよう、日本語と英語を併記しています。この書が世界平和の連帯を結ぶ一助となれば、これ以上の喜びはありません。

二〇一六年十月

広島女性平和委員会　総合委員長　品川　俊子

委員長　渡辺　浩子

# 目次　女性たちのヒロシマ――笑顔かがやく未来(あした)へ

はじめに ……… 3

広島被爆地図‥証言者の被爆地点 ……… 12

新しい生命の誕生のとき
いつも恐怖を抱いた　　河田 和子 ……… 14

ケロイドに苦しみ懸命に生きた体験を
戦争を知らない子らに語り伝える　　森田 節子 ……… 34

原爆で満身創痍に。この苦しみを
誰にも味わわせたくない
　　　　　　　　　　　山中 恵美子 ……… 58

命あることに感謝し
少しでも人の役に立つ生き方を
　　　　　　　　　　　清代 律子 ……… 82

母は娘たちを被爆者にさせないため
原爆手帳の申請を拒否した
　　　　　　　　　　　上土井 多子 ……… 98

重度の貧血に苦しみながら
食堂や市場で働き続けた
　　　　　　　　　　　鈴木 信子 ……… 112

姉の死を無駄にしないために
国内外で平和訴え被爆証言
　　　　　　　　　　　岡田 恵美子 ……… 126

絶望から使命を見いだし
若者とともに核廃絶を世界に訴える　　松原 美代子……144

「広島が全滅です！」
通信室から原爆を第一報　　岡 ヨシエ……160

爆心地から一・五キロの病院で
閃光を感じ轟音を聞いた　　山口 幸子……178

麻酔なしで眼球を切除された
母の絶叫が今も耳に　　竹岡 智佐子……192

戦争の報道に胸を痛め
被爆体験を語ることを決意　　土本 幸枝……212

「生き残ったことに感謝しようね」
母の言葉を胸に平和活動を持続　佐藤 廣枝 ...... 228

広島を訪れる外国人に
英語で被爆体験を伝える　小倉 桂子 ...... 246

むすびにかえて ...... 264

口絵写真提供　広島青年平和委員会（SGI-世界平和の樹）
　　　　　　　読売新聞社（オバマ演説）
　　　　　　　PIXTA（折り鶴）

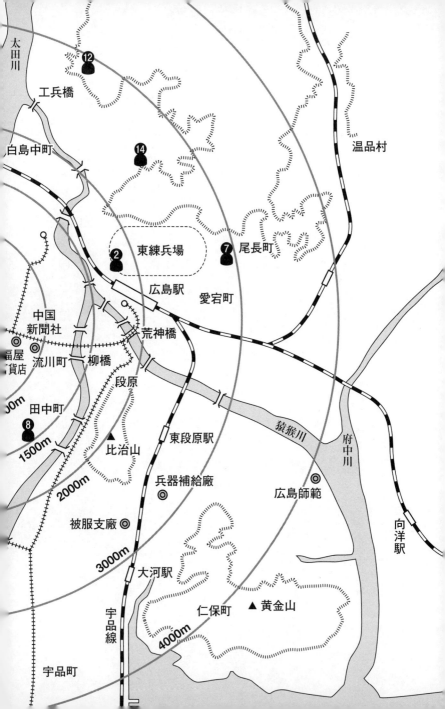

# 新しい生命の誕生のとき いつも恐怖を抱いた

## 河田和子さん

かわだ・かずこ　一九三一年（昭和六年）九月生まれ。広島県立広島第一高等女学校（現・広島皆実高校）二年のとき、爆心地から二・五キロの飛行機工場で被爆。父は自宅で爆死。母と必死で生き抜くが、体調不良が続く。結婚し、命懸けで二人の子どもを出産。被爆のことは話すことを避けていたが、五年前に「被爆証言」を依頼され初めて語った。「命を大切に」という気持ちでボランティア活動を続け、知的障がい者の支援で知られる国際民間ボランティア団体「パイロットインターナショナル日本ディストリクト広島パイロットクラブ」会員となる。第十二代日本代表を務める。広島市南区在住。八十五歳。

# 被爆の影響なのだろうか
# 出産時に血が止まらない

「このままでは母体が危険です！ 出産は諦めてください」
緊迫した声で医師にそう告げられたとき、私は全身から力が抜けるような気がしました。

一九六〇年（昭和三十五年）――。二人目の子どもを妊娠し、四カ月目に入ろうとしていたときのことです。中絶を余儀なくされる現実を突きつけられれば、母として悲しくない訳がありません。けれど、私は正直、ホッとしたのです。

毎日、強烈な吐き気で何も喉を通らず、水さえ受けつけない。布団から起き上がる力もなくなってくる。体は痩せ細り、私はまるで重病人のような状態でした。苦しく辛い日々だったのです。避けられなかったこととは

河田和子

いえ、「かわいそうなことをしてしまった」と、今も心が痛みます。

中絶の一件の一年半ほど前に、私は長女を出産しましたが、かなり重いお産でした。妊娠中は悪阻（つわり）がひどくて食べられないだけでなく、一日中、船酔いしているように気分が悪く、たびたびお腹（なか）が張って、横になっても仰向（あおむ）けになっても、どんな姿勢をとっても、苦しくてたまりませんでした。

そんな状態に必死で耐えていたのですが、出産四カ月ほど前、庭の雑草を抜いているとき突然、出血したのです。広島大学病院に緊急入院し、一カ月ほどで退院しましたが、出産三日前に異常を感じ、再び入院しました。肉体的な苦痛は相当なものでしたが、担当の教授が女専（広島女子専門学校、現・県立広島大学）の恩師だったことで、精神的には安心して出産に臨みました。

そして、大量出血しながらも長女を出産。それでも担当医はすぐに「元

気な赤ちゃんでしたよ!」と知らせてくれました。

当時、「被爆者夫婦には奇形児が生まれる」という風評が飛び交い、巷では原爆による小頭症児が生まれたというニュースが話題になっていました。夫も私も被爆していたので、初めはずいぶん心配しました。

でも、「心配してもしょうがない。授かった子はどんな子であれ、私たちの子ども。大切に育てていこう」と夫婦で話し合い、それ以降は、そういう心配は一切しないと決めていたのです。

ともあれ、元気な赤ちゃんと聞いて、心底ホッとしたことを覚えています。

その一方で、異常なほどの激しい悪阻と、出産時の大量出血を考えると、「今は元気だけど、のちのち、この子に何か起こるのでは?」と漠然とした不安に苛まれていました。出産後に両親が被爆者であるために「経過観

河田和子

察の必要があります」と医師に告げられ、そのまま一カ月間入院。私はもちろん、夫も毎日、会社の帰りに病院に立ち寄り、血液検査などのデータを提供しました。緊迫した状況が続きましたが、信頼していた恩師や担当医が最善を尽くしてくださったので、とても心強かったです。

一カ月後、医師、医療スタッフに見送られ、長女を抱いて晴れて退院することができました。

二人目の子どもの中絶という辛い経験を経て、一九六一年（昭和三十六年）に長男を出産しました。長男を妊娠中のときの悪阻は、以前に比べてひどくはなかったのですが、このときも産後の出血がひどく、またしても「このままでは母体が危険」という状態になりました。

背中とお腹に大きな拍子木（ひょうしぎ）のような木を当てられ、ちょうどサンドイッチのように体を挟（はさ）まれました。板の隅（すみ）には穴が開いていて、紐（ひも）を通して固

定されています。止血補助と先生に言われましたが、止血になるのか、何も分からないまま、ただ、耐えるしかありません。わが子の小さな命とわが命を守りたい一心で、脂汗を浮かべながら、ただ、耐えるしかありません。

血が止まらなくなることと原爆との因果関係は分かりませんが、私は出産のたびに大量出血し、「瀕死の状態」になっていたのです。被爆後は歯茎からの出血、抜歯の際の出血などに恐怖を抱き続けていました。

## あまりの大きな衝撃に人間らしい感情も失う

あの日は、朝から暑い日でした。

雲一つない青空を、低い爆音とともに敵機B29爆撃機が白い飛行機雲を引きながら飛んでくるのが見えました。私は地元の袋町国民学校から第一

河田和子

県女（県立広島第一高等女学校）に進学し、二年生になったばかりの十三歳でした。学徒動員で、爆心地から二・五キロ、己斐（現・西区）の飛行機の工場に通い、ジュラルミンの部品を磨いていたように記憶しています。
「空襲警報」が解除になっているのに、爆撃機が飛んでいるのを不審に思って、みんなが工場の窓に近寄っていきました。その瞬間、オレンジ色の閃光が走ると同時に、大地震が起きたかのように工場が激しく揺れたのです。爆発音は聞こえませんでした。私はとっさにその場に伏せ、何が何だか分からないまま、すぐにみんなと一緒に山に向かって逃げました。
しばらくすると、頬にぱらぱらと何かが当たりました。見ると、黒くて油のようにべとついた雨が降ってきたのです。ガスタンクが爆発したらしい、黒い雨はそのせいなのかと、私は漠然と思っていました。
雨に打たれながら山の中でひたすら助けが来るのを待っていると、友人

たちの家族が次々に迎えに来て、一人また一人と帰っていきます。爆心地から遠く離れた所に住む人たちでした。

爆心地から近い大手町（現・中区）のわが家からは、誰も迎えに来ません。帯状に燃え広がる広島の街を、私はうずくまったまま身を震わせて見つめていました。

やがて、友人のお父さんが迎えに来たので、私も一緒に連れられて山を下り、燃えさかる街を後に、夜通し歩いて地御前村（現・廿日市市）の疎開先に向かいました。地御前には父の実家があり「何かあったら地御前に」とあらかじめ父の兄弟たちで決めてあったのです。

その途中で見た光景は今でも忘れることができません。顔、背中、手足が赤黒く焼け爛れ、皮膚が剝けてダラリと垂れ下がり、まぶたが塞がった、およそ人間とは思えない被爆者の群れ。生きた屍のようにさまよう人、人、人……。私はその行列と一緒になって、地御前に向かっていました。

河田和子

「水を! お水をください!」「助けて! 助けて!」切羽詰まった声、懇願する声が今も耳朶から離れません。

焼け爛れた赤子を背負った母親が、行列の後ろから付いてきました。どう見ても子どもはすでに死んでいます。わが子の死を信じまいとするかのように、その母親はしきりに子どもを振り返りながら歩き続けているのです。やがて力尽きた母親は、道端にうずくまり、ついに列から取り残されていきました。みんな茫然自失の状態だったのでしょう。誰も助ける人はありませんでした。

疎開先に向かって歩いていると、民家から出てきて、ザルに入れたトマトを差し出してくれる人もいましたが、誰もがそれを手に取る気力さえなく、暗がりの中を無表情に、ただ歩き続けたのでした。

一方、私の母はその日、たまたま疎開先の地御前村にいました。地御前

の実家に預けていた荷物の一部を取りに来ていて、警戒警報が出て帰れなくなり、難を逃れたのです。

地御前の疎開先にたどり着いた私は、やっと母と再会したというのに、ホッとしたとも嬉しいとも何とも感じませんでした。あまりに大きな衝撃を受けたとき、人は感情すら失うのでしょうか。自分の中で何かがプツリと切れたかのように、そのときの私は無感覚で何の感情も湧かなくなってしまっていたのです。

## 父の遺骨を前に
## 初めて思い切り泣いた

父はといえば、伯父、伯母とともに自宅にいました。父は兄弟三人で事業を営んでおり、兄弟で財産を共有し合うほど仲が良く信頼し合っていま

河田和子

した。
　あの日も同じ敷地内に住んでいた父の兄と兄嫁が、父と一緒に被害に遭ってしまったのです。爆心地から二キロの範囲は鉄筋の建物が二、三棟焼け残っただけで、周囲はすべて焼け野原になりました。広島駅から宇品港（現・広島港）がまっすぐ見えたほどです。大手町四丁目（現・二丁目）の自宅は爆心地から五百メートル。父たちが生きているはずがありません。
　翌日、母と私は早朝から、親戚の人たちと一緒にまだ燻ぶっている大手町のわが家の跡に行き、瓦礫を掘り返したり、市内を歩き回ったりして、すでに遺体になっているであろう父と伯父、伯母を捜しました。
　付近にはおびただしい数の死体が転がっていて、足の踏み場もないほどでした。男女の見分けもつかない、まるで丸太のような焼死体。鼻を突く異臭が漂うなか、一体一体転がすようにして私は顔を確認していきました。生焼けの焼死体は人怖いとか気持ち悪いとか、そんな感覚もないままに。

間ばかりではありません。戦時下、大本営が移設され軍都であった広島だけに、多くの軍馬も死んでいました。

結局、三人の遺体は発見できませんでした。原爆投下から三日後、ようやく市内の火災も下火になると、兵隊たちの手によって転がっていた死体が集められ、穴を掘り、組み上げられた丸太の上で茶毘に付されました。丸太に火がつけられ、だんだんと大きな炎に……。火の勢いが増すと「プスッ」という異様な音を発して遺体のお腹が割れ、飛び出した炎の色の内臓が、むくむくと盛り上がっていきます。

その光景を、母と私は茫然と眺めていました。

それから約一カ月後に「枕崎台風」と呼ばれる大きな台風が広島を襲いました。川が氾濫して市街地は洗い流され、あれだけ掘り返しても見つからなかったというのに、玄関の敷石付近から遺骨が二体だけ地上に出てき

河田和子

たのです。私たちは、これが父と伯父だと判断して弔いました。伯母は依然、行方不明のままです。

原爆投下からずいぶんと日は経っていましたが、そのときまで私には何の感情も起きてきませんでした。この夜、二つの遺骨を前にして、私は母と抱き合って初めて泣きました。

思い切り流した涙が凍りついた心を解かしたのでしょうか。翌日から私に人間的な感情が蘇ってきたのです。

## 母の愛に支えられ
## 健康を取り戻し教師に

このころから、私の体に変調が出始めました。高熱が続き、最初は歯茎から、次に喉からの出血で、口の中はいつも血泡だらけでした。下血も止

まらず、髪の毛がどんどん抜け始めました。後に原爆症と診断されるのですが、当時は原因が分かりません。歯茎と喉の出血のときは「ジフテリア」、下血のときは「腸チフス」ということで「法定伝染病」にされてしまいました。

隔離する施設も医者も薬もなく、地御前の実家の納戸で横になっているだけの闘病生活でした。納戸は隔離病棟となり、私はそこから出ることは許されません。近所には私が「法定伝染病患者」であることは伏せてあるので、私の吐いた物や汚物類は母が深夜、こっそりと裏の竹林に埋めにいっていました。それがいつの間にか「竹林に女の幽霊がでる」と近所の噂になってしまったのです。

母はどこで聞いてきたのか、「ドクダミ草が病に効果がある」と言って、毎日、野に生えているドクダミ草を摘んできて、生葉を焙烙で炒り、やか

んで煮出して飲ませてくれました。
　臭みの強いドクダミ草の液を水代わりにガブガブ私に飲ませ、お粥まで
ドクダミ草の汁で煮るほど、母のすることは徹底していました。
　すると、不思議なことに三カ月余りで、私は学校に戻ることができるま
でに回復したのです。「絶対に娘を助けてみせる」という母親の一念が通
じたかのようでした。私は母の愛情とドクダミ草のおかげで、奇跡的に回
復することができたと思っています。今でもドクダミ草の白い花を見ると、
「命」を感じるのです。

　大手町のわが家は焼けてしまったので、その後、私と母は御幸橋近くの
伯父のバラック小屋に身を寄せました。
　被爆後、初めて学校に集まった日、多くの友達の訃報を知らされました。
学校に残っていた上級生や先生、土橋（現・中区）の建物疎開に駆り出され

ていた一年生二百八十人は直接被爆で全員死亡したのです。

「○○さんも亡くなった。△△さんも亡くなった」と聞かされると衝撃は大きく、次は私に「その日」が来るのではないか、という不安が重くのしかかって、長い間消えませんでした。

生き残った同級生も皆、同様の思いを抱えているのです。「あの日」のことについては、いまだに話し合ったことはありません。各自がバラバラに逃げたので、その人なりの「あの日の出来事」があったはずなのに、それを話すことが怖い。

「あの日、あなたはどうしたの？」と聞くだけで、いまだに身を震わせて拒否反応を示す人もいるほどです。被爆者だけが持っている「漠然とした不安感」。それはいまだに消化されてはいないのです。突然に身内や友人、日常を失った喪失感（そうしつかん）を抱えているのです。

また、孤児（こじ）になった人たちも多くいました。当時、第一県女といえば広

河田和子

島でも名門の女学校。将来の夢に向かって勉学に励み、誇り高く生きている生徒がたくさんいました。ところが学校に戻ってみると、「〇〇さんは家族全員が亡くなり孤児になった」「△△さんは弟と二人だけになって遠くの親戚に引き取られた」といった話を数え切れないほど聞かされたのです。勉学への道や夢が、突然断たれてしまった彼女たちの無念さを思うと、私の心は激しく痛みました。

その後、私は広島女子専門学校へと進学。当時の私は虚弱体質でガリガリに瘦せていました。母はとても心配し「激しい運動はダメ」と言って、一切運動をさせてくれません。「箱入り娘」の私でした。

物が不足していた時代なのに、母は体に良いといわれる食べ物を一生懸命、用意してくれました。それなのに、食欲がなくて少しだけしか食べられません。卒業と同時に、教師として浜松（静岡県）に赴任してからは、寮生活で生徒と同じ給食を食べ、クラブ活動に汗を流すうちにみるみる丈

夫になっていきました。

　七年後、結婚のために広島に帰りました。彼は県女時代の恩師の息子でした。恩師である姑はとても評判の良い人で、母も『三国一の花婿』と乗り気です。という言葉はあるが『三国一の姑』というのは、なかなかいないよ」と

　夫は爆心地から二キロほどの千田町（現・中区）の学校で被爆。私は二・五キロの己斐の飛行機部品工場で被爆。お互い被爆しているのは知っていましたが、当時はまだ、それほど放射能の影響について理解されていなかったので、その後何が起こるか考えもおよびませんでした。二人の子どもたちは、両親の被爆の影響もみられず、元気に成長しました。私たちが被爆者であることは子どもたちに敢えて話してきませんでしたが、姑が語り部をしていましたので、当時の模様を何度も話していました。それで、

河田和子

何となく知っていると思います。

　被爆を体験したことによって「命を大切にする」というのが、私の大きなテーマになりました。一九二一年（大正十年）、アメリカで国際民間ボランティア団体「パイロットインターナショナル」が設立され、一九五一年（昭和二十六年）に日本で初めて「東京パイロットクラブ」が設立されました。広島では一九九二年（平成四年）に「広島パイロットクラブ」を設立しました。知的障がい者を支援するクラブで、先天性のダウン症や発達障がいのある人たち、後天性の事故や病気によって脳に障がいを負った人などさまざまです。

　もちろん、障がいのある人たちの直接的なかかわりは専門のスタッフがやりますが、私たちは社会へのアピールや講演、イベント活動などでの資金調達をして障がいのある人たちが地域社会で普通に生き生きと暮らせる

ように、さまざまな奉仕活動をしています。

アメリカに本部があるので、コンベンションなどで何度か行きました。「アメリカが落とした原爆でひどい目に遭ったあなたが、なぜアメリカのボランティアに？」と聞かれます。「憎しみを超えてこそ、平和を生み出せる」と答えています。

「平和」を願うのはどこの国民も同じです。人種や国境を超えて、人間として平等に授けられた「命」の尊厳こそ、平和の根源ではないでしょうか。

河田和子

# ケロイドに苦しみ
# 懸命に生きた体験を
# 戦争を知らない子らに語り伝える

## 森田節子 さん

もりた・せつこ　一九三二年（昭和七年）十一月生まれ。十二歳のとき、爆心地から約一・七キロの東練兵場で被爆し、両腕に大火傷を負う。結婚後、広島を離れ大阪などで暮らす。広島に戻った五十六歳から「被爆を語り継ぐ会」や「広島県原爆被害者の会」などで被爆証言活動を始める。二〇一〇年（平成二十二年）からは「広島平和文化センター」の被爆体験証言者としてニューヨーク、パリ、中国など世界各国で証言活動を行っている。広島市東区在住。八十四歳。

# 「臭い! うつる!」といじめられた日々

　銭湯に入ると、刺すような視線が集中しました。露骨に私のそばから離れる人、離れたところから好奇の目でじっと見る人……。その人たちの表情には、驚きと恐怖が溢れていました。
　私の両腕と左太腿には、赤く醜く盛り上がったケロイド状の傷痕があるのです。
　「気にしない」と自分に言い聞かせ、私は淡々と体を洗い続けました。
　けれど、銭湯のご主人に、「お客さんが、うつるんじゃないかと気味悪がっている。商売に影響するので、来るならお客さんのいない閉店間際にしてくれへんか」と言われたときはショックでした。ここは広島ではなく、大阪だというのに。「知り合いのいない大阪なら、被爆したことを知られ

森田節子

ず、穏やかに暮らせるかもしれない」と、私は夫の転勤に、かすかな希望を抱いて大阪にやって来たのです。

仕方なく、銭湯が閉まる時間ギリギリに行くようにしましたが、それもだんだん煩わしくなって、結局、台所の流し台にお湯を張って行水するようになりました。惨めでした。この醜いケロイドに、私は苦しめられ続けました。

終戦後、県立広島第二高等女学校（現・広島皆実高校）から、できたばかりの男女共学の新制国泰寺高校へ入学しました。第二県女は、広島女子専門学校（現・県立広島大学）の付属校なので、そのまま女子専門学校に進学という選択もあったのですが、校舎も同じで顔見知りの先輩や同級生もいるので、少しでもそこから離れたかったからです。顔や頭に大火傷を負い、女性として筆舌に尽くしがたい苦しみを抱えた

同級生を見るのは辛く、私自身、体に大火傷を負いながら「顔に火傷がなくていいね」と言われることも耐えがたかったのです。

当時、比治山に米国のABCC（原爆傷害調査委員会）ができたばかりでした。授業中に日本人の通訳を連れて米兵がジープでやって来ると、私一人が呼び出されます。二人の米兵に挟まれ、ABCCに連れていかれ、形ばかりの血液検査と体力測定の後、裸にされてケロイド痕を何枚も写真に撮られるのです。

十七歳の多感な年ごろだっただけに、泣き出したいほど恥ずかしく悲しかった。病名も治療法も告げられず、何かの実験台にされたという屈辱感しか残りませんでした。以後、何度、検査の呼び出しがあっても、私は行きませんでした。

疎開から戻ってきた大柄な生徒や、戦闘帽を被ってくる男子生徒もいて、「臭い！（ケロイドが）うつる！」と、いじめられたこともあります。気の

37　森田節子

強い私は、睨みつけて言い返したりしましたが、家に帰ると将来を悲観して、睡眠薬を飲んで自殺未遂を起こしたり、死に場所を求めて夜の海へ飛び込んだこともありました。

「このケロイドさえなければ！」と何度恨めしく思ったことか。

## 救助の伝令隊として
## 必死に歩き続けた

広島に原爆が投下されたとき、私は県立広島第二高等女学校（現・広島皆実高校）一年でした。入学当初から上級生は勤労奉仕に出ていて、新学期だというのに校舎はガランとしていました。六月ごろからは、戦況の悪化に伴って授業がなくなり、勤労奉仕だけになっていました。

その日、私は、広島駅の北側にある爆心地から約一・七キロの東練兵場

で、朝八時から勤労奉仕の草取りをしていました。食料増産のため、広い練兵場も見渡す限りのイモ畑になっていたのです。
「あっ、落下傘が!」
突然、同級生の一人が叫びました。
顔を上げようとした瞬間、熱い光が全身を包んだかと思うと、激しい爆風に吹き飛ばされ、私は意識を失いました。気がつくと異様な臭いが立ち込め、雑草に火がついて燃えていました。一人また一人とゆっくり立ち上がる様子は亡霊のようでした。その服はボロボロに焦げ、煙が出ています。隣で一緒に草取りをしていた同級生は、爆風で四、五メートルも飛ばされていました。
空を見上げたため、顔に火傷を負った子は顔全体が腫れ、瞼も垂れ下がって目が見えない様子。斜めから熱線を受けた子は片側だけが赤く剝け、皮膚が垂れ下がったまま歩いています。

脇腹から飛び出した腸を押さえている子、飛び出した目玉を手のひらで支えている子……。倒れている友達を起こしてあげようと手を握ると、彼女の手の甲の皮膚が私の手にくっ付いてきました。

担任の女の先生は顔から体半分に大火傷を負っていましたが、それでも気丈に「早くこっちに来なさい！」と、みんなを山の神社（広島東照宮）に誘導しました。この神社の境内は、草取り作業に入る前にみんなが手荷物を置いた場所でした。何も考えることができずに、必死で山を上り、「熱い」「痛い」と感じだしたのは東照宮に着いてからでした。

火傷を冷やそうと、手荷物の中の水筒を取り出しましたが、自分ではどこが火傷しているのかさえ分かりません。お互いに火傷に水を掛け合って冷やしました。手の皮が剥けて、水筒の蓋を開けられない子が何人もいました。

私の上衣の左袖がちぎれそうになっていました。引っ張ってみると、左

腕の付け根から指先まで長手袋を脱いだように、皮膚がズルリと剝けたのです。
肘から血がダラダラと流れていました。引っ張った方の右手も、グローブのように腫れ上がっています。左太腿からお尻にかけてもモンペが焼け、大火傷を負っていました。

先生が「歩ける人はいますか？」と聞き、三キロ離れた宇品（現・南区）の学校に救助を頼みに行くよう言いました。私たちは四、五人で出かけました。痛みに耐え、互いに励まし合いながら必死に歩きました。
私たちが「救助を頼みに行こう」と東照宮の階段を下りかけると、下の方から、逃げてきた人々の群れが階段を上ってくるところでした。肌が剝けて真っ赤になっていたり、煤けて黒ずんでいたり、とても人間とは思えない姿でした。見ることさえも怖くて、顔をそむけてしまいまし

41　森田節子

た。ものすごい悪臭が漂っています。
三十分ぐらい経ったころ、私は急に吐き気を感じ、大量の汚物を吐きました。
広島駅は潰れていて、「0番線」と呼んでいた宇品線越しに駅の反対側を見ると、街は炎と黒煙で先が見えません。川に架かった木の橋はほとんど落ち、かろうじて残っている猿猴橋は、欄干が壊れ、電車が途中で止まっていました。

私たちは宇品線の線路伝いに南に向かうことにしました。途中、捨てられたマネキン人形のように、数人が防火用水槽から首だけを突き出して死んでいるのが見えました。
大州（現・南区）の鉄橋の手前でエプロン姿の婦人たちが、「どこの学校？頑張って帰りんさいね！」と声をかけてくれ、大きな餅箱におにぎりを入

れて配っていましたが、とても食べられません。それは灰にまみれたおにぎりだったうえ、私は吐き気がひどくて口に入れることができないのです。絶えず、胃液とともに吐瀉物が口の端からダラダラ流れている状態でした。

大州の鉄橋は這って渡りました。そのころになると、火傷が痛くてヨチヨチ歩きしかできません。鉄橋の下の川を大勢の大人や子ども、馬などの死体が流れ、途中の橋桁に引っかかっていました。悪夢か、地獄か、とても現実とは思えませんでしたが、「とにかく、学校に戻って、東照宮に残してきた友達の救助をお願いしなくては！」との信念を持ち、強い使命感と責任感だけに支えられて、私たちは歩き続けました。

途中で人に会うたびに、「学校に知らせてください！ 第二県女の生徒が東照宮で救助を待っています」と声をかけましたが、誰も「それどころ

43　森田節子

ではない」といった感じで通り過ぎていきます。そのころになると、一緒に歩いていた友達も動けなくなったり、他の道を行ったりと、いつしかバラバラになってしまいました。

被服支廠(ひふくししょう)(現・南区、軍服や軍靴などの製造施設)を過ぎて学校の近くまで来ると、水をたたえたレンコン畑が見えました。緑の青々としたハスの葉を見たときは、まるで突然、天国に来たような気持ちになり、みんなで次々と水の中に入りました。熱い体に水の冷たさが気持ち良く、今思うと泥水だったのでしょうが、思い切り水も飲みました。

「救助の伝令隊(でんれいたい)」はもう二、三組あったようですが、途中で橋が落ちていたり、道路が遮断(しゃだん)されたりしていて、学校にたどり着けたのは、比治山の東側を通っていちばん遠回りをした私たちだけでした。

やっとの思いで学校にたどり着くと、第二県女の木造校舎の屋根は潰れ

ていました。イモ畑になった広い運動場には、無数の筵が敷かれ、焼け爛れた女生徒たちが累々と寝かされています。音楽室や作法室を埋め尽くしているのは、大火傷の人、今にも死にそうな人、すでに死体になっている人……。山に残してきた生徒たちより、はるかに重傷の人たちばかりでした。

山に残してきた級友たちは、触ると皮膚がくっ付いてペロリと剝ける状態の火傷でしたが、ここにいる人たちは熱線が体の奥まで入ったためか、触ると肉ごとくっ付いてくるのです。火傷をした女生徒が「オシッコがしたい」と言うので、先生が「これにしていいですよ」と生け花用の水盤を持ってきました。後で見ると、その水盤のふちには彼女のお尻の肉片が張り付いていたのです。学校内は混乱していて、私たちのことを報告できるような状態ではありません。何ともいえない死体の臭いが教室中に充満していました。

## 壮絶な治療を見て
## 母は「いっそ娘を死なせてやって」

　私は急にお母さんに会いたくなり、学校から歩いて十分ほどの自宅に向かいました。夕方の四時近くでした。通りは誰も歩いておらず、静まり返っていました。左足を引きずりながらボロボロになって帰ってきた私は突然、顔中血だらけになった近所のお母さんたちに取り囲まれました。

　爆心地から約三・七キロのわが家一帯は、爆風で家は倒れ、人々の顔や体には吹き飛んだガラスが刺さり、どの人も血だらけだったのです。建物疎開（そかい）の作業に出たわが子を心配して、往来まで様子を見に出ていたお母さんたちがワッと駆け寄り、口々に「せっちゃんが戻ってきたんだから、うちの子も絶対戻ってくるわ」と歓声を上げました。私はその声を聞いたとたん、安堵（あんど）からか、意識が遠のいていったのです。

気がついたときは家の中でした。わが家も二階の屋根が抜け、星が見えていました。私を覗き込んだ母の顔も乾いた血がこびりついて、すごい形相です。近所の人たちの手で体に張り付いた衣類をハサミで切って脱がせてもらい、バケツで薄めた消毒薬で、レンコン畑の泥や火傷跡などを丁寧に洗ってもらいました。

また、近所の人たちが配給の貴重な天ぷら油を持ち寄って、体中に塗ってくれたのです。爆風で壊れ、足の踏み場もない部屋に、私一人が横になれるだけの隙間をつくり、ゴザを敷いて寝かせてくれました。

翌日から四〇度近い熱が一週間続き、医者からは「生きているのが不思議です！」とサジを投げられました。てっきり死んだと思っていた娘が生きて帰ってきたので、父は「兵隊に行った息子たちに代わる家の跡取りとして、どんなことをしても、この娘は死なせない！」と決意したそうです。

47　森田節子

私の上には五歳間隔で四人の兄がおり、全員が軍人だったのです。その後、兄たちは全員、生きて戻ってきました。

日清、日露戦争で衛生兵の知識を身につけた父は、薬も医療器具もないなか、私の火傷の傷口にひたすら天ぷら油を塗り、あせも予防の天花粉を振りかけて、包帯が肌に直接くっ付かないようにガーゼを巻いてくれました。このガーゼを剝がされるときが耐えられないのです。激痛は脳天まで突き抜けました。血膿で固まったガーゼは、ゆっくり剝がしても痛みは同じですから、父は私を押さえつけ、一気に剝がすのです。血が飛び散り、私は泣き叫び気絶しました。

その後、また油を塗り、天花粉を振りかけ、ガーゼを巻く。これの繰り返し。油や天花粉がなくなると、しまいにはキュウリをすりおろして塗ったのです。いつ終わるともしれない壮絶な治療に、母は「私の方が気が狂

いそう。いっそ、娘を死なせてやってください」と神に祈ったそうです。父はもっと辛かったと思います。

この治療法をめぐって、毎日、父と母の口論は絶えなかったのですが、他に有効な治療法はなかったのです。私の汚れ物を洗う母の手は紫色に腫れ上がっていました。私の体からは相当悪いものが出ていたようです。

後日、このガーゼの取り換えの繰り返しで大量の血が出たことが良かったと判明。「出血しなければ、汚れた血膿で体内から腐ってくるところだった」と言われ、被爆後すぐに東照宮の森で吐いたことも良かったようです。

当時、集団疎開から戻ってきた甥や姪たちが「せっちゃんの部屋は臭くて入れない」と顔をしかめるほどでした。体内からのリンパ液が血膿と

なって出るため、その臭いは強烈だったのです。

火傷の跡は、何度も傷口のかさぶたが破れ、やがて薄い皮膚が醜く赤く盛り上がりケロイド状になるのです。二、三カ月経ったころ、やっと赤く薄いケロイドの皮膚ができてきて、出血も止まりました。結局、左太腿、左腕の内側から指先までと右の二の腕の外側から肘までに真っ赤なケロイドが残ったのです。そして、草抜きでうつむいた姿勢でにかけて真っ赤なケロイドが残ったのです。不思議と背中はひどくありませんでしたが、それでも全身の三分の一を火傷したので、これ以上範囲が広がっていたら、助からないところでした。

十月ぐらいになって、やっと学校に戻れましたが、級友の無残な死を聞いて胸が潰れるような思いでした。三年生を終えるころから、顔に火傷跡のケロイドがある生徒は、ほとんど学校に来なくなりました。

「せっちゃんは顔にケロイドがないからいいわね」と仲の良かった友達から言われるたびに、かえって辛く、何とも言いようがありませんでした。
「髪は女の命」といわれます。頭の真ん中が火傷によって禿げたり、髪の毛が抜けて坊主頭になった子は、どんな思いで耐えたのでしょう。彼女たちは、だんだんと口を利くこともなくなりました。

失明して学校に戻ってきた子もいました。火傷の爛れで顔が曲がってしまった子も。彼女が貧血を起こして倒れたときは、曲がった口がどうしても開かなくて、呼吸をさせるのに苦労しました。指がくっ付いて鉛筆を握れなくなった子が、おどけるようにして、指を見せる姿を見るのも辛く、悲しい復学生活でした。

# 夫と励まし合いながら懸命に生き抜いた

　そんなある日、一人の男性が母親と一緒に「嫁にもらいたい」と訪ねてきました。わが家の向かいに、銀行の金庫や門扉を作る工場があり、そこに勤め、宇品線で通勤していた一歳年上の男性に、私は見初められたのです。最初は、私が被爆していることを知った彼のお母さまが「嫁に来ても家業の農作業はできないだろう」と反対したようですが、彼の説得で折れ、訪ねてこられたのです。彼も中学二年のとき被爆していました。
　父は初めは「一人娘なので遠くにはやれない！」と反対していましたが、最後には「嫁にもらってくれるだけでありがたいことだ」と許してくれたのです。私が十九歳、夫が二十歳で結婚しました。二人とも被爆していたので「お互い支え合って生きていこう」と話し合いました。

当時、被爆者の結婚には悪い噂が多く、たとえ、お見合いの話が出ても「被爆している女の人との結婚はダメ！どんな子どもが生まれるか分からない」などと言われるのでした。体にケロイドがあるなしというより、「被爆」そのものが敬遠されるようになってきたのです。

このころから「広島に落とされた新型爆弾は原子爆弾で、放射能の影響がある」と知られてきたからです。健常者との結婚が無理と分かり、納得して被爆者同士で結婚する人たちが増えてきました。こういった結婚に対しても、ずいぶん酷いことを言われました。

「被爆者夫婦の間には奇形児が生まれる」

聞こえてくるのは嫌な話ばかり。

そんなことから、夫に大阪転勤の話があったときは、二つ返事で承諾しました。ところが、夫は被爆の影響のせいか、とても疲れやすいのです。

大阪に出てからも、「ご主人が気分が悪くなって駅で休んでいるので、迎

53 森田節子

えに来てくださゝい」という駅員さんからの電話が何回もありました。診察してもらっても原因が分かりません。

私も風邪（かぜ）をひきやすい体質でしたが、風邪薬を飲んで済ませていました。広島にいなかったため原爆症などの情報に一切触（ふ）れることもなく、あまり不安を感じなかったことは、ある意味で良かったのかもしれません。

その後、夫は大阪で電気製品に付ける商標を作る下請け会社を設立。夫と二人、励まし合いながら頑張りました。私は教員免許をとったり、デザインの勉強をして、デザイナーとしてファッションショーを手伝ったり、充実した日々を過ごしました。大阪、東京を転々として広島に戻ってきたのは五十歳半ばのことです。

そのとき、原爆症で亡くなる方が、続いていらっしゃることを知りました。私のケロイドは薄くなりましたが、逆に原爆症への不安は強くなりま

した。

広島に帰ってきてから、知人の紹介で修学旅行生たちに被爆体験を語るようになりました。もう二十年以上続けております。最初は十分も話すと涙が出て話せなくなったのですが、真剣な目をして聞いてくれる子どもたちに励まされて、続けられています。後日、感想文を送ってくれる生徒さんもいて、その率直な感想文を読んでいると「今まで生かされた甲斐があった」と思います。

二〇一〇年（平成二十二年）に日本被団協（日本原水爆被害者団体協議会）の代表としてNPT（核不拡散条約）再検討会議に参加するためにニューヨークの国連本部へ行きました。こんなことを言うと申し訳ないのですが、会議そのものにはあまり興味はありません。何年経っても核廃絶ができない指導者たちに期待は持てないのです。何よりも、子どもたちと話すことで、次世代の彼らが手を取り合って核をなくしてくれるかもしれないのです。

森田節子

「子どもは平和の発信地」だと思います。イギリスに行ったときも、現地の人にお願いして学校でお話しさせていただきました。

二〇一五年（平成二十七年）八月に肝臓がんを手術しましたので、体調を見ながらの活動になりますが、これからも世界へ、子どもたちへと語り続けていきます。

# 原爆で満身創痍(まんしんそうい)に。この苦しみを誰にも味わわせたくない

## 山中恵美子 さん

やまなか・えみこ 一九三四年(昭和九年)三月生まれ。江波国民学校六年生のとき、眼科に向かう途中、爆心地から約一・三キロの住吉神社で被爆。血小板減少症、原爆白内障、甲状腺がん、脳腫瘍のほか、さまざまな原爆症と闘いながら生き抜いた。結婚し三人の娘の母となる。三人は母親の被爆の影響からか、がんを患うが、いずれも克服した。二〇一一年(平成二十三年)三月、ピースボートによる「ヒバクシャ地球一周証言航海」プロジェクトで外務省非核特使として十三カ国、十四会場の大学・学術機関で被爆体験を語った。呉市吉浦在住。八十二歳。

## 私の被爆の影響か
## 三人の娘もがんを患う

　一九七六年（昭和五十一年）のことです。大学に入学したばかりの長女の左目の下に、突然、泣きぼくろのような黒いシミができました。しばらくすると、鼻の下にも同じようなものが……。義母が「きれいな顔なのに、かわいそう。病院でとってもらおうね」と、地元の整形外科病院に連れていってくれました。

　二ミリほどの小さなホクロに見えましたが、メスを入れると、すでに一センチほどの根を張っていたそうです。皮膚がんでした。

　父は全身がんに侵されて亡くなり、その後、私も血小板減少症、原爆白内障、虚血性心疾患と、次々に原爆症を発症したのです。幸い、三人の娘たちは病弱ながらも、それぞれが学校に通うまでに成長していました。そ

れでも「子どもたちに何も起きなければいいけど……」と、私はいつも不安を抱えていました。

悪い予感が最初に的中したのが、長女のがんだったのです。そして、この後、下の娘たちにも私の被爆の影響と思われることが次々と表れるようになりました。次女は「陽に当たると倒れる」と言うので心配になり、病院で診てもらったところ、再生不良性貧血と診断されたのです。三女も大学二年の十九歳のとき、あまりに腹痛を訴えるので病院で診察を受け、卵巣がんを告げられ、二年後には甲状腺腫瘍も発症しました。

子どもが病を発症するたびに深い苦しみに苛まれ、心の中で「ごめんなさい」と、何度手を合わせたことか。私もたくさんの病気に罹りましたが、自分が病気になるのは仕方のないことでも、子どもの病気は代わってやりたくても叶いません。

母親としてこれほど辛いことはありませんでした。

「娘たちが病を克服して、それぞれの幸せをつかんでほしい」
私の願いは、ただそれだけでした。

私が最初に原爆症と診断されたのは一九六二年(昭和三十七年)。子育て真っただ中のころでした。小さな切り傷でも血が止まらず、指に傷ができると紫色になるまで、傷口の根元を輪ゴムで止めていました。血小板減少症だったのです。一九七〇年(昭和四十五年)には原爆白内障で手術。常に体調はすぐれませんでしたが、夫と協力して一生懸命、子どもたちを育てていました。

虚血性心疾患と診断されたのは、長女が高校生だった一九七四年(昭和四十九年)。疲れやすく、すぐに横になる日々でした。外を歩くと足元がふらつき、川の流れを見たり、車が私の横を通っただけで引き込まれて倒れそうになるほどでした。

山中恵美子

その二年後から、長女をはじめ、次女、三女が相次いで発病したのです。

幸い手術は成功し、娘たちは無事に病を乗り越えることができました。

ところが、ホッとする間もなく、今度は私に甲状腺がんが見つかったのです。二〇〇五年（平成十七年）のことでした。甲状腺は喉仏の下にある、蝶が羽を広げたような形の器官です。右は全摘、左は一部だけ残して取り除き、喉の前の筋肉と気管も切除しました。

そのため、声が出なくなり、四十日間の入院中から筆談で言いたいことを伝えるしかありませんでした。

乗り越えても、乗り越えても、「これでもか」と、次々に襲いかかる被爆の後遺症。心は弱り、今にも折れそうでした。「こんなことで負けてたまるか！」と、自分で自分を奮い立たせ、出ない声を振り絞るように叫んでいると、何と徐々に声が出るようになっていったのです。

## 強烈な光と爆風で一瞬にして意識を失う

　一九四五年（昭和二十年）八月四日、江波国民学校六年だった私は、四年生の弟と二人で倉橋島（現・呉市）の疎開先から、二泊三日の予定で広島市内の江波（現・中区）の実家に帰省していました。

　数日前から、朝起きると瞼が開かないほど目ヤニがひどくなったため、広島県庁の近くにある三宅眼科で治療してもらおうと思っていたのです。八月四日の夕方に実家に帰り、五日、六日と三宅眼科で治療を受け、六日の夕方には疎開先に戻る予定でした。

　六日の朝、自宅からバスで二十分ほどのところにある三宅眼科に行くため、私は「江波バス停」からバスに乗りました。舟入の「一軒茶屋」辺り

山中恵美子

まで来ると警戒警報が発令され、それが空襲警報に変わったため、私は乗っていたバスから降ろされました。

しばらくすると、空襲警報が解除になったので、私は歩き出しました。

ところが、住吉橋を渡り住吉神社まで来たところで、履いていた下駄の鼻緒が切れたのです。近くの建物の陰で鼻緒をすげ替えようとしていると、工場の建物から出てきたおじさんが「暑いから、中で結びんさい」と言って、すげ替え用の麻紐を出してくれました。

麻紐を受け取り、鼻緒をすげ替えようと屈んだ瞬間、太陽が落ちてきたかと思うほどの強烈な光を浴びせられたのです。爆風で体は押さえ込まれ、息もできなくなって、そのまま気を失いました。

爆心地から約一・三キロ地点でした。建物の壁に守られたため、私は奇跡的に大火傷を負わずに済んだのです。

気がつくと、私は大量の瓦礫に埋もれていました。

「助けて！ 助けて！」と大声で叫ぶと、瓦礫の隙間から、焦げてボロボロになったゲートルを巻いた軍靴が見えました。前掛けをかけたその人は「どこじゃ、どこじゃ」と叫びながら、瓦礫をどけて手を差し伸べてくれました。

その手をつかんだとたん、ズルッと相手の手の皮が剝けたのです。相手はすぐに手の向きを変えて、お互いの指と指を引っ掛けるようにして引っ張り出してくれました。

瓦礫に火がついて、燃え始めているところもありました。幸い、私のいた場所の近くに火は出ていませんでしたが、急いでその場を離れました。目の前には、異様な光景が広がっていました。まだ午前中なのに、辺りは薄暗くなり、くしゃくしゃに髪を振り乱した人、引き裂かれたような衣服を身にまとった人、半裸の状態の人、異様な姿をした人たちがウロウロと

逃げ惑っているのです。
「とにかく、家に帰らなくては」と、江波の方向を探しているうちに、もの凄い勢いで火の手が迫ってきました。
炎の勢いは驚くほど早く、今にも飲み込まれそうです。ジリジリと体が焦げていく感覚を振り払うように、私は泣きながら土手を走りました。無我夢中で走り、吉島刑務所の塀まで来て、やっと火の手から逃れることができました。またしても、厚い壁に助けられたのです。
「おーい、江波に帰る者はおらんかぁ」
突然、大きな声が聞こえました。声のする方向を見ると、顔見知りのおじさんが、江波から救助に来た船で叫んでいたのです。知り合いに会えたことにホッとして、私は再び泣きながら船に駆け込みました。
船の中には数人のおじいさんとおばあさんが乗っていました。顔は真っ黒く煤けて、髪の毛は逆立っています。よく見ると意外と若い人のようで

した。おそらく私も、おばあさんに見えたことでしょう。

　江波のわが家に着くと、家は崩れ、誰もいません。辺りを捜していると、近所のおばさんに出会いました。「お母さんは海宝寺の横穴防空壕に避難したかもしれない」と言うので、急いで行ってみましたが誰もおらず、家族を捜していると、やっと、母と四人の弟たちに会うことができたのです。近くの防空壕に避難していたのでした。

　一番下の弟は、生まれて九十日目の乳飲み児です。母は背中から首にかけて火傷を負いながらも、必死で子どもたちを守っていました。

　夜になって、兵隊さんが「防空壕は危ないから山に逃げなさい」と知らせに来ましたが、私たち家族は疲れ果てていて動く気力もありません。防空壕にいた三、四世帯の近所の人たちも同様のようで、その表情には深い絶望感がにじみ出ていました。

山中恵美子

誰も無口でした。
「ここで一緒に死にましょう」
みんなの思いは同じでした。

その夜は、一晩中、街が燃える炎で昼間のような明るさでした。大八車やリヤカーが通る音、被爆者の泣き声や呻き声、子どもが親を、親が子を、死に物狂いになって捜す声が、ひっきりなしに朝まで聞こえていました。

翌七日の朝、兵隊さんがトラックでおむすびを運んで来てくれたので、それを食べ、壊れて流れっぱなしになっている蛇口から水を飲みました。
「お父さんや親戚、親しくしていた人たちはどうしただろう」と思いながらも何もできず、私たちは途方に暮れていました。
ですから、呉から伯父たちが船を雇って、私たちを捜しに来てくれたときは、一筋の光を見る思いでした。「広島に新型爆弾が落ちたと聞いて、

すぐに迎えに来たけど道路が寸断されて江波までたどり着けんかったけえ、船を頼んできたんじゃ」と伯父が言い、私たちはすぐに船に乗り込みました。本川から海へ出るまでは、川に浮いている幾つもの死体にゴツゴツとぶつかって、船はなかなか前に進みません。私は震えるような気持ちで船に揺られていました。

伯父の家に着くと、父もやって来ました。父は兵器補給廠（武器弾薬の集積・補給）に勤めていて、暁部隊（陸軍船舶司令部）に行く途中、電車の中で被爆したのです。「住吉橋で兵隊と一緒に川に浮いている死体の引き揚げ作業を手伝ってきた」と父は言いました。
ところがその後、父は目が見えなくなり、全身がんを発症したのです。古い浴衣布で作った父のオムツが、腸が溶けたような大量の血膿で染まっていたことを今でも覚えています。病院の洗い場では、同じような状態

の患者の家族たちが、血で真っ赤になったオムツを洗い、干していました。「この先どうなっていくのやら……」と、みんな一様にため息をつきながら。

次々に人が死んでいきました。父も十年余り後、五十三歳で亡くなりました。

被爆後、私も体調を崩し、最初はひどい下痢に悩まされました。次に髪の毛が抜け出し、坊主頭になってしまいました。弟たちも同様に頭髪が抜けて坊主頭なので、それほど恥ずかしさも感じなかったのです。人に聞かれても「(髪は)ピカドンに食べられた」と、みんなを笑わせていました。

被爆しても無傷で元気だった人が、翌朝、突然、全身に小豆大の斑点が出て亡くなる。またある人は、耳、鼻、歯茎から出血して、あっという間に亡くなる。そんなことが次々と起きていました。

70

私も下痢、発熱、歯茎からの出血、鼻血など原爆症特有の症状が続きました。被爆時に、近くの工場が吹き飛んだとき、私は無数のガラス片を浴びたのですが、体に刺さった大きなガラス片は江波陸軍病院で抜き取ってもらったものの、戦争が終わった後も、ときどき、背中や腕に赤い腫瘍ができ、膿をもってとても痛痒くなりました。
家族にカミソリで腫瘍を切ってもらうと、チョコレート色のガラス片がポロッと出てくるのです。それは一九七七年（昭和五十二年）ごろまで続いたのです。

## 夢破れた青春と夫との出会い

被爆してからは病弱で、研屋町（現・中区紙屋町辺り）の水野病院で入退

院を繰り返しました。治療のおかげで徐々に健康になり、十八歳で福屋百貨店に勤めるまでになりました。終戦から八年余り。世の中は新しい日本の幕開けを感じさせる息吹に満ちていました。

このころ、高校の先輩の紹介で、二歳年上の広島大学の学生とお付き合いをするようになりました。私は彼が語る「観光立国の夢」に、うっとり聞き入っていました。ところが、私は肺結核を発病し、再入院です。本の好きな彼は、ニーチェや石川達三など、自分が感銘した本を持ってお見舞いに来てくれました。二人は病室でいつまでも語り合いました。

やがて、外交官を目指していた彼から「試験に合格したら外務省勤務になる。東京で一緒に暮らそう」と、プロポーズされたのです。「卒業式には着物を着て列席してほしい」と言われ、参列しました。そこで初めて、福岡の彼のお母さんを紹介されました。その後、何度か福岡のご実家にも伺いました。私の人生の最高の瞬間でした。

あるとき、私は彼のお母さんに呼ばれました。福岡の実家に伺うと、お母さんは改まった様子で、私にお金の包みを差し出しました。そして、「息子には絶対言わないでほしい」と念を押してから、「私としては、どうしても広島で被爆したあなたを、うちの嫁として迎えることはできない」と言われたのです。

あまりにも思いがけないことに激しい衝撃を受け、目の前が真っ暗になりましたが、必死でこらえました。そして、お金を丁重にお断りして、黙って身を引くことを約束しました。

「豊後水道に身を投げたら、遺体は沖まで流され人目につかないだろう……」

広島に帰る船の中では、死ぬことばかりを考えていました。

「いつ飛び込もう」「いつ飛び込もう」と迷っているうちに、広島に着い

てしまったのです。彼には電話で「私は肺結核の体でいつどうなるか分からない。だから、どうしても結婚する気持ちにはなれません」と告げました。彼からは「急な心変わりの理由を知りたい」と何度も問い詰められました。私は「彼にお母さまを恨ませるようなことをしてはいけない」と思い頑として理由は言いませんでした。

その直後、彼のお父さまから「本当にすまない！」と詫びる長いお手紙をいただきました。母にだけ破談の理由を話しましたが、母は「そんなことを言うなら、こっちの方からお断りだわ」と激怒していました。

その後は、せめてもと思い、被爆したのは住吉神社（爆心地から約一・三キロ）ではなく、爆心地から約三キロ離れた江波の自宅ということにしました。

父が三菱造船の元請けを営んでいたので、母は元従業員などに私の見合

いの相手を探してくれるよう頼んだようです。ある日、職場に母から電話があり、父が危篤だと告げられました。

私は驚いて、実家に急ぎました。息せき切って玄関の扉を開け、「ただいまー」と声をかけてから家に入ると、知らない男性がいるのです。何と、母が見合いの相手を呼んでいたのでした。

「私には好きな人がいます！　それに、まだ結核も完治していませんので」と断りましたが、その人は「あなたの気持ちが済むまで、いくらでも待ちます」と言うのです。別れたばかりの彼のことで頭がいっぱいの私は、胸のレントゲン写真まで見せて断り続けました。

その男性は私が帰ってきたときの「ただいまー」の一声を聞いて「この人と結婚しよう！」と決めたと言うのです。結局、その一途な気持ちに惹かれ、二十三歳で結婚。妻となりました。

嫁入りの前に、彼からもらったたくさんの恋文を、おくどさん（＝かま

山中恵美子

ど）で焼きました。新婚旅行から帰ったら、別れた彼が自殺未遂したことを知りました。あまりにも辛い出来事でした。

被爆者が健常者と結婚するのはとても困難です。夫には気に入ってもらったけれど、結婚する前に、夫と義母との間ではこんなやりとりがあったことを後で知りました。夫が義母に私の被爆のことを話すと「女の（体が）弱いのは一生の不作だよ」と言われたそうです。その言葉に対して夫は「体の弱い人が結婚して強くなったり、強かった人が逆に弱くなったりすることはよくある。こればっかりは富くじのようなもんだ」と反論したとのこと。義母は「分かった！　でも、他の人に言うたらいけんよ」と言って、認めてくれたそうです。

こうして私は山中家に嫁ぎ、二年目に長女を妊娠したものの、結核がまだ治っておらず、胸に空洞があったので、医師からは「産んだら母体が持

たない」と言われたのです。夫も「子どもより、あなたに元気でいてほしい。出産は諦めよう」と言ってくれたのですが、せっかく授かった子どもです。どうしても産みたかった。

血小板減少症の兆候があったのか、医師からは「病気のため、帝王切開はできない」と言われました。陣痛が起きても体力がないので、すぐに疲れて眠り込んでしまいます。「眠り産」は産道で胎児が挟まれた状態になり命を落とすことが多いので、とても危険なのです。

結局、三日三晩かかって、二〇〇〇グラムの長女を出産しました。生まれたとき、長女の頭は七福神の布袋さんのように長細かったこと、その姿が愛おしくてたまらなかったことを思い出します。しかし、出産で無理をした代償は大きく、体調を崩し寝込むことが多くなりました。そんな私と赤ん坊を、夫や義母が温かく世話をしてくれました。

その後、私は三人の娘の母となることができたのです。

被爆から七十一年経ちました。それぞれに子どもが生まれ、今私は七人の孫のおばあちゃんです。娘たちも健康を取り戻し、全員結婚しました。

一九九五年(平成七年)八月十五日の「終戦記念日」、広島の被爆者遺族代表として日本武道館で献花させていただいたことは忘れられません。式典が終わってから美智子皇后陛下から優しいお言葉をかけていただいたこととも感激でした。

二〇一一年(平成二十三年)、ピースボートによる「ヒバクシャ地球一周証言航海」プロジェクトで外務省非核特使として十三カ国、十四会場の大学・学術機関で被爆証言をさせていただきました。この年の三月十三日にはスイスのジュネーブにある国連本部でも証言させていただきました。

「もう二度と、悲惨な歴史を繰り返してはならない」

「平和のために役に立つのなら、思い出すのも辛いけれど、私は自分の体

験を語ろう」

そんな精いっぱいの思いを込めて被爆体験を語りました。

ところが、語り終えた直後に私は倒れてしまったのです。以前から、足がもつれてよく転ぶので気になってはいました。帰国して国立呉医療センターで脳腫瘍と診断され、前頭葉の手術を受けました。

幸いにも、手術後は順調に回復していますが、あの原爆で私の体は文字通り、満身創痍になっていたのです。

こんな苦しみは、金輪際、誰にも味わってほしくありません。

十数年前になりますが、孫娘が作文の県大会でグランプリ賞をとったことがありました。内容は「広島の原爆」についてで、娘から私の被爆のことを聞いていたらしく「頑張って生き抜いてくれたおばあちゃんに感謝しています」という内容でした。孫の代までしっかりと被爆体験が受け継がれていることを感じて嬉しかったですね。

山中恵美子

思い出すのも辛い被爆体験を話すのは、本当は嫌なことです。
それでも、「体験を後世に伝える」のが私の役目と思って、今も修学旅行生などに語り続けています。また、「呉原爆被害者友の会」の理事を引き受けて早いもので三十年になりました。

# 命あることに感謝し少しでも人の役に立つ生き方を

## 清代律子 さん

せいだい・りつこ　一九二七年（昭和二年）十一月生まれ。十七歳のとき、爆心地から一・六キロの広島女子高等師範学校（現・広島大学）で被爆。大火傷を負い、実家のある尾道市で治療。洋裁学校に通い、後に結婚した。第二子が生後十七日目に亡くなる。三十一歳のときに離婚し、喫茶店を営みながら子どもを育てた。施設訪問のボランティアを続け、二〇〇四年（平成十六年）に福山市から表彰を受ける。福山市松永町在住。八十九歳。

# 体育教師になる夢が
# 原爆でメチャクチャに

「広島なんかに行くんじゃなかった！」
激しい後悔に、私は長い間苛まれました。
教師になることを夢見て、尾道から広島の女子高等師範学校に進学したのに、たった二カ月で傷だらけになって実家に戻ってきたのですから。

私は、姉と五歳年下の弟の三人姉弟の真ん中で、がんぼ（おてんば娘）と呼ばれるほど活発な少女でした。子どものころからの夢は、体育の教師になることでした。私が尾道高等女学校（現・尾道東高校）を卒業した年、広島で初めて女子教員を養成する女子高等師範学校ができました。私はぜひ進学したいと思いましたが、戦争で学校の先生が足りなくなったためです。寄宿舎生活になるため学費のほかにお金がかかり、経済的にも容易なこと

清代律子

ではありません。

ところが、父は私の望みを叶えるためにお金を出してくれたのです。父は藁を原料とした縄や筵の商いを手広く営んでいて、わが家が経済的に恵まれていたこともありましたし、教師をしている義兄（姉の夫）が、私が教職に就くことを勧めてくれたことも、私の進学を後押ししてくれました。

尾道から広島女子高等師範に行ったのは私一人でした。

それまで私は広島に出たことがなかったので、入学式の前に父が学校まで付いてきてくれ、入寮の手続きなどもすべてやってくれました。親元を離れ、寮生活が始まりました。新設校でしたが、校舎の建設が間に合わず、間借りしての開校だったため、入学は六月からでした。

教室で「女子師範生の心構え」を聞いていることが多かったと記憶しています。夢に向かい、青春の第一歩を踏み出そうとした、まさにそのときでした。一発の原爆によって、私の夢は無残にも打ち砕かれたのです。

# 熱線と爆風で倒れた校舎の下敷きになり意識を失う

 あの日は、朝早くから蟬が鳴き出し、暑い一日の始まりを告げていました。登校の準備をしていると、「警戒警報」発令の鈍いサイレン音が鳴り響きました。私はすぐに防空頭巾を被り、薬、日用品、懐中電灯などを入れた「非常袋」を肩に掛けて、運動場に掘られた防空壕へ走りました。防空壕の中では、級友たちも防空頭巾の上から手で頭を押さえ、膝を曲げて丸くなり、避難姿勢をとっていました。誰もが無言です。
 やがて、警戒警報解除になると、やっとみんなに笑顔が戻り、ぞろぞろと校舎に帰りました。私も二階の教室で先生を待ちました。

清代律子

一時間目が始まる少し前。八時十五分。

カメラのフラッシュのような強い光が、大きく広く「ピカッ」と光った瞬間、何が起きたのかと思う間もなく、私は意識を失いました。学校は爆心地から一・六キロ地点でした。気がつくと、強い熱線と爆風で倒れた校舎の下敷きになっていました。周囲は薄暗くてよく見えず、背中の上には太い木材がずっしりと覆い被さっています。

隣の席の同級生の名前を呼んでみましたが、返事はありません。体中が痛くて、火傷の火膨れのためか、右半身が熱くぶよぶよしています。

「何とかここを出なければ！」と、必死に体を動かしているとスポッと体が抜け、上の方にぼんやりとした明るさを感じました。

校舎の屋根から抜け出て見た街は、高い建物がなくなり、辺り一面が広場のよう。見慣れた広島の街は跡形もなくなっていたのです。

先生の一人が瓦礫の中で仁王立ちになって、凄い形相で「早く逃げろ！

「東へ逃げろ！」と叫び、崩れた校舎からはすでに煙が上がっていました。校舎の瓦礫の下から、ヨロヨロと這い出してきた四、五人の級友たちと一緒に、私は東へ向かって逃げました。彼女たちは火傷を負い、大怪我をしていました。顔や手足にガラスが突き刺さり、だらだらと血が流れているのに、応急手当をする余裕がありません。布で傷を押さえながら、必死で校内を出たのです。私の席の横の窓が開いていたので、私は砕けたガラス片を浴びずに済んだのでした。

往来は、さらに酷いありさまでした。顔中血だらけで息も絶え絶えの人。半裸で狂ったように子どもの名前を叫んでいる母親。全身大火傷で泣きながら母親を求めてさまよう子ども。体の皮膚がべろりと剝けて「熱い、熱い！」と呻く人。丸太のような死体が、あちこちに転がっていました。髪の毛は逆立ち、顔と体は煤けて男女の見分けもつかないのです。

清代律子

途中、軍隊の救護所があったので入りましたが、中はひどい負傷者ばかり。そして、どこから運ばれてくるのか、大勢の死体がトラックに積み込まれていました。

ジリジリ照りつける夏の暑さのなか、思わず吐きそうになるほどの嫌な臭いや、右上半身の肉が抉り取られたような激しい痛みにじっと耐え、順番を待ちました。やっと、私の番になり、両腕、首、顔に油をべっとり塗られ、右手を三角巾で吊ってもらいました。

救護所の出口で、乾パンと金平糖を配っていました。甘い金平糖を口にすると力が出てきたので、みんなと海田市駅に向かいました。校舎の下敷きになったせいで体のあちこちが痛み出し、特に息をするたびに肋骨が痛みました。首も腫れて顔を上げるのも辛いのです。

それでも、友達と離れてしまうのが怖くて、必死で付いていきました。みんな不安で、誰一人として口を開く人はいません。無言で、暑さの中を

歩き続けました。学校を出たのは朝でしたが、救護所で手当てを受けたあと、海田市駅に着いたときには、夕暮れになっていました。

駅はいつ来るともしれない汽車を待つ人で大混雑でした。みんな、「広島でどんな空襲があったんだろう？」と話し合っています。逃げてくる人たちも、少しずつ増えてきました。陽がとっぷり暮れたころ、ようやく汽車が入ってきました。敵機に見つからないよう、灯りをつけていません。真っ暗な列車はたちまち満員に。私たちも必死で乗り込み、やっと広島を離れることができたのです。しかし、列車は「本郷止まり」でした。本郷駅前の旅館に行き「広島に落ちた爆弾で怪我をした」と話し、私たちは泊めてもらうことができました。

尾道の実家に無事を知らせるため、宿の電話を借りると、電話口には母が出ました。「原子爆弾」ということはまだ知らなかったので、母には

清代律子

「爆弾でちょっと怪我をしたけど、歩けるので、明日朝一番の汽車で帰ります」と話しました。

一緒に逃げてきた友達は「やっと手足を伸ばせる」と横になりましたが、私は体が痛くて横になることもできず、椅子にもたれたまま夜明けを待ちました。

翌朝、心急くまま一番列車に乗り込みました。本郷駅からは、仕事や学校に行く人で満員に。日常生活の風景がそこにあり、広島の惨状が嘘のようでした。髪はボサボサで顔に火傷を負い、腕を三角巾で包んだ私は、恥ずかしくて車内の隅で小さくなっていました。

やっと尾道駅に着きました。駅に迎えに来ていた父の姿を見るなり、私はころげるように駆け出すと、「お父さ〜ん」と抱きついて大声で泣いたのです。

「おお、よう帰ってこれたのう!」と言った父は、火傷跡に油をべったり塗った私の姿を見て、茫然としていました。
「母さんも待っとる。早う帰ろう!」と言うのが精いっぱいのようでした。
こうして、八月七日朝九時過ぎ、やっとの思いで疎開先の三成(現・尾道市)の家に到着したのです。家に着いて真っ先に飲んだ冷たい水の美味しさは、今も忘れられません。

母も弟も私の火傷を見て、「こりゃ、大変だ。痛かろう」と大騒ぎです。普通の火傷と違って原爆の熱線による火傷は傷口が深く抉られて、中から嫌な臭いの膿が出てくるのです。その臭いにハエが飛んでくるので、私はいつも母が吊ってくれた六畳蚊帳の中に入っていました。

翌日、尾道の病院で診てもらいましたが、医者も原爆による火傷の治療法は分からず、通常の火傷の薬をもらっただけ。近所の人から「キュウリ

は熱を取る効果がある」と聞いた母は、擦り下ろしたキュウリを毎日、傷口に貼ってくれました。被爆したとき、上は体操着で下はモンペという服装でした。不思議なことに服は全く焼けていなかったのです。火傷は体操着から出ていた両腕、そして顔、首、肩の右側に集中しており、肩と腕にはケロイドが残りました。

## 生後わずか十七日で逝(い)ってしまった次女

私が広島女子高等師範学校に進学したのは、義兄の勧めでもあったので、父はあからさまに言いませんでしたが、「広島に出すんじゃなかった」という悔(く)やむ思いはあったと思います。私も「広島には二度と行きたくない!」と、その後は尾道に留(と)まりました。

当初、父は私が結婚することは無理だと思っていたようです。私が一人で外出ができるようになると、「手に職を付けておいた方がよい」と、尾道の洋裁学校に通わせてくれました。

一年半ほど経（た）ち、顔のケロイドが目立たなくなると、「できることなら結婚させてやりたい」という親心だったのでしょう。私はまだ十九歳でしたが、「できることなら結婚させてやりたい」という親心だったのでしょう。

二十歳の誕生日の一カ月前に、私は見合い結婚をしました。相手は義兄の弟で、私より六歳年上でした。かなりの弱視だったので兵隊にとられず、軍属として南方方面に行き、尾道に帰っていたそうです。
「被爆した者は早死（はやじ）にする」「被爆者には奇形児が生まれる」などという噂（うわさ）が流れていたので、父は「嫁にもらってくれるのなら誰でもよい」との焦りもあったのではないかと思います。

戦後の物のない時期でしたから、近所を気遣（きづか）って派手（はで）な結婚式はしませ

93　清代律子

んでした。それでも、夫は紋付き袴、私は着物を着て写真館で「結婚写真」を撮りました。

結婚して三カ月余りで、私は成人式を迎えました。式典は尾道の土堂小学校の講堂で行われました。顔の火傷は目立たなくなっていましたが、首にはまだ赤い痕が残っていたので、襟の高いブラウスを着て出席。女学校時代の同級生と久しぶりで再会したのですが、「広島での被爆」のことを知られるのが怖くて、早々に帰ってきました。その後も長い間、夏でも長袖の洋服で通しました。

父は、私たち夫婦の新居も用意してくれました。私は広島でのことは「わずか二カ月間の悪夢だったのだ」と心に決め、家事に専念。何事もなく暮らしましたが、二年後に妊娠したときはさすがに不安になりました。誰にも相談することができませんでしたが、「奇形児が生まれたら、そ

のときはそのときだ！」と弱い自分を叱咤し、腹を決めたのです。出産は大勢の人がいる病院ではなく、家に産婆（現在の助産師）さんに来てもらったので、気は楽でした。無事、元気な女の子が生まれ、「被爆したけど、私の場合は影響なかった」と、ひと安心でした。

その後、再び妊娠して二人目の女の子が生まれました。やはり、産婆さんに来てもらって自宅で出産。ところが、産婆さんが帰ってから赤ちゃんの容体が急変したのです。ヒクヒクと体を痙攣させて、生後十七日目に亡くなってしまいました。驚きと悲しみで言葉も出ませんでした。「ひょっとして被爆のせい？」と私は急に不安になったのです。
夫から私の被爆のことで何か言われたことはありません。私が被爆したことは知っていたけれど、自分も弱視だったので問題にしなかったのでしょうか。

結婚当初、父は私を慰めるように、よく夫のことを「ひょっとすると成功するかもしれん男だ」と言っていましたが、「逆に、まったくダメになるか、どっちかだな」と声をひそめることもありました。

父が心配した通り、夫は何をやってもうまくいかず、そのたびに父に援助を頼み、そして酒に溺れたのでした。苦労の連続の結婚生活でしたが、三十一歳のとき、八歳の長女を連れて協議離婚しました。

数年後、濃い茶色の尿が出るようになり、それが何日も続くので病院で診てもらうと「甲状腺が悪いのではないか」と告げられました。ともかく、あの原爆で私の人生がメチャクチャになったことだけは確かです。

その後、父が資金を出してくれたので、尾道駅前に喫茶店「ロマン」を開店。二十年間続けました。父には苦労のかけ通しでした。今でも申し訳ないという気持ちと感謝の思いしかありません。

五十七歳のとき、ボランティア活動の誘いがありました。あのとき死んでいたら何をすることもできません。「元気で生きているからには、少しでも誰かのお役に立ちたい」と思い、引き受けました。以来、ボランティアグループのメンバーとして月に二回、特養ホームへ訪問させていただき、食事介護、清掃、シーツの取り替えなどをやりました。

活動が二十年を超えた二〇〇四年（平成十六年）には、福山市から表彰されました。その後もしばらく続けていましたが、八十歳を過ぎたころから体力的にも厳しくなってきたため、今は退（ひ）いています。

多くの人を苦しめる戦争は二度と起こしてはいけない、核のない平和な社会を築いてほしいという深い願いを込めて、現在、「福山市原爆被害者友の会」の語り部（かたべ）として、被爆体験を語らせてもらっています。今後はさらに若い人たちに継承していきたいと思っています。

# 母は娘たちを被爆者にさせないため原爆手帳の申請を拒否した

## 上土井多子 さん

かみどい・かずこ　一九三九年（昭和十四年）六月生まれ。原爆投下時は六歳だった。爆心地から十五キロ以上離れた可部上市（現・安佐北区）に疎開していたが、母親と一緒に、被爆した人たちを介抱した。母親も自身も肝臓障害、がんなどを患う。父は復員後、兄弟を捜すために爆心地付近を歩き回り、後に死亡。広島市佐伯区在住。七十七歳。

## 放射能の影響か
## 母娘とも体調不良に

「絶対に三人の娘たちを被爆者と知られてはならない!」と、母は「原爆手帳(被爆者健康手帳)」の申請を、断固拒否しました。「医療費が無料になる」など、さかんに「原爆手帳の申し込み」の宣伝が行われていましたが、母は一切耳を貸しませんでした。「被爆したことを知られて婚家から実家に帰された」とか「被爆が原因で婚約が破談になった」という話があちこちで聞かれるようになったからです。

いつの間にか、私たち姉妹は「被爆は自分たちとは無関係」と思うようになっていました。私はその後に起こったさまざまな病状も被爆とは無関係だと思い、妊娠しても子どもが生まれても放射能の影響に不安を感じることもなく、七十年余りを過ごしてきました。それでも、あらためて振り

上土井多子

返ってみると、あれは放射能感染の影響だったのかな、と思うことがずいぶんありました。

最初の出来事は原爆投下から四年後、私が小学校四年生のときです。肝臓障害で、シーツがまっ黄色になる日が数日続いたことがありました。皮膚や白目だけでなく、汗までも黄色になるほど、ひどい黄疸が出たのです。生理が始まってからは、ひどい生理痛で学校や会社を休まざるを得ませんでした。

社会人になってからは、突然四〇度近い高熱が出て立っていられず、横になると数時間で嘘のように元に戻るということがしょっちゅうあり、「きっと私は異常体質だ」と思っていました。七十歳を過ぎてからは子宮肥大と卵巣肥大で、子宮と卵巣を摘出。母が亡くなった年と同じ七十二歳のときは膀胱がんを患い、手術しました。

被爆当時、生後八カ月だったすぐ下の妹は、数日後に風邪をひいたような状態になったかと思うと、みるみる悪化して仮死状態で病院に運ばれました。両足が三倍の大きさに腫れ上がり、切開して血膿を搾り出すと「バケツ一杯にもなった」と母が言っていました。一カ月以上入院し、どうにか命を取り留めた妹は、退院してからも病弱でした。学校にあがると、母は担任の先生に「この子は生きていてくれるだけで十分なんです。だからこの子に宿題は出さんといて」と頼んだほどです。

妹の症状も被爆者の介抱を続ける母に背負われたまま、数日を過ごしたことと無関係ではないと思うのです。

母は胃がん、胆管がんを発症し、二年余りの入院生活の後、七十二歳で亡くなりました。胆管がんの治療費は高額で、「原爆手帳」さえあれば治療の費用が無料になり、経済的に助かったと思うのですが、母は絶対に申

請手続きをしませんでした。

胆管が詰まると、胆汁を煮詰めて丸薬のようにして包み、飲みやすくして母に飲ませました。胆汁が消化器官に流れなくなると命にかかわることもあるため、体内に戻す必要があったのです。胆汁を煮詰めるとき、とても臭くて閉口しました。

## 爆心地から十五キロ離れた可部上市に疎開

父は桐の下駄や箪笥の加工材を手広く商っており、一時は職人さんが六十人以上もいたそうです。工場は本川町（現・中区）にあり、千田町（現・中区）に自宅があったのですが、当時、母と私と妹は可部上市（現・安佐北区）に疎開していました。

八月五日に、荷物を取りに千田町の自宅に行く予定でしたが、汽車は鈴なりの満員状態で「とても生後八カ月の妹を連れていくことはできない」と諦めたのです。もし乗っていたら、私たちは確実に命を落としていました。

母は面倒見のいい人で、妹が生まれる寸前まで町会の班長を引き受け、大きなお腹を抱えたまま「警戒警報発令！」などと町内を触れ回っていました。焼夷弾で家屋が燃えたときの消火道具として、水を含ませて使うモップのような「火叩き」がありましたが、母は町会分の「火叩き」を保管し手入れもしていました。

疎開先の可部上市は、爆心地から十五キロ以上も離れています。当時、私はよく鏡を持ち出して遊んでいたようですが、あの日、一瞬「ピカッ」と光ったので、母はてっきり私が鏡で遊んでいると思い「いけんよ！鏡

103 　上土井多子

で遊んじゃ」と注意したと言います。可部上市では、ガラス戸が割れたりという原爆投下の影響はほとんどなく、むしろ誰も気がついていなかったというのが実情でした。

本来、私たち家族は被爆の影響などなかったはずなのです。疎開したのは三月二十九日。最後の疎開引っ越し馬車に荷物を積みました。ところが、面倒見がよかった母を頼って、疎開後も千田町にいたころの近所の顔見知りの人たちが「住み心地はどう？」などと絶えず訪ねてきていました。そんな関係が続いていて、被爆した千田町の人たちが母に助けを求めて、続々とやって来たのです。その人たちを介抱するうちに、母と私たち二人姉妹（三番目の妹は戦後に誕生）は、二次被爆したのだと思われます。私は当時六歳でした。

## 被爆者を介抱する母を手伝い、走り回った

原爆投下後、最初に来たのは洋裁学校の先生の子どもで、二人兄弟の弟さんの方でした。その日の午後だったか、可部に向かう馬車に乗ってきて、「ただいま!」と疎開先のわが家に元気よく入ってきたのです。

彼は裏の川に魚とりに行くほど元気だったのですが、夜になって高熱が出ました。「しんどいよ! 痛いよ!」と唸り出し、翌日も一日中唸り続けて、次の日の朝、冷たくなっていたのです。顔といわず腕といわず、紫斑が出ていました。あれほど健康そうで、顔にも体にも火傷一つなかった彼が、三日も経たぬうちに亡くなったことは、大変ショックな出来事でした。

そのころはすでに、千田町で被爆して逃げてきた人たち十数人が、私た

上土井多子

ちの疎開先の家に来ていました。女性と子どもばかりで男の人はいませんでした。母は妹を背負ったまま、濡れタオルを配ったり、焼けた衣類を取り換えたりと、被爆者の介抱に追われました。私も母を手伝い、被爆者の人たちの間を走り回っていたのです。

紫斑が出て亡くなった弟さんの死と前後して、彼のお兄ちゃんもやってきました。彼は全身大火傷で、目と鼻と口の部分を少し空けただけで、顔を包帯でグルグルに巻いた姿で現れました。ギョッとしましたが、そのあと、彼は生き延びたのです。

「包帯のお兄ちゃん」に続いて、社会人になっていた彼のお姉ちゃんも、辿り着きました。二人の弟たちを捜して、あちこちの救護所を回っていた彼女は、母に「おばちゃん、ここにおったらいけんよ。被爆した人の空気を吸うたらいけんと言うてたよ」とここにおったらいけんよと知らせてくれました。救護所を回るな

かで聞いてきたらしいのです。

母は、すぐに近所の空き家を三軒借りて、家族連れをそこに移し、私と妹は隣の大きな農家に借りた一間に寝泊まりしました。

知らせてくれたお姉ちゃんも紫斑が出て、翌日亡くなりました。もう一人、中年の女性も亡くなり、子どもたちだけが残されました。

後日、包帯を巻いていた「お兄ちゃん」に会いました。私は気づかなかったのですが、向こうから母に声をかけてきたのです。すでに包帯は取れていましたが、両耳は溶けてなくなり顔の両側に穴が二つ開いているだけでした。鼻も片方が穴だけになっており、顔全体はケロイドで赤く引きつっていました。私はそのケロイドの顔を見ているだけで気持ち悪くなりました。

彼がなぜ助かったのかというと、顔の傷口に湧いたうじ虫が放射能の悪

いものを血膿ごと食べてくれたのが良かったそうです。

可部上市の奥に大林病院とお寺があり、被爆者を受け入れていました。そこに向かうオート三輪に乗った人が、八百屋の前に止まって「何でもいいからボロ布を分けてくれ！」と叫んだことがありました。乗っている人たちはほとんど衣類が焼けて裸同然でした。

運ばれてくるのは、生きている人ばかりではありません。大八車に満載された死体が川の中州まで運ばれていました。川が深いので中州まで大八車を入れられず、鳶口で死体を魚のように引っかけて、中州に放り投げているのです。そんなことができるのは、子どもや小柄な女性の死体だったからではないでしょうか。

なかには、まだ息があって呻いたり、身を捩ったりする「死体」もあったそうです。今でも、中州と鳶口を見ると、あの光景を思い出してぞっと

します。中州に運ばれた死体は並べられて、重油をかけ焼かれていました。風が吹くとその臭いで何も喉を通りません。避難してきた人は五人亡くなり、他の人たちは病院に運ばれたり、軽傷の人は親類を頼って出ていったりして、四、五日で誰もいなくなりました。

父は八月半ばに九州の連隊から復員。すぐに本川町の工場に様子を見に行ったところ、職人さんたちは折り重なって亡くなっており、被爆後、二週間経っていたので、腐敗していたということでした。父は五人兄弟の長男だったので、兄弟やその家族を捜しに、何日も爆心地を歩き回ったため入市被爆し、五十六歳で亡くなりました。

## 新居に引っ越し
## 被爆を封印した

一九四八年（昭和二十三年）七月三十一日、私たち家族は、疎開先の可部上市から広島の幟町(のぼりちょう)の新居に移り、私は幟町小学校に転校し、三年生の二学期から復学。幟町に来てからは、母は二度と可部には行こうとしませんでした。また、「原爆」という言葉を口にすることもありませんでした。近所の人たちも、わが家は疎開していたということしか知らないので、原爆が話題になることもありません。

たまに原爆が話題になったときにも、母は絶対に話に乗りませんでした。一度だけ、原爆手帳をもらった人が「医療費がタダになるので助かるわ」と話したところ、「娘がいるからねぇ……」と、ぽつり漏(も)らしたことがありました。被爆者の介護をして二次被爆したことを自覚していたから

でしょう。

 母は、「可部」や「原爆」とは無関係、といった感じで日常を過ごしていました。その徹底ぶりは恐ろしいほどで、私たちも母の前では「可部」のことは絶対に口にしませんでした。母は体重三十五キロの痩(や)せた体で、何回も輸血することがありましたが、そんなときでさえ「被爆とは無関係」で通しました。おかげで、私は三十歳で結婚するときも、八年後に娘を授かったときも、何一つ不安を感じないで過ごしてきました。

 「不安」が一番「残酷」なことを、母は知っていたのかもしれません。

# 重度の貧血に苦しみながら食堂や市場で働き続けた

鈴木信子 さん

すずき・のぶこ　一九二五年（大正十四年）二月生まれ。二十歳のとき、爆心地から約一・七キロの千田町（現・中区）にあった婚家で被爆。全身に浴びたガラス片が、長い間体に留まり、たびたび切開して取り出した。戦後、重い貧血に苦しみながら、夫の母が営む食堂を手伝う。訳あって夫と離婚後、やっと見つけた職場で重い貧血のため倒れそうなときも必死で働いた。一九五六年（昭和三十一年）に再婚。廿日市市佐方在住。九十一歳。

# 三十三年経っても
## 体内からガラス片が出てきた

体の中に埋もれていたガラス片が、何かの拍子に表面の方に浮いてくるのでしょうか。体内をあちこち移動して、突然、思わぬ場所から飛び出してくる。それが神経に触って、ちくちくと痛痒(いたがゆ)くなり、触ってみると皮膚の下に硬い異物のシコリを感じるのです。

最初はそれほど気にならなかったのですが、だんだん痛痒さがひどくなってくるので病院で診てもらい、メスを入れると五ミリぐらいのガラス片がぽろっと出てきます。何回ぐらい切ったでしょう。はっきり数えていませんが、四、五回は取り出してもらったと思います。

最後に切ったのは一九七八年（昭和五十三年）です。広島市民病院で、左膝(ひざ)の外側からガラス片を取り出しました。

鈴木信子

「三十三年も足に入れとって、ダイヤモンドになって出てくるのならいいのに、ガラスのままじゃ何にもならんわな」。そう言ってお医者さんが笑いました。

私にとって、あの日から三十三年という歳月は、長いようでもあり短くも感じられました。

貧血にも悩まされました。戦争が終わり、夫の母が営む食堂を手伝っていたころです。生理になると貧血はさらにひどくなり、本当に辛くて困りました。ちょっと物を取りに二階に上がろうと思っても、眩暈がして足元が覚つかない。二階に上がったはいいけど、ふらふらして階段から落ちそうになったこともありました。

その後、訳あって離婚。生活のために働くところを探しましたが、なかなか見つからず、やっと、知人の紹介で中央卸売市場に勤めることにな

りました。

市場では年に一回、保健所の検診車が来て健康診断をしてくれるのです。私は必ず貧血で再検査となり、病院で検査を受けるのが当たり前のようになっていました。

職場では、注文が来ると「この日にあの品が何個、これがいくつ」というようにみんなと協力して、その日のうちに急いで袋詰めをしなければなりません。私の体が弱いことは店の人たちも知っていたので、「無理するな」といたわってくれましたが、私は大工の娘で、仲間と心を合わせて一つ一つの仕事を仕上げる父の背中を見ていますから、自分だけ休むなんてできません。

立っていられないほどだるくて、横になりたくてたまらないときも、我慢して一生懸命に働き続けたのです。でも、今はこう思っています。「逆に、それが私を丈夫にしてくれた」と。

鈴木信子

# 全身にガラス片を浴びて裏庭に放り出された

一九四五年（昭和二十年）、私は二十歳で見合い結婚をしました。夫は同い年で、一週間後には出征して岩国の連隊に入るという慌ただしい結婚でした。

当時はそういう結婚も珍しくなかったのです。

お舅さんは消防署に勤めていて、建物疎開の家屋解体で忙しくしていました。嫁ぎ先には精神的に不安定で寝たきり状態の義兄（夫の兄）がいました。国民学校高等科のとき、胸元に蛇を投げつけられたのがきっかけで、狂ったように泣き出し、それ以来おかしく気の小さい人だったらしく、なっていったのです。

日頃は義兄の下の世話をし、空襲警報が鳴ると義兄を背負って防空壕へ逃げるのが、私の役目でした。戦争が激しくなり、終戦の一カ月ほど前に

義母は義兄を連れて五目市（現・佐伯区）に疎開していました。

あの日、私は千田町の赤十字病院の裏手にある婚家にいました。義父は朝早くから加古町（現・中区）の建物疎開作業に出かけていました。食事を終えた私は、畑に行くためモンペに着替えようとしていました。

その瞬間です。大きな衝撃を受け、気がついたら肌着のシュミーズ一枚という姿。着替えの途中で裸足のまま裏庭に放り出されていたのです。

「ピカッ」という光も「ドーン」という音も聞いていません。

全身にガラスの破片を浴びて、白いシュミーズは血だらけでした。何が起こったのか分からないまま、「ともかく逃げなくては！」と土手に上がりました。右足から血が噴き出しています。

南大橋（爆心地から一・七五キロ）を渡るときは足からの出血がひどく、意識が朦朧としていて、橋から落ちそうになる寸前で、ハッと気がつき、

鈴木信子

人に助けてもらって渡りました。
「土手の下に下りなくては！」と、私は必死で下りて川に泊めてあった船の陰に隠れました。船のそばには、死んだ孫を抱きしめ「息子にどう詫びたらいいのか」と、肩を震わせているおばあさんがいました。高等科ぐらいの男の子が泣いているのでそばに行ってみると、その脇で母親らしい女性が亡くなっていました。顔に傷もなく、美しいままで。

そのときのことは、おぼろげな記憶しか残っていません。言葉を交わしたことも覚えていませんが、近くの工場の人なのか、「己斐（現・西区）まで行ったら、五日市の工場へ行くトラックが待っているので乗せていってあげる」と言ってくれたところをみると、どうやら五日市に義母が疎開していることを、私は話したらしいのです。

己斐に向かって歩きだしたものの、途中で貧血を起こして気分が悪くなり「ここで放っておいて！」と叫んだことは、はっきりと覚えています。
しかし、それから己斐に行ったのも、どんな車に乗せてもらっていたかも、あまり記憶にないまま、その夜は、五日市の工場に泊めてもらっていたのです。

翌朝、私は五日市の義母の疎開先に向かいました。「お義母（かぁ）さんは大丈夫だろうか」「ちゃんと会えるのだろうか」。不安でいっぱいになりながら土手を歩いていると、思いがけず、義母とばったり出会ったのです。私は思わず抱きつき、わあわあ泣きました。

一カ月後、体中にガラスが刺さった私を義母が大八車（だいはちぐるま）に乗せて廿日市（はつかいち）（現・廿日市市）の病院に連れていってくれました。病院の中は、被爆した人でごった返していました。どんな人たちがいたのかよく覚えていません

鈴木信子

が、私の前にいた三十歳代の男の人の胸には拳くらいの大きさの穴が開いていて、今にも死にそうな様子でした。

私の右膝の後ろには、二センチ大のガラス片が埋まっていました。爆風は北から南へ吹き抜けたので、私の体に埋まっているガラス片も右側に集中していました。ガラスを浴びてから一カ月以上経っていたので肉にしっかり食い込んでいるのです。

それを取り出してもらったときの、あの痛み。今思い出しても震えがくるほどです。麻酔なしで足をザクザク切って取り出したのですから。

義母は私が五日市に行った日から、建物疎開に行ったお舅さんを広島市内であちこち捜し回り、ついに似島（現・南区）の方まで行って、そこで亡くなっていたことを突き止めました。私の足のガラス片の治療はそのため一カ月後となってしまったのです。その間も私は足を引きながら、義兄の

世話に追われていました。

広島市内に住んでいた義父の妹のお母さんは、孫をかばいながら亡くなったそうです。自分は黒焦げで、胸にしっかりと抱え込んだお孫さんも、気の毒なことに生焼けになって発見されたと聞きました。

## 戦地から戻った夫は
## 働こうとしなかった

戦争が終わり、一カ月後に夫が戦地から戻ってきました。

一九四七年（昭和二十二年）の春過ぎたころに、義母は宇品の電停前で食べ物を売り始めました。義母は昔、千田町で食堂を営んでいたのですが、戦況が厳しくなり、売る物がなくなったため休業していたのです。何かしないと食べていけません。戸板に果物を並べて売ったり、お米はないので

鈴木信子

副食ばかりです。おからのおにぎりも売っていました。その後、再び食堂を始めました。

夫とは、結婚して一週間しか一緒に生活したことがなかったので、互いに性格も何も分かっていませんでした。ともに暮らして分かったのは、夫は働くことが嫌いな人だということでした。復員しても働くところのない時代でしたが、夫は職を探そうともせずに、ぶらぶら遊んでばかりでした。食堂がどんなに忙しくても、手伝おうとしません。子どものころから、食堂がどんなに忙しくても、手伝わないのが当たり前と思っていたようです。町内の夜店でカキ氷を始めたころは、面白がって一、二回手伝ってくれましたが、すぐに「きつい！」と言ってやめてしまい、それっきり。働いたのを見たのはそのときだけです。

翌年に長女、その三年後に次女が生まれました。お産は比較的安産で彼

爆を気にしたことはありません。食堂が忙しく、そのうえ寝たきりの義兄の世話もしなければなりませんので、それどころではなかったのです。その義兄も一九四八年（昭和二十三年）十月に亡くなりました。

夫は親しい女性がいたようで、しょっちゅう家を空けていました。ある日、夫が「下の娘を着替えさせて」と言うので着替えさせると、次女を連れて女性のところに行ってしまいました。私は「娘たちのためにも辛抱しよう。いつか夫も変わってくれるかもしれない」と自分を励ましながら我慢していました。しかし結婚から七年後、とうとう耐えきれずに離婚しました。

一九五二年（昭和二十七年）、娘二人は婚家に引き取られ、私一人で実家に戻ってきたのです。

私の父は大工でした。いつもは三滝（現・西区）の現場に行くのですが、

その日に限って腹痛を起こし、爆心地から一・五キロの自宅にいたため、爆死してしまいました。

母は江波(えば)(現・中区)の三菱工場(爆心地から四キロ)に働きに出ていて無事でした。母はすぐに父や姉、私を捜しに市内を回りました。歩きに歩き、疲れ果てて、焼け残った本川(ほんかわ)小学校に入って眠ってしまったそうです。翌朝、起きると仰天したと言います。学校中におびただしい死体の山ができていたのですから。

八月六日のことをお話しするたびに、胸がチクチク痛みます。まるで体内に潜(ひそ)んでいるガラス片が、じわりと浮いてきたかのように……。

# 姉の死を無駄にしないために
# 国内外で平和訴え被爆証言

## 岡田恵美子さん

おかだ・えみこ　一九三七年（昭和十二年）一月生まれ。八歳のとき、爆心地から約二・八キロの尾長（現・東区）の自宅で被爆。その後、再生不良性貧血に苦しむ。当時十二歳の姉は建物疎開の作業に出かけたまま戻らず、どれほど捜しても遺骨や遺品が見つからないため、両親は姉の生存を信じたまま亡くなった。姉の死をきっかけに、平和を訴える活動に参加。被爆体験を語るため、核保有国のインド、パキスタンも訪れた。広島市東区在住。七十九歳。

## 戻らぬ姉の生存を
## 信じ続けた両親

あの日、「行ってきます！」と元気に建物疎開の作業に出掛けた十二歳の姉の美重子は、いまだに戻ってきません。姉が行ったのは、爆心地から八百メートルの土橋（現・中区）でした。両親は三カ月間、毎日、焼け跡や救護所を捜し回りました。

建物疎開先にも何度も足を運びましたが、遺骨はおろか遺品らしきものさえ見つけることができませんでした。

「第一県女（県立広島第一高等女学校、現・広島皆実高校）の生徒の何人かは、己斐国民学校へ避難した」と聞けば、わずかの希望を胸に飛んで行き、「逃げる途中で、天満川に落ちた子が何人かいた」と知ると、その辺り一帯を何日も聞いて回りました。似島（現・南区）に、多くの負傷者が運ばれ

岡田恵美子

ていたことを知ったときは、似島まで見に行ったりもしましたが、手掛かりさえつかめないのです。
捜しに行くところがなくなっても諦めきれず、二葉山の麓にある七カ所の寺院、仏閣、神社で、毎日お百度参りをしていました。
ただ、姉を捜すことに必死で、私たちのことは眼中になかったようです。両親はただ私と弟たちはそのころ、両親と話をした記憶がありません。戦時中だったので家族写真もなかったのです。しばらく経って、姉が七歳ごろに始めた日舞の稽古の姉の思い出となる写真すらありませんでした。
写真を親類からもらうと、両親は愛おしそうに眺めていました。
せめて、何か「姉の持ち物」と分かるものが土橋の焼け跡から見つかれば、気持ちの整理もついたでしょう。
「美重子は怪我をして、どこかで治療を受けているのかもしれない」
「そのうち、ひょっこり帰ってくるのでは？」

何の遺品もないだけに、落ち着かない日々を過ごしていました。結局、両親はずっと姉の生存を信じ、死亡届も出さないまま亡くなりました。両親も姉も本当にかわいそうでした。

私が物心ついたころから、日本はずっと戦争、戦争でした。私たちは毎日、出征（しゅっせい）する兵隊さんを「万歳、万歳！」と小旗を振りながら見送っていたのです。

母の着物を解いて作ったモンペ服の上下に防空頭巾（ずきん）という格好で、国民学校へ通いました。学校では空襲警報が鳴るたびに防空壕（ごう）へ逃げ込んだり、運動場で手旗信号を習ったりで、机に向かって満足に勉強した記憶はありません。ラジオで東京、大阪をはじめ全国の空襲を知り、B29爆撃機が飛んでくるたびに怯（おび）えていました。健康な男性はすべて兵隊にとられた広島の地で、残された女たちが消火のためのバケツ競争や竹槍（たけやり）の訓練に励んで

いたのです。

戦況が厳しくなると、国民学校初等科三年生から六年生は先生に引率されて山奥のお寺などに疎開。高等科の生徒は、空襲の火災が周辺に広がるのを防ぐために建物を取り壊す建物疎開の作業に駆り出されていました。

## 放射能の影響で再生不良性貧血に

当時、私は八歳で、尾長国民学校三年生。父は松本商業学校（一時工業学校と改称された。現・瀬戸内高校）の教師で、自宅の三軒隣に学校がありました。あの日、父は生徒を引率して早朝から建物疎開の作業で出かけていました。父と姉が出掛けたので、母と私、五歳と三歳の弟の四人は、尾長（現・東区）の自宅で朝ご飯を食べていました。

午前八時過ぎ、飛行機の爆音がしました。警戒警報が解除になっていたので、二人の弟は「日本の飛行機が飛んできた！」と、庭に出て飛行機に向かって手を振りました。真っ青な空に飛行機の翼がキラキラ光っているのが見えました。

そのとき、「ピカーッ」という凄い光と「ドーン」という衝撃が。気がつくと、私は吹き飛ばされて庭の地べたに叩き付けられていたのです。家の壁は崩れ、柱は「くの字」に折れています。ガラスの破片が刺さった頭から血を流しながら、母が必死の形相で家から出てきました。私はてっきり焼夷弾が落とされたと思ったのです。

自宅は爆心地から約二・八キロ。上の弟は軒の下にいたので無傷でしたが、庭に出ていた下の弟は背中から腕、足にかけて大火傷を負って、大声で泣いています。着ていたランニングシャツと半ズボンは、焦げてボロ布のよう。火傷がひどく、首から左腕にかけて焼け爛れていました。後にケ

ロイドが残り、夏でも首と腕を隠(かく)すために襟(えり)の高い長袖(ながそで)シャツを着ていました。

わが家だけでなく近所の家も崩れ落ち、周囲は瓦礫(がれき)の山。朝の食事時で火を使っている家が多かったので、あちこちの家が燃え出し、街全体が火に包まれることになったのです。とりわけ、かわいそうだったのは、母親が建物の下敷きになり、そこに火が迫ってきたときに、「母ちゃんを、母ちゃんを助けて！」と、叫びながら助けを求める子どもです。しかし、どうしてあげることもできません。

火事は広範囲にわたりました。倒れた柱に挟(はさ)まれて逃げ出せないまま、焼け死んだ女の子の「ギャーッ」という悲壮な叫びは、今も耳の奥に残って離れません。

逃げる道中、衣服が焼けて裸同然の人、皮膚が垂れ下がり、目玉が飛び

出して動けなくなった人、性別が分からないほど火膨れがひどい人たちが「水をください！　水を！」と、呻いているのです。けれど、やがて動かなくなりました。

広島市内が燃えているので、周辺の人たちは火の来ない東練兵場へ逃げてきました。私も血だらけの母と火傷を負った弟たちとともに逃げ込みました。私は有毒なガスを吸い込んだのか、息苦しくて何度も吐きました。

東練兵場の中は、もの凄いありさまでした。顔がザクロのように割れ、血だらけになった瀕死の人、腕が裂け白い骨まで見えている人、腸が飛び出したまま死んでいる人……。死体や怪我人の間を、たくさんの迷子が泣きながら母親を捜しています。幼い子どもの黒焦げの死体もありました。性別も分からないほどで、顔を見ると目玉が飛び出していました。至る所に何百という死体が転がっており、死体を運ぶ人や、その死体に重油をかける人が無言で作業を兵隊たちが多くの死体を焼いていました。

しています。異様な光景でした。中には、まだ息のある人もいたようです。時折聞こえてくる「ギャーッ」という断末魔の声に、私は耳を塞ぐ気力もないまま茫然としていました。

苦しくて動けなくて、私は母たちと東練兵場の原っぱに横たわり、多くの死体の中で一晩を過ごすしかありませんでした。ゴオー、ゴオーと音を立てて、広島の街は燃え続けました。真っ赤に燃える衝撃的な光景を見たので、今でも私は夕焼けが嫌いです。

翌朝、川に架かっていた木の橋の多くは焼け落ちていました。

一晩、練兵場にいて、翌日、崩れたわが家に戻ると、知らない人たちがたくさん避難していました。二日ほどして父方の祖母が訪ねてきたので、西高屋（現・東広島市）にある父の実家に避難することにしました。

母は「美重子が戻ってくるかもしれないのでここに残る！」と言うので、

私と弟たちが祖母と一緒に西高屋を通る貨物列車に乗り込みました。どこへ運ぶのか分かりませんが、貨物列車には死体が満載されていました。そのころから、私の体調は悪くなっていきました。歯茎から出血し、口の中は血だらけ。死体の臭いに胸がムカムカし、体がだるく起きていられない状態でした。ずっと横になったまま、「たいぎー（だるい）、たいぎー」と、唸っていたのです。後に、白血球が減る「再生不良性貧血」と診断されました。放射能の影響でした。

貨物列車が向洋駅近くまで来たとき、警戒警報が鳴って止まったのですが、降りて逃げる気力もありません。結局、一時間近くかかって西高屋に着いたのでした。

父の一番下の妹と、姉一家三人が亡くなっていましたので、祖母は仏壇に手を合わせ「酷いよのう、酷いよのう。あのピカドンさえなかったら」

岡田恵美子

と死ぬまで言っていました。

三カ月くらい経って、両親が尾長の自宅から、ようやく西高屋に避難してきました。さんざん姉を捜し回った末のことでした。ある日、金だらいに母の着物が入っていたので、洗濯しようとポンプで水を勢いよく注ぐと、みるみる水が真っ赤になりました。そのとき母が妊娠して流産していたことを知ったのです。

当時、火傷の薬だといって「人骨の粉」が出回りました。何も薬がないので、死体の骨を砕いて粉にしたものを薬として売っていたのです。弟たちもそれを火傷の傷口に塗っていました。

父が学徒を引率した建物疎開の場所は、比治山の東側でした。山の陰だったので直接の被爆は免れ、父は段原商店街で負傷者の手当てを手伝っていたそうです。実家に戻ってきたのは、原爆投下から三日後のことでした。

# 世界の子どもたちに平和教育が必要と実感

終戦後、県北の三次（現・三次市）の疎開先から戻ってきた子どもたちが「お母ちゃん、お母ちゃん」と、亡くなった母親を捜して焼け跡をうろうろしていました。このような原爆孤児が広島には二千人いたとも、六千五百人余りいたともいわれています。生き残った孤児たちの、その後の五年間は「もう一つの戦争」でした。

ひもじいお腹を抱えて街中をうろついても、食べられそうな物はありません。そんな孤児たちにヤクザが食べ物を与え、その代償にピストルを持たせて「強盗しろ。人殺しをしてこい！」と強要したそうです。売春をして飢えを凌いでいた十二、三歳くらいの孤児の女の子たちもいたようで、

岡田恵美子

そうしなければ生きられなかったのです。

原爆投下から一カ月後に広島を襲った枕崎台風では、多くの孤児たちが増水した川に流され、亡くなりました。橋の下をねぐらにしていたためです。また、冬の寒い夜、猿猴川の橋の下では、何十人もの孤児たちが一塊になって凍死しているのも発見されました。

翌年四月。新学期になり、私は通っていた尾長国民学校に行ってみましたが、すでに校舎は焼失していました。仕方なく、近くの尾長天満宮に向かいました。学問の神様を祀っている神社で、お正月に張り出された書き初めを見に行ったり、試験のたびにお参りに行ったりしていた、私にとっては馴染み深い場所でした。天満宮の石段に腰かけていると、一人、二人と同級生が集まってきました。

「生きとったんね！」

お互いに声をかけながら、無事を喜び合いました。その数は十人余りでした。

戦後三年経っても、川に入るとまだ人間の骨が足に当たることがありました。川底まで回収の手が回らず、流された遺体はかなり長い間、放置されたままだったのです。

子どもの行方不明者が多く、川底からベルトのバックルや学生服の金ボタンが発見されるたびに、「うちの子どものでは?」「孫のではないだろうか?」と、多くの人たちが確認に押しかけました。

一九五〇年(昭和二十五年)に母が亡くなりました。火葬場で母の骨を拾おうとしましたが、放射能の影響か骨は脆くなっていて、箸で挟むことができません。頭蓋骨がキラキラと光るので、何だろうと見ると、頭に刺さったガラス片がまだ残っていました。教師として子どもたちに軍事教育

岡田恵美子

をしてきた父は、戦後、「申し訳なかった。すまなかった」と、人の顔を見ると頭を下げ続け、母を亡くした後は腑抜けのようになってしまいました。

私が平和を訴える活動を始めたきっかけは、母が亡くなり、遺品を整理していたとき、偶然、三枚の便箋に書かれた姉の手紙を見つけたことです。予科練に入隊したばかりの従兄にあてた手紙には、「銃後には、もう晩秋の気候となりました。（中略）恂様が元気で凱旋なさるときは、他所へ帰ったように思われるでしょう。建物疎開で家は壊れ、練兵場にはイモがたくさん植えてあるので、昔の広島のようには思われません」（編集注＝現代文に改めました）と綴られていました。

当時、十二歳で第一県女の一年生だった姉はとても気持ちが優しくて、私と二人で陸軍病院に慰問に行き、蓄音機のレコードに合わせて一緒に日

本舞踊を舞ったこともありました。また、わが家は戦前では珍しくオルガンがあって、姉が弾くオルガンに合わせて、私と弟が童謡や唱歌をよく歌いました。

姉の遺骨も遺品もありません。この手紙だけが形見です。初めてこの手紙を読んだとき、心の底から「原爆が憎い」と思いました。姉の死を無駄にしないためにも、私は原爆の恐ろしさを訴えていこうと決めたのです。

それからは、広島平和記念資料館の来館者への解説をしたり、原爆の悲惨さを伝える「ヒロシマピースボランティア」の活動に参加しました。さらに、この活動の一環で「ヒロシマ世界平和ミッション」という「世界に被爆を語る」ことを趣旨とした平和運動に参加。二〇〇五年（平成十七年）二月、「被爆証言」の講演のために、インドとパキスタンを訪問しました。インドでの講演が終わり、会場を出た私の目はあるものに釘づけになり

ました。十二、三歳くらいのみすぼらしい女の子が赤ん坊を抱いて立っていたのです。抱いているのは、明らかに彼女の子どもです。また、立派な軍施設の脇で、食べ物はないかと、ゴミを漁る裸足の女の子たち。パキスタンでも同じ光景を目にしたとき、広島の原爆孤児たちと二重写しになりました。あのような悲惨な子どもたちを見るのは、もうたくさんです。子どもは地球の宝物なのですから。

インドでは学校でも講演させていただきました。子どもたちに「お隣の国のパキスタンの子どもたちとも仲良くしようね」と言うと「嫌だ！だって敵だもの！」と言うではありませんか。両国の関係には複雑な歴史があるとはいえ、「みんなと仲良くする」という教育ではなく、「敵だから注意しろ！」と教えられているのです。驚きました。

未来ある子どもたちのためにも、世界中で平和のための教育が必要だと痛感した瞬間でした。

# 絶望から使命を見いだし
# 若者とともに
# 核廃絶を世界に訴える

## 松原美代子 さん

まつばら・みよこ　一九三二年（昭和七年）八月生まれ。十二歳のとき、爆心地から一・五キロの鶴見町（現・中区）で被爆。顔、両手、足に大火傷を負い、瞼は閉じず、肘は曲がったままだった。二十歳のとき、大阪で形成手術を受けた。米国の平和活動家バーバラ・レイノルズさんと世界平和巡礼に同行し、核実験反対を十四カ国で訴えた。広島平和文化センター退職後、「ヒロシマの心を伝える会」を設立し、核廃絶運動に奔走する。広島市南区在住。八十四歳。

# 鏡に映った顔を見て衝撃で涙が止めどもなく流れた

こっそり鏡台を覗いた瞬間、あまりのことに声も出ませんでした。薄暗がりとはいえ、そこに映っていたのは今までの私の顔ではなく、まるで赤鬼。赤く腫れ上がって引きつった皮膚に覆われた顔でした。特に目の周りは熟したトマトのように崩れ、眉毛もありません。

「これが、私…？」。絶望感に襲われ、悔し涙が止めどもなく流れました。

私は被爆し全身に大火傷を負いました。その日のうちに人の助けを得て、わが家に戻ってきたのでした。顔の火傷が気になり、何度も母に「鏡を見せて！」と頼みましたが、母はいっこうに鏡を持ってきてくれません。体に負った火傷の傷は深く、まだ思うように歩けませんでしたが、ある日、私は這うように鏡台に向かったのでした。

松原美代子

「もっと丁寧に治療してくれたら、こんなことにはならなかったのでは」と、母に八つ当たりしたことは二度や三度ではありません。やり場のない悲しみと怒りは、母にぶつけるしかなかったのです。
「お前に代わって、私が原爆を受けりゃあよかったのにねえ」
「いっそ、あのとき死んでいた方がよかったんかねえ」
母はこう言って、私が嘆き悲しむたびに一緒に泣くのです。後で知ったのですが、私が死の瀬戸際でうなされていたとき、母は自分の大切な着物を背負って田舎に行き、それを売って私の治療費に充てていたそうです。そのことを聞いてからは「母の前では決して泣くまい！」と決めました。

　七カ月の自宅治療を終えて、再び登校してみると、約二百五十人いた学友は、わずか五十人足らずになっていました。

## 「あんた一人で逃げて！」と涙を浮かべて、その場に崩れた友

　あの日、広島女子商業学校（現・広島翔洋高校）一年だった私は、爆心地から一・五キロ離れた鶴見町（現・中区）に、建物疎開の後片づけに行っていました。私たち一、二年合わせて約五百人の生徒と教師十一人は、比治山橋（ひやまばし）のたもとの集合場所に向かいました。雲一つない澄み切った夏空が広がる、爽（さわ）やかな朝でした。

　鶴見町の作業場に着くと、私はお弁当箱と救急箱が入ったかばんを作業小屋に入れました。そこには、出動命令を受けた各地域の国民学校、女学校の低学年による動員学徒や、各職場の国民義勇隊員（ぎゆうたい）が続々と集まってきていました。

　私たちは四人一組になって、壊れた屋根瓦（がわら）や木片、釘（くぎ）などを集めて笊（ざる）や

籠に入れ「よっしゃ、よっしゃ」と掛け声をかけながら運んでいました。

そのとき、親友の船岡さんが「あっ、B29の音がする！」と叫んだのです。

警戒警報は解除されていたので「そんなはずはない！」と思って空を見上げると、白い飛行機雲の先に、かすかにB29爆撃機の翼が見えました。目を凝らすと、尾翼の辺りが「ピカッ」と光り、オレンジ色とも青白い色とも見えました。あわてて地面に伏せたとたん、私の隣で「ドカーン」という轟音がしました。とっさに、私が狙われたのだと思いました。

どれくらい経ったのでしょうか、気がついて周りを見渡すと、土煙が立ち込め、薄暗くて何も見えません。隣にいた船岡さんも、四人一組で作業していた友達も爆風で飛ばされたのか、近くにいないのです。

だんだんと足元から薄明るくなってきたので、ふと自分の体を見て驚き

ました。「白い色は敵機から目につきやすいから」と、茄子紺に染めた上衣とモンペが熱線で焼けて、胸と腰の辺りの布地がボロ布のように残っているだけ。白いズック靴はそのままでしたが、足の甲が火傷で腫れ上がり、はち切れそうです。痛くてたまらず、その場で裸足になりました。

あらためて体中を見直すと、両手、両腕、両足と顔に大火傷を負っていました。皮膚は赤く腫れてセロハンのようにツルリと剝け、真っ赤な肉肌に。両手の指や腕の皮膚はボロ布のように垂れ下がり、血が滲んだまま黄色に変色しています。

あの瞬間、眩しかったので右手を顔の前にかざしたせいか、特に右手がひどく火傷していました。恐ろしくなって、暗闇の中を瓦礫につまずき、転びながらも夢中で逃げました。かすかに前が透けて見えるようになり、たどり着いた先は橋のたもとでした。

橋のたもとには、たくさんの被爆者が身を寄せ合っていました。ほとん

どの人が、着ているものを熱線で焼かれて裸同然です。黒く煤けている肌からは血が流れていました。歯だけを白く残してあとは黒焦げになった死体もあります。

川は、真っ黒な煙か霧のようなものに覆われて、その中で大勢の人が呪文のように一斉に声を上げています。それがまるで海鳴りのように響いて聞こえるのです。

私も体の熱さに耐えきれず、川の中に入っていきました。「松原さんじゃない？」と誰かから声をかけられましたが、顔に大火傷を負い、腫れあがった首とあごの区別もつかなくなった相手は、見ただけでは分かりません。声の様子で、ようやく同じクラスのみっちゃんだと分かりました。川の中は、私たちのように火傷で顔の判別ができない人がたくさんいました。

私はここで初めて冷静になり、爆弾は私だけを狙ったものではなく、みんながやられたことを理解しました。そうこうするうちに、今、来た方向から火の手が上がり、こちらに迫ってきそうでした。あわてて、みっちゃんと川から出て土手の上まで這い上がりました。

多くの人が夢遊病者のように右往左往しています。水を飲もうとしたのか、防火水槽に首を突っ込んだまま死んでいる人もいます。傷ついた人々があちこちで座り込んでいました。電車の架線は切れて垂れ下がり、電柱も折れて倒れていました。

荒神橋のたもとまで来たとき、みっちゃんが目にいっぱい涙をため、私をじっと見つめてこう言いました。

「私はもう歩けない。あんた一人で逃げて！」

そして、彼女はその場に崩れてしまったのです。

友を背負って救護所に連れていってあげたいけど、自分もこのまま座り

込みたいほど疲れきっていました。後ろ髪を引かれる思いで、黙ってその場を離れるしかありませんでした。三日後、みっちゃんは両親に見つけ出されましたが、手の施しようもなく亡くなられたそうです。今でも思い出すと、私の胸は張り裂けそうになるのです。

ガラス戸の破片が道路まで散乱している段原商店街を抜け、母校の広島女子商業学校を通って、出身校の大河国民学校付近まで来ました。しかし、熱さと火傷の痛みで、私はとうとう歩けなくなり民家の軒下に倒れ込んでしまいました。そのとき、浜村の叔母さんが通りかかり、私を背負って家まで運んでくれ、その後、近所の山の避難場所まで連れていってくれたのでした。

四日間、四〇度近い高熱と下痢が続き、歯茎からも出血。髪の毛は半分抜けました。何度も意識が朦朧として死の淵をさまよっていました。

担架に寝かされ大河国民学校の救護所まで治療に通いました。火傷は顔、両手、両腕、足まで広がっていました。

膝(ひざ)は後遺症で、伸びたまま曲がらなくなる恐れがあるといわれました。膝を固まらせないために、医師が膝の関節を折り曲げるのですが、かさぶたが破れ、血が噴(ふ)き出します。その痛さといったら「いっそ殺して！」と叫びたいほどでした。

## 原爆で失明した孤児たちの保母として懸命に働く

終戦後、広島はどこも食料難でした。私は火傷で変形した不自由な手でサツマイモの蔓(つる)を剝いたり、少しでも家計の足しになればと洋服のボタン付けの内職をしたりしました。

「体が弱い」「顔にケロイドがある」という理由で、就職先はありません。仕事がないうえに、被爆者は「放射能の影響でいつ病気が発症するか分からない」「結婚しても障がいのある子どもが生まれる」などという絶望的な噂が流れ、結婚話もまずありませんでした。

このような差別のなか、辛く暗い気持ちで生きていた私に「大阪で手術を受けませんか」と誘ってくれた人がいました。キリスト教流川教会の谷本清牧師が、八十人以上の「原爆乙女」に治療を受けさせるという運動のなかで、私にも声をかけてくださったのです。私が二十歳のときでした。

大阪で手術を受けることになり、私は症状が軽い方だったらしく、最後の治療組でした。結局、七カ月間で十二回の形成手術を受けました。左目の周りにメスが入れられ、瞼が閉じられるようになったときの嬉しさは、たとえようもありませんでした。それまでは、まばたきもできず、ゴミが入りゴロゴロして痛かったのです。

また、曲がった肘や指は、自分の太腿の肉を移植するなどして手術を繰り返した結果、伸ばせるようになりました。この喜びのなか、母がいつも言っていた「他人には良くしてあげなさい。必ずあなたに還ってきます」という言葉を思い出しました。

そして私は結婚を断念し、生涯を「人のために生きよう」と決意したのです。

ちょうどそのころ、この手術の機会をくださった谷本牧師が、原爆で盲目になった孤児たちの施設を設立し、私はそこで働かせてもらうことになりました。盲目の孤児は、最初は三人でしたが、たちまち三十人に増えました。原爆で突然、盲目になったのですから、それはかわいそうでした。ボタン一つかけるのも、一人でオシッコに行くのもままなりません。肩につかまり、手を引いてもらわなければ動くことさえできないのです。

あのとき、原爆を直に見たことで失明した子もいました。「パーンッと熱線が一本の線になって目の前を走ったと思ったら、もう目が見えなくなっていた」と、ある子どもは話してくれました。

子どもたちの世話をすることで、私はやっと自分の生きる意味を見いだしたのです。目の見えない子どもたちの保母（現在の保育士）として私は懸命に働きました。

いつしか私は、原爆について深く考えるようになりました。「戦争や原爆を造り出すのは人間だ。だからこそ人間が本気になって戦争や核兵器を憎み、核兵器廃絶を訴えなければ、また人間は同じ過ちを繰り返す」と思い、自分の人生を核兵器廃絶活動に捧げる決心をしたのです。

盲目の孤児たちの施設に八年間勤めた後、臨時雇用で、市役所で原爆手帳発行の仕事をすることになりました。本当は、銀行に勤めるのが夢で女

子商業学校に入ったのですが、被爆したためにそれも叶いませんでした。

それでもバカにされたくない一心で、私は勉強しました。市役所の人の許可で広島大学の聴講生になったのも、このころです。特に英語に関心があったので、本を買って独学を続けました。

その後、広島平和文化センターに勤めることになり、核実験反対の抗議文を英文で書いて、世界へ発信する部署に配属されたので、独学の英語の勉強が役に立ちました。

広島平和文化センターに二十七年間勤務し、一九九三年（平成五年）に退職。その後は、毎年のように、インド、イギリス、ノルウェー、グリーンランドなどで「被爆体験」を語ってきました。

一九九六年（平成八年）、多くの人に原爆や核問題について学んでいただき、「核兵器廃絶」「恒久平和への願い」を世界に伝えたいとの思いから、大学生、教師など若い世代を中心とした平和学習グループ「ヒロシマの心

を伝える会」を設立しました。会の活動として、広島を訪れる米国の公立学校の教育者を、広島市立高校の授業参観に招待しており、「平和」「歴史教育」について日米教師の意見交換の場も提供しています。ホームページを立ち上げ、インターネットで海外の人たちとの交信も始めました。

実は、広島平和文化センターに在職中の一九八八年（昭和六十三年）九月に、私は乳がんの手術を受けました。五カ月間休職したのですが、このとき発見された胃の三つのポリープは「常に検査の必要がある」と医師は言います。正直言って、再びがんになるのではという不安に、常につきまとわれています。

それでも私は、被爆体験を語り、核廃絶を訴え、戦争の愚かさを一人でも多くの方に分かっていただきたいのです。不安と闘い、不安に負けず、

これからも訴え続けてまいります。

# 「広島が全滅です！」通信室から原爆を第一報

## 岡ヨシエ さん

おか・よしえ　一九三一年（昭和六年）一月生まれ。比治山高等女学校（現・比治山女子中学・高等学校）三年のとき、学徒動員で中国軍管区司令部に配属。通信学徒として任務に当たっていたとき、爆心地から〇・七キロの地点で被爆。壊れた通信室から、直通電話で福山連隊に原爆投下の第一報を伝えた。若くして亡くなった級友たちのためにも真実を伝えたいと「証言活動」を続けている。広島市中区在住。八十五歳。

# 被爆証言をする場所は
# 級友と戦った地下司令部で

　私は、一九九一年（平成三年）九月に、初めて「被爆体験」を語りました。それまでにも、いろいろな方から「被爆証言をお願いしたい」との依頼はあったのですが、ずっと断り続けてきました。思い出すのも辛いのに、言葉にして語るなんて、とても私にはできないと思ったからです。

　しかし、あるとき、東京の公立中学校の三年生を受け持つ先生から「当時の岡さんと同年齢の子たちに語っていただきたい」と熱心に頼まれ、その言葉に心を動かされました。

　初めての証言に際し「あのとき、ともに戦った学徒たちと一緒にいた場所でなら」と、広島城内に今も残る半地下の「中国軍管区司令部（作戦司令室・通信室）」跡地をあえて選んで話をしました。

161　岡ヨシエ

ところが、友達のことを思い出しながら話しているうちに、何度も言葉を詰まらせてしまったのです。最後には、とうとう涙が出てきて止まりませんでした。辛い思い出の染み込んだ部屋で語っていると「彼女がここにいて……」「あの人はこっちにいた……」と、みんなの顔が次々に浮かぶのです。

その日は、どうにか話し終えて自宅に戻ったのですが、たった一回話しただけなのに、ストレスからか血小板の数値が下がり、「血小板減少症」が再発したのです。医師からは「安静にするように」と注意され、二年間の静養を余儀(よぎ)なくされました。

六十三歳のとき、ようやく症状が安定したので「証言活動」を再開しました。この年齢まで生き延びたのは、あそこで亡くなった同級生の代わりに「何があったのか」を伝える使命が、私にはあるからだと気がついたからです。

証言活動を再開すると「学校や施設でもお話をしてください」といった依頼も受けるようになりました。私はみんなといた地下司令部の跡地で話すことを大切にしています。剥き出しのコンクリートの四角い部屋は、天井も低く煤けて、今は通信機材も椅子も机も、各部屋の扉さえなくなり、そこには湿った空気が流れているだけ。話を聞く生徒さんたちにとっては、決して快適とは言えないかもしれませんが、ここで話していると、亡くなった同級生たちも一緒になって語ってくれているような気がするのです。

当時、私は比治山高等女学校三年でした。学徒動員で中国軍管区司令部に配属されていました。広島城のお濠の土手の中に、上空からは分からないように半地下の壕が掘られており、そこが全中国地方へ指令を出す「司令作戦本部」になっていました。

四月七日、比治山高等女学校の学生のうち五十人が選抜され、一部の軍

人しか入ることの許されない「作戦本部」に通信学徒として配属されたのです。

さらに四十人が追加され、九十人の態勢で勤務に就くことになりました。三十人ずつの三班三交代制で、朝八時から夕方五時までの日勤班、夕方五時から翌朝の八時までの夜勤班、もう一班は、夜勤明けの休日という態勢でした。夜勤の場合でも、朝七時半から始まる大本営前庭での朝礼には出席します。その後、近くの宿舎で午前中は勉強。そして、午後から夜勤に備えて仮眠をとるのでした。

司令部の入り口に一番近い部屋では、二十五人が耳にレシーバーを付け、中国地方全二十数カ所の監視哨から入ってくる「敵機が飛来」などの情報を聞いてキーに打ち込みます。打ち込んだ情報は、作戦本部にある地図上のランプの点滅となって伝えられます。

二番目の部屋には通信部隊の兵隊たちがいました。三番目の部屋に、通

信学徒四人が壁に向いた格好で二列になって、作戦本部からの命令を各部隊へ直通電話で伝えます。同じ部屋の反対側には、交換機があり、作戦本部から指令が出ると、NHK（日本放送協会）、県庁、軍需工場などの専用直通電話につながる交換機のコードを接続して、一斉に警報を伝えるのです。その操作をするのが私の任務でした。

扉の下に小さな小窓があり、指令が出るときはブザーが鳴って、そこからメモが出てきます。その内容を私を含め五人の通信学徒が専用直通電話で各所に連絡するのです。「警戒警報」は「ケハ」、「空襲警報」は「クハ」。「10ケハ」というと「10時警戒警報発令」という意味になります。

一番奥の部屋にある作戦本部には、厚い木の扉が付いていて誰も出入りができません。参謀や将校たちは反対側の専用出入口から出入りしていました。

広島は軍都と呼ばれ、広島城の周囲は軍隊の施設だらけでした。他の都

市は空襲が続いているのに、なぜ、軍都の広島には空襲がないのだろう、と私は疑問に思ったものです。実際、爆撃機が飛んでこないので、私たちの勤務は七月末から夜勤は三十人が前半・後半に分かれて、十五人ずつの態勢となりました。

## 「新型爆弾にやられた!」と呻(うめ)くように叫んだ負傷兵

原爆投下前日の八月五日、私は夜勤の前半組に当たっており、午後五時に日勤組から仕事を引き継いで、午前一時までの任務に就きました。夜半、「敵機、豊後(ぶんご)水道北上中」との情報が入り、私は「ケハ」に続く「クハ」指令をNHKや各部隊へと流していました。指令を受けた方は、それぞれが警報サイレンを鳴らして市民や関係者に知らせるのです。

午後十一時ごろから兵庫・西宮、翌六日午前三時、愛媛・今治、四時には山口・宇部に次々と百から百二十機のB29爆撃機の大編隊での空襲があり、「総員部署につけ！」との号令が。

仮眠中の後半組も起こされ、私も午前一時に交代する猶予もなく、一睡もせずに任務に当たることになりました。

明け方ようやく静かになったので、近くの宿舎に急いで戻り、ご飯にお味噌汁をかけてかき込み、地下壕に戻って日勤の交代要員を待ちました。

朝八時を過ぎても交代要員が来ないのでジリジリしていると、突然「広島東方、B29三機」との通報がありました。それなのに、作戦本部からは「ケハ」も「クハ」も出ません。

八時十三分、やっと作戦本部の扉のブザーが鳴って小窓から「ケハ」（警戒警報発令）のメモが出されました。私は交換機に向かい、一度に数本のコードを挿して各軍需工場などの相手を呼びました。いつものことなので、

167　岡ヨシエ

さほど緊張もしていませんでした。

一斉に出た相手に「広島、山口、警戒警報……」と言いかけたとたん、真っ白い閃光が激しく目を刺したのです。

「事故だ!」そう思った瞬間、私は意識を失いました。四、五分くらい経ったでしょうか、少しずつ意識が回復すると、私は灰色の霧の中にいました。

机は横倒しになり、椅子は壊れ、私は座っていた場所より三メートルほど飛ばされていて、体の上には交換機が載っかっているのです。部屋の中は、まるで人の気配がありません。もうもうたる灰塵の中で目を凝らすと、部屋の隅に目と耳を押さえた学徒の板村さんがいました。彼女は瞼をわずかに切っただけで、無事のようでした。

私たちは何が起こったのかも分からないまま、外に出ました。最初に目

168

に入ったのは、敷地内にあった三つの建物です。司令官のいた一号庁舎、将校たちの二号庁舎、講堂として使っていた三号庁舎が押し潰され、木屑と壁土が山のように積もっていました。焼夷弾なら火事になるはずなのに、火も出ないで建物だけが潰れていたのです。

なぜだろうと不思議に思いながら、私は一人、お濠の土手に駆け上がりました。広島市にはもともと中国新聞社と福屋百貨店くらいしか高い建物はなく、他は木造の民家が多かったのです。広島市内は見渡す限り赤茶色の瓦礫の街と化していたのです。まだ火は出ていませんでした。宇品の港が目の前にあり、似島が見えました。土手の下で、負傷した兵隊が「新型爆弾にやられた！」と呻くように叫んでいるのが聞こえました。

通信室に戻ってみると、「今はそれどころではありません！」と板村さんが受話器に向かって話しています。「四国軍管区司令部」からの電話

169　岡ヨシエ

だったようです。

広島が全滅状態なのに電話が通じる? と思いながら床に散乱した受話器をとってみました。最初の二、三機は壊れていてつながりません。諦めずに試していると、福山連隊の直通電話がつながったのです。

「広島が全滅です!」

「ん?……。今、何と言った? 全滅と言ったか?」

「はい、全滅しています」

「なぜ全滅になったのだ? 全滅の理由を言いなさい」と言われ、答えに窮しましたが、とっさに負傷した兵隊が叫んでいた言葉を思い出しました。

「新型爆弾にやられました!」

そのとき、パチパチという木の爆ぜる音がして、火の手が迫ってきました。急いで外に飛び出すと、崩れた一号庁舎の建物の下敷きになった兵隊が、這い出そうともがいています。

板村さんと二人で駆け寄りましたが、太い柱が組んだように重なってビクともしません。私たちの手には負えそうもない、と思ったところに傭員の松井さんが来られ、三人で頑丈な棒を差し込んでテコの動きで柱を起こしました。少しずつ上がった隙に、兵隊は体を捩るようにして這い出したのです。

しかし、喜び合っている余裕はありません。火の手はそこまで迫っているのです。朝礼をしていた大本営の前にも学徒は一人もいません。火の勢いは強く、周りは乾燥して髪の毛は今にも燃え出しそうです。服も熱くなって顔も真っ赤に火照り、私たちはたまらず大本営前の池に飛び込みました。頭から泥水を被っても、すぐにカラカラに乾いてしまうのでした。

板村さんと二人、火に包まれて死を覚悟していました。

# 幼年学校の仮救護所で重症者の看護を手伝う

　昼間なのに辺りはどんよりと薄暗く、不意に大粒の真っ黒い雨が降ってきました。泥水のような雨で、土砂降りの豪雨です。全身びしょ濡れになりながら池の中で佇んでいました。
　四十分ほどで雨は嘘のようにやみ、その雨のおかげで、火は消えました。その黒い雨に感謝しましたが、それが空中の放射能を含んだ怖い雨ということを当時は知るすべもありません。その雨にあたって、後に原爆症の症状が出た人はたくさんいます。

　雨が上がってみんなを捜しに広島城の天守閣の反対側に回ってみると、三人の学徒が石の上に座っていました。普段は上衣に名札が付いているの

で名前が分かるのですが、衣服がビリビリに破れていて名札が読めません。
一人は顔が二倍に腫れて目も潰れ、一人は首が後ろにガックリと折れ意識がほとんどありません。もう一人は浜岡さんだと分かりましたが、彼女の右肘の関節は砕け内側の骨と肉がはみ出していて、今にも取れてしまいそうに腕がぶら下がっていました。しきりに水を欲しがるのですが、飲み水なんてどこにもありません。
「後で戻ってくるから、ここで待っていて」となだめ、「みんなはどこ?」と聞くと、浜岡さんは「あっち!」と力なく指さしました。その方向には軍人専用の城東橋が架かっており、その先に軍人を教育する幼年学校がありました。
私は立ち上がり、そちらに向かいました。城東橋を渡りかけたとき、「ドボーン」という水音が聞こえました。とっさに「浜岡さんでは?」と思い、祈るような気持ちで戻ってみると、彼女はすでにお濠に浮いていた

岡ヨシエ

のです。水が飲みたくて、お濠に身を乗り出して落ちたのでしょう。

夕方、山口、岡山から救護の看護兵が来ると、負傷した学徒二十人、兵隊三十人が担架で次々と運ばれ、幼年学校の場所にできた仮救護所に収容されました。

私たちも看護のため、収容された学徒を診て回りました。「水、お水を飲ませて！」と皆が言います。看護兵は初めは「火傷の者に水を与えると死ぬからイカン！」と言いましたが、水を飲まなくても怪我人は次々と亡くなります。「どうせ死ぬのなら、最後に水を飲ませてあげよう」と思ったのでしょうか、看護兵が「一口ずつ飲ませてやれ」と静かに言ったので、私はやかんに水を汲んできて飲ませてあげました。
背中に二十センチほどの棒切れが刺さったまま、軍幹部が真っ青な顔をして座り込んでいました。脳天に穴が開いた兵隊さんは、呼吸するたびに

頭の中の肉がヒクヒク動いていました。空を睨んだまま目を剝いて死んでいる人、お腹が破れて腸がはみ出ている人。救護所は重症者でいっぱいでした。

陽も暮れかかったころ、同じ班だった古池さん、宮川さん、森田さんたちが戻ってきました。皆で再会を喜び合い、板村さんと私を入れて生存した五人で通信室に戻って雑魚寝しました。

救護所の方からは、「お母さ～ん」と叫ぶ、若い兵隊さんの声が聞こえてきます。その悲愴な声を聞きながらも、疲れ切っていた私たちは眠ってしまいました。

翌日、五人で救護所に手伝いにいくと、たった一晩経っただけなのに、学徒や兵隊の火傷にうじ虫が湧いて、体が真っ白に見えました。娘たちの安否を聞いた学徒のお母さんたちもやって来ました。傷ついた娘を抱いて必死に呼びかける母親。ボロボロと流す母親の涙が

岡ヨシエ

顔に落ちて意識を取り戻した学徒は、「お国のために役立って逝くのですから、泣かないで」と笑顔さえ見せて息を引き取ったのです。

八月十五日の終戦までに、救護所に収容されていた二十人の学徒は全員息を引き取りました。大阪から将校と下士官が来て、亡くなった上官の代わりに指揮をとりました。

八月十八日、破壊された司令部で解散式が行われ、下士官からの「ご苦労であった」の一言で、私たち五人はそれぞれ親の元に戻りました。互いに「二学期に学校で会おうね！」と言って別れましたが、自宅に戻るなり、高熱、下痢、そして、地の底に引きずり込まれるような倦怠感といった原爆による症状で、私は二年間の自宅療養生活を余儀なくされたのです。

生き残った私の使命は、任務に最後まで責任を感じながら亡くなった級友たちの冥福(めいふく)を祈り、彼女たちの生きた証(あか)しを証言すること――。そう心に決め、私は自分を奮い立たせ「証言活動」を続けているのです。

# 爆心地から一・五キロの病院で閃光(せんこう)を感じ轟音(ごうおん)を聞いた

## 山口幸子さん

やまぐち・さちこ　一九三三年（昭和八年）四月生まれ。広島赤十字看護専門学校（現・日本赤十字広島看護大学）一年の十二歳のとき、広島に原爆が投下される。当時、爆心地より一・五キロの看護学校の炊事場にいたが怪我はなかった。三原市の実家に戻り、後に結婚。原爆症の症状も出ず、自身を被爆者と思ったことはなかったが、申請の条件を満たしていたため被爆者健康手帳の交付を申請。八十歳を過ぎて胆嚢がん、大腸がんなどを患う。三原市糸崎在住。八十三歳。

# 従軍看護婦になるため
# 赤十字看護専門学校へ

　私は三原市で塩田を経営する両親のもと、三人姉妹の三女として生まれました。姉妹の中でも一番、おてんばだった私は、学校から帰ると毎日のように塩田脇の大きなシュロの木に登りました。そこから町を眺めるのが大好きだったのです。

　子どもが娘ばかりだったため、父は「わが家から兵隊が出せずお国に申し訳ない。せめて娘の一人でも従軍看護婦にして、お国のためになれば」と考えたようです。とびきり活発だった私が女学校を卒業すると従軍看護婦になるために、広島赤十字病院（現・広島赤十字・原爆病院）の中にある広島赤十字看護専門学校に行かされました。

　当時、看護専門学校では女学校を卒業後、二年間の教育を受ける甲種と、

179　山口幸子

## ごろごろ転がっている
## 死体の中を逃げた

一九四五年（昭和二十年）八月六日の朝、私はちょうど炊事当番に当たっ

尋常高等小学校を卒業後、四年間の教育を受ける乙種がありました。
広島赤十字病院の三階の半分が女子寮になっていて、三十余人が入寮。入りきれなかった十数人は別寮といって、病院脇の平屋の二間に分散して入っていました。看護学校一年生の私は別寮で暮らしました。
寮生は別寮に併設された一階の食堂で食事をします。食堂の隣には炊事場があり、調理係のおばさんたちの他に三、四人の寮生が一週間交代で炊事当番に当たり、朝六時から食器を並べたりお茶の入ったやかんをテーブルに出したりしました。

ていました。七時の朝食が終わると、寮生は各部屋に戻っていき、私は炊事当番の平岡さんと並んで食器を洗っていました。そのときです。突然「ピカッ」と何かが光ったのです。光線は、それほど大きくは感じなかったのですが、次の「ドーン」という激しい音に、私は寮に爆弾が落とされたと思いました。

というのも、一週間ほど前にB29爆撃機が飛んできて大量のビラを撒いていったからです。寮の前にはチラシがドサッと塊で落ちてきました。婦長さんがバケツを持って出てきて「触ってはいけません！読んではいけません！」と叫びながら、ビラをバケツに回収していましたが、いたるところに散らばっているので、手に取らなくとも読めます。ハガキ大のビラには煙突のある工場のイラストが描かれていて、日本語で「市民と戦っているのではない。近日中に爆弾を投下する。即座に退避せよ」と書かれていたのです。

食器洗いをしていた私は「ドーン」という轟音を聞くと、とっさにご飯を炊く大釜のふちの下に飛び込みました。一緒に食器を洗っていた同級生は下敷きになって亡くなってしまいました。天井の梁が落ちてきて、照明が消え、辺りは真っ暗です。そのうえ、窓の外も夜のような暗闇なのです。建物が崩れていて、どこがどこだか分かりません。
「お父さん、お母さん、助けてぇ！」と、私は必死で叫びました。
やがて、両親が近くにいるわけがないと気づき、「ここは神様だ」と思い直して「神様！　助けてぇ！」と叫び続けました。
窓の外も黒い霧に包まれたように真っ暗なのに、時々、霧の隙間から「シャー」と筋のような白い光が差し込んできます。恐怖で口の中は乾き、声も出せません。それでも「このまま閉じ込められていては大変！」と思い、大声で叫んでいると、幸いにも、誰かが瓦礫をどけてくれたのです。

私は足元に気をつけながら、急いで外に出ました。外に出ると、黒い霧のようなものがゆっくりと上がっていて、足元の一メートルくらいが明るくなっていました。徐々にですが、霧が晴れ、黒い幕が上がっていくように周囲が明るくなってきました。

辺りを見て驚きました。顔中血だらけで倒れている人、片腕がちぎれて呻いている人、衣類がすべて焼けてしまって腰にベルトだけを締めている人、皮膚がドロドロに焼け爛れた赤ちゃんを抱いた母親、皮が剝けて頭の前後の見分けがつかない人など、悲惨な状態の人々が目の前にいるのです。死体もごろごろ転がっています。

そのうちに、あちこちから火が出て燃え出しました。火傷で真っ黒になった人たちが、どちらに行っていいか分からず、うろうろしています。兵隊がさかんに「航空隊へ逃げろ！」と叫んでいました。

航空隊がどっちなのか分かりませんでしたが、ともかく、人が行く方へ付いていきました。

地面が熱く焼けているので、履いていた靴のゴム底はたちまち溶けてしまいました。道路に散らばっている下駄の片方と軍靴の片方を見つけて履き、火のないところをうろうろしながら夜明けを待ちました。

翌朝、病院へ戻ってみると、私のいた別寮は消失していました。

また、隣の山中高等女学校（現・広島大学）からも火が出て、一晩のうちに焼け落ちていました。焼け落ちた女学校の体育館に入ってみると、看護専門学校の友達の一人が平均台に力なく座っていました。顔中にガラスが刺さり、噴き出した血が顔に幾筋にもなって、それがそのまま乾いているのです。

三階の女子寮の窓が吹き飛び、ガラスの破片でみんなが大怪我を負ったと聞きました。私のいた炊事場の窓ガラスは金網が張ってあったので、ガ

ラス片を被らずに済んだのでした。

　病院の前で、赤ちゃんにおっぱいを飲ませたまま黒焦げになっていたお母さんの死体を見たら、急に怖くなり私は三原の実家に帰ろうと思いました。

　しかし、どこを歩いても、行く先々の橋が焼け落ちて行き止まりなのです。私は渡れる橋を探しながら歩きました。しばらく行くと、道端に机が置かれ、兵隊さんが「罹災証明書」を発行していました。私が「三原に帰りたい」と話すと、名刺大の藁半紙に無造作に「罹災証明書」と書いて渡してくれました。それを持って歩き、やっと向洋駅に着いたのです。

　数日前に大阪から暁部隊（陸軍船舶司令部）の兵隊が応援に来ていて、昨日の朝、護国神社前で整列しているところに原爆が投下され、大勢の兵隊が亡くなったということでした。向洋ではどこで用意したのか、死体を入

山口幸子

れたたくさんの棺が次々と貨車に積み込まれているところでした。棺には一人一人の所属と名前が書かれていました。

私が手書きの罹災証明書を見せると、「棺と一緒でいいなら」と言われました。私は、山のように積まれた棺の間にもたれ掛かるようにして座り、貨車に揺られていました。三原駅に着くと、無人のはずの貨車から私が降りたので、駅にいた人たちが驚いて集まり「広島から来たんか?」「向こうはどうなっとる?」と、たちまち質問攻めです。私は人々から逃れるように家へと急ぎました。

家に帰ると、母は目を丸くして驚き「広島は全滅したと聞いたが、よう戻った!」と泣き出しました。父も看護学校に行かせたことを後悔し「すまんかったのう、すまんかったのう」と泣いていました。

広島赤十字病院は原爆投下後、すぐに被爆者の治療に当たっていました。

多くの医師や看護婦が亡くなったので人手が足りなくなり、私にも病院に戻るよう再三、電報が届きました。あまりに悲惨な光景を目の当たりにした私は、とても行く気になれませんでした。電報が来るたび、ぐずぐずしていると父が代わりに出かけて、詫びていたようです。

「一度は顔を出さんといけんよ！」と父に言われ、三カ月後の十一月四日に、大量の大豆とはったい粉を持って、父と一緒にやっと病院に挨拶に行きました。そこで初めて、多くの同級生が犠牲になったことを知ったのです。私は衝撃を受け、深く冥福を祈りました。

## 不安なく暮らしていたが八十歳でがんを発症

三原の実家に戻った私は、以前から習っていたお茶とお花の稽古に再び

山口幸子

通いました。ある日、年配のお弟子さんから「いい人がおるけど、会ってみなさらんか?」と言われました。相手の人は二歳年上で海の予科練（よかれん）といわれた「人間魚雷」に乗っていた人で、出撃直前に終戦となり、中止命令が出たため生き延びることができたそうです。そして、終戦の翌年に、三原に戻ってきました。

当時、わが家は塩田を持っていて少々裕福でしたので、紹介した人が思い直したのか、相手に「あそこ（私の実家）は金持ちじゃけえ、断られるかもしれん。もう一人、たばこ屋の娘でいい娘がおるけん。そっちを紹介しようか?」と言ったそうです。

負けん気の強い彼は、この一言にカチンときたらしく、「たばこ屋の娘はいらん。塩田の娘にしよう」ときっぱり決めたようです。そして、私たちは結婚しました。

夫は被爆していませんし、私も確かに爆心地から一・五キロの病院にいましたが、炊事室ですから、正確に「被爆した」といえるのかどうか分かりませんでした。だから、被爆は他人事のように感じていました。そんなふうですから、私が目撃した原爆投下直後の広島の街の様子を夫に話しても「そうなんか！ すげえのう！」と感心するだけで、私と被爆は無縁と捉えていました。

歯茎からの出血や髪の毛が抜けるといった、原爆症特有の症状も出なければ、大きな病気をすることもなかったため、私自身も被爆とは無縁と考えていたのです。長女を身ごもったときも何の不安もなく、無事出産しました。

戦後三十年を過ぎたころ、たまたま女学校時代の友達と出会いました。彼女は県庁で、被爆当時の書類の整理をしていて、「あの日、広島駅を汽

車で通過し、入市被爆として原爆手帳を支給してもらった」という話になり、「あなたは爆心地付近にいたんだから十分な対象者よ。手帳を申請した方がいいわよ」と言われたのです。
「当時、広島にいたことを証明してくれる人」が必要だと知り、広島赤十字病院の谷口婦長を捜したところ、ご高齢でしたが健在でした。当時のことを証明していただいて、私は「原爆手帳」を手にすることができたのでした。
 ところが手帳をいただいてから、大腸がん、肝臓がんを相次ぎ発症。肝臓がんの手術のとき、肝臓を三分の一、胆嚢も摘出しました。原爆との因果関係ははっきりしませんが、「原爆が体に影響を及ぼしたのでは」という不安は拭い去ることができません。
 二度と被爆者を出さないよう、世の中が平和であることを祈るばかりです。

# 麻酔なしで眼球を切除された母の絶叫が今も耳に

## 竹岡智佐子 さん

たけおか・ちさこ　一九二八年（昭和三年）二月生まれ。女学校を卒業したばかりの十七歳のとき、爆心地から約三キロの己斐上町（現・西区）の自宅で被爆。陸軍病院の看護婦長（現在の看護師長）を務めていた母は、眼球が飛び出す重傷を負い、目について語らぬまま生を終えた。被爆体験を、一九八二年（昭和五十七年）にニューヨークでの国連軍縮特別総会・対話集会をはじめ、ロシアの大学でも二〇〇一年（平成十三年）に証言。現在は、広島市の被爆体験伝承者となった娘とともに広島平和記念資料館の被爆体験証言者として活動。広島市安佐南区在住。八十八歳。

# 母はギュッと口を結んで目のことは「言いたくない！」

母・リョウの枕元に義眼が置かれているのを、私は何度か目にしたことがあります。それは、ちょっと見ると飴玉みたいでした。

戦後、すぐのころですから「義眼の収納ケース」などという物はありません。眠る前には、金平糖などが入った小さな紙箱に綿を敷いて、取り外した義眼をその中に入れるのですが、ちょうど良い紙箱が見つからないときは小皿に載せて、枕元に置いて眠るのです。

義眼は目ヤニで白く汚れることもあるので、母は水で丁寧に洗っていました。慣れてくると、洗う水がないときなどは、クルッと横を向いてパクッと口に含み、舐めてきれいにして何食わぬ顔で、義眼をはめていました。

193　竹岡智佐子

母が義眼を使い始めたころは、義眼を入れようとする気配を感じるや、私は他の方を見たり、席を立ったりと、その仕草をなるべく見ないようにしていました。何となく、かわいそうな気がして……。

当初は母も義眼のことはずいぶん気にしていました。お友達やお医者さんのところに行くときは、必ず顔を斜めにして義眼の右目が写らないように、さりげなく避けていたのです。みんなで写真を撮るときなどは、必ず顔を斜めにして義眼の右目が写らないように、さりげなく避けていたのです。お友達やお医者さんのところに行くときは、必ず孫の真里子を連れて、見えない右側を歩かせ、杖代わりにしていました。また、目の形に合った義眼を作るのは難しく、何度も作り直したようです。

義眼は完全な球形ではなく、後ろ側は少し窪んでいます。ちょうど入れ歯をはめる歯茎のように。

右目の中はメスできれいに神経まで抉り取られ、赤い傷跡のある空洞のまま固まっています。

あるとき、私は思い切って"あのときのこと"を聞いてみました。母はギュッと口を結んだまま長い沈黙が続きました。

そして一言、「言いたくない!」と。母は六十二歳でこの世を去りました。とうとう、「母の右目」については、本人の口から気持ちを聞くことができませんでした。

## 全身血まみれの友に声をかけられて

一九四五年(昭和二十年)八月、私は陸軍病院の看護婦長をしていた母(当時四十二歳)と、己斐上町(こいうえまち)(現・西区)で暮らしていました。私は山中高等女学校(現・広島大学)を卒業したばかり。女学校を卒業すると陸軍か海軍の仕事をすることが義務づけられ、女子挺身隊(ていしん)として天満町(てんまちょう)(現・西区)の軍需工場となった東洋製罐(せいかん)で、人間魚雷(ぎょらい)「回天(かいてん)」の部品を造っていました。大きなヤスリで面取りという部品の凹凸(デコボコ)を平らにする作業をやってい

竹岡智佐子

たのです。

「回天」は一人乗りの魚雷です。国民学校高等科を卒業したばかりの十四、十五歳の少年兵を、わずか三カ月間の特訓で敵の戦艦に体当たりさせる、いわば「海の特攻隊」が乗る人間魚雷です。

八月五日は徹夜作業でした。夜明け前に「女子挺身隊の人たちだけ、今日は家に帰ってゆっくり休んでください」と言われ、私は工場を出ました。夏の夜空は戦争なんて嘘のように真っ青で、まだ星が輝いていました。

もう二、三カ月も休みがなかったので、挺身隊の同僚の香川さん（愛称・ホコちゃん）、大塚さんと私の三人で「今日は暑くなりそうだから、一休みしたら包ケ浦に海水浴に行かない？」と約束しました。

包ケ浦海水浴場は一度、機銃掃射を受けて遊泳禁止になっていたのですが、私は女学校時代に水泳部員で、水泳が得意だったこともあり危険を気に留めなかったのです。

八時十五分に己斐駅（現・西区）に集合と決めていたので、急いで洗濯などの用事を済ませ、玄関を出るとき、もう一度、ポケットから手鏡を出して自慢の長い髪の三つ編みを確認しました。

その瞬間です。
「ピカッ」という凄(すご)い光とともに「ドーン」という音を聞いたまま私は意識を失いました。己斐上町の自宅は、爆心地から約三キロの場所でした。気がつくと、家から三十メートルも離れた裏のサツマイモ畑に倒れていました。
「何でこんなところに？」
わが家を見ると、屋根瓦(がわら)も窓も吹き飛んで、家は傾いているのです。近所の家も同様でした。家に入ろうと思っても、体がぶるぶる震(ふる)えて足が立ちません。ふと、頭に手をやると、ヌルッと頭から血が流れていました。

竹岡智佐子

空には真っ黒い、雲か煙か分からないものが、不気味にむくむくと渦を巻いて広がっていきます。周りは、ガラスの破片が背中に刺さった人、飛んできた木片の古釘がお腹に刺さった人など、血だらけの怪我人でいっぱいでした。

道路に出てみると、坂の下から黒い塊がぞろぞろ上がってきました。よく見ると、火傷を負い、髪の毛が逆立った煤けた人の群れでした。肌は赤く剥け、皮膚はワカメを引き揚げたように、肩から腕を伝って指先から垂れ下がり「助けて、熱いよ、喉が痛い、お水ちょうだい」と叫びながら上がってきます。

家から出てきた近所の人たちも、あまりの酷さに「死ぬんじゃないよ！どこから来たの？」と声をかけていました。少しでも日差しを避けて家の軒先に入ろうとした人々も、その場に倒れ込み、バタバタと死んでいきました。喉の奥まで焼けて、声の出せない人もたくさんいました。

少し時間が経つと、辺りは日が暮れたように暗くなり、真っ黒い雨がザーザー降ってきました。その雨水は腕や足に当たると、大豆ほどの丸く黒いシミとなってこびり付くのです。

突然、群衆の中から女の人がふらりと立ち上がり、「チイちゃん」と私に呼びかけました。「あら、私の名前を呼んだけど、あんた誰？」と私は尋ねました。全身真っ黒焦げで髪の毛も逆立ち、頬が裂けて血がダラダラ流れています。体のあちこちに穴が開いていて、そこからも血が流れ出ています。一緒に海水浴に行こうと約束したホコちゃんだったのです。

彼女は約束の時間までに己斐駅に行こうと電車に乗り、駅に着く直前に、吊り革につかまったまま被爆。気がついたら川の中に落ちていたとのこと。川を這い上がって、私のところまで逃げてきたのです。海水浴に行く約束をしたもう一人、大塚さんは軽い怪我で済みましたが、ホコちゃんはその

竹岡智佐子

後、行方不明になってしまいました。

私は家に戻りましたが、陸軍病院で看護婦長をしている母が心配になり、翌朝、まだ街は燃えていたので、防空頭巾を水で濡らして頭から被り、水筒を下げて捜しに出かけました。その日まで母は、病院に泊まり込んで一週間以上も家に帰っていませんでした。外地から負傷した兵隊が大勢送られてきたため、看護に明け暮れていたのです。

陸軍病院のある相生橋まで来て、川を見ると満潮時で増水した川の中にびっしりと死体が浮いています。それも川底まで重なり合っていて、川の水が見えないほどです。川に一晩浸かった焼死体は、ぱんぱんに膨れ上がり、顔もドッジボールのように丸くなって、人相まで変わってしまっています。

この死体の中に母がいるかもしれない。そう思った私は、何度も川に向かって「お母さ〜ん」と呼んでみました。ふと川向こうを見ると、三人の

男の人が、汚れて真っ黒になったふんどし一つで、川に浮いている死体を川岸に引き揚げているところでした。三人は衛生兵で「自分たち三人だけが生き残ったのが申し訳ない」と必死の形相でした。

私はそばに行き、「母を捜している」ことを告げると、一人の男の人がこう言いました。

「この病院にいた人たちはほとんど生きとらん。今朝までは何百人か生きていたが、口や鼻や耳から血を噴いて次々と死んでいった。今生きとる何十人かの人たちも目も見えず、耳も聞こえなくて死ぬのを待つばかりだ」

母が死んだなんて信じたくはありませんでしたが、せっかく捜しに来たのだからと、川岸に引き揚げられた死体を確認させてもらうことにしました。母の目印は三本の金歯。二本の木片を使って死体の口をこじ開け、金歯を捜しました。どの顔も人間の顔ではなくなっています。死体の唇は五センチも膨れ上がっていて、なかなか口が開かないのです。それでも、怖

竹岡智佐子

いとも気味が悪いとも思わず、必死で四、五十人の死体の口をこじ開けました。

けれど、母は見つかりませんでした。

## ようやく見つけた母は息をするのもやっとの状態

鷹匠町(たかじょうまち)(現・中区)の近くに、叔母(母の兄嫁)と国民学校四年生の従妹(いとこ)が住んでいたことを思い出し、行ってみることにしました。爆心地の近くなので、どの家も跡形もなく焼けたり崩れたりしていました。墨で叔母の家の名前が書かれた防火水槽を見つけ、その辺りをズック靴の先で掘り返すと、出てきた屋根瓦や小石はまだ熱いのです。従妹にあげた私の服の切れ端が出てきましたあちこち掘り返していると、

た。さらに、向かい合った状態の大人と子どもの白骨が出てきたのです。一瞬のうちに焼けてしまったのか、きれいな白骨でした。
何ともいえない思いで立ち尽くしましたが、気を取り直し、私はハンカチに二人の骨をいくつか包んで、持ち帰りました。
翌日も母を捜しに、今度は赤十字病院まで行きました。途中、川の近くに転がった焼死体にかぶりつく二、三匹の大きなドブネズミを目にしました。
病院前の広場まで来ると、大勢の人が集まっています。死体の山が三つできており、まだ火をつけていない死体の山を見て母を捜しました。それを見たら辛くて居たたまれなくなり、私は家に帰りました。
五日目の夜。気分が悪くふらふらしました。それだけでなく、頭に手をやると、ばさっと手のひらいっぱいに髪の毛が抜けてきたのです。
両腕には、いつの間にか卵大の薄紫色の斑点が三つも四つも浮き出てい

竹岡智佐子

「このまま私、死ぬのかな？」と、急に不安になりました。

六日目の朝、近くの農家の高林のおじいさんが一緒に捜してくれるというので、少しふらふらしましたが、舟入の方向に行ってみました。

舟入病院の焼け跡に立っていた人が「江波国民学校（現・中区）に、負傷者がたくさん運ばれていったよ」と教えてくれたので、行ってみると、国民学校の中は廊下も歩けないほど死んだ人でいっぱいでした。そのうえ、どの教室も火傷と死体の臭いで息ができないほどなのです。暑さで火傷の傷口も死体も腐り、真っ白いうじ虫が湧いていました。重なっている人の顔は崩れて、骨まで見えています。

私は母の名前を呼びながら、重なって死んでいる人の顔をあっちへ向けたり、こっちへ向けたりして確認しました。

各教室を回りましたが、母はどこにもいません。最後の教室に入ると、並べられた机の上に、顔や体を包帯で巻かれた人たちが丸くなって寝かされていました。それは、まるで包帯で固めた死体のようでした。

私は高林のおじいさんと一緒に母を捜しました。

「チイちゃん……」

私の前で、丸くなった"包帯"が私の名前を呼んだような気がしました。

「あんたの名前を呼んだのなら、お母さんだろう。金歯の確認をしてみよう」と高林のおじいさんに言われ、ぐるぐるに巻かれた包帯の口の部分をゆるめ、覗き込みました。

すると、金歯が見えたのです。

「お母さんに違いない！」

確かめようと、私はその人の丸くなって曲がっている足を伸ばしました。

すると、ふくらはぎから白色の看護婦の制服が覗いたのです。その制服の

205　竹岡智佐子

裾を引っ張ったとたん、ばらばらと何百匹といううじ虫がこぼれ落ちました。傷口から入り込み、骨まで食い込んでいたのでしょう。私は悔しくて涙が出そうでした。

　高林のおじいさんが、母に食べさせようと持ってきたトマトをポケットから出して、母の口元に持っていきました。六日間、何も食べていない母は、トマトを口に含むとゆっくりと口を動かしました。その夜は母のそばにいて、一晩中、母にたかるハエを一匹ずつ取りました。それは大きなハエで、母の肉に食らいついてなかなか取れないのです。指先に力を込めて引っ張り取ると、母の皮膚を口いっぱいにくわえたままでした。

　翌朝、高林のおじいさんが大八車(だいはちぐるま)を引いて迎えに来てくれたので、母を家に連れて帰りました。母の右半身は火傷で真っ黒に焦げていて、左半身はガラスの破片がいっぱい刺さっていました。近所のおばさんたちが外で待っていてくれ、母を大八車から家に運び入れてくれて部屋に寝かせると、

母の包帯をぐるぐる外し始めました。

そのとき、「ギャー」という叫び声が。

驚いて母の顔を見ると、右の眼球が飛び出しているのです。顔中にガラスが刺さり、鼻も折れて白い骨まで見えていました。

母は息をするのもやっとの状態だったのです。

戸坂国民学校（現・東区）には陸軍病院の薬学部が疎開していて、医者もいて薬もあると聞いたので、自転車に取り付けたリヤカーに母を乗せ、三時間かけて連れていきました。ところが、着いてみると「つい先ほど、医者も看護婦も血を吐いて死んでしまった」と兵隊に告げられたのです。途方にくれる私に、その人は「軍馬を診ている獣医が一人生き残っている」と教えてくれました。

私は母を助けたい一心で、診てもらうことにしたのです。教室の真ん中

竹岡智佐子

に筵を敷き、母はそこに寝かされました。
「今から手術をします」
獣医さんの声と同時に、母が動かないよう三人の兵隊が馬乗りになって押さえました。獣医がメスを持って母の枕元に立ちました。その姿を見るなり、母は「この手術は受けません！やめてください！」と言うのです。看護婦長を務めていた母は獣医を見て、どんな手術をされるかが分かったようです。獣医は母に「眼球の奥の方で両目の神経はつながっているので、このままにしておいたら、やがて左目も腐ってきて失明する。急いで右目をくり抜いて内部を消毒しなければ！」と言いました。麻酔薬も痛み止めもないのです。
そこで私は「今、飛び出した右目を取り除かなかったら両目とも見えなくなるのよ！」と必死に母を説得しました。そして手術が始まりました。
それ以上は見ていられなくて、私は廊下へ出ました。

ドア越しに聞こえる母の絶叫、呻き声、暴れる物音……。

母の右目は麻酔もなしに、抉り取られたのです。聞いていられないほど残酷(ざんこく)な悲鳴が、一時間余りも続いたでしょうか。私はその場にしゃがみ込み震えながら、「助けて、母を助けて！」とひたすら祈るしかありませんでした。内科医だったら、おそらく手術はしなかったでしょう。獣医だからこそできた手術だったと思います。

その後、死ぬまで目のことを話そうとしなかった母。母を思い出すたびに、原爆は体だけでなく心も深く傷つけ、誰にも癒やすことはできないのだ、とつくづく思うのです。

戦争が終わって一年後、大竹の引き揚げ援護局に勤めていた私は、同じ職場の竹岡と縁あって結婚しました。最初に生まれた子は弘訓(ひろのり)と名づけました。色の白いかわいい男の子でした。近所の人たちも来て、みんなで喜

び合いました。私たちにとって何よりの希望でした。

しかし、生後十八日目のこと。二時間前まで元気にお乳を飲んでいた赤ちゃんが急に苦しみ始め、亡くなったのです。赤ちゃんの胸からお腹にかけ、自分の腕と同じ、薄紫色の斑点がビッシリと出ていました。病名は「原爆症」と診断され、戦争が終わってからも、原爆はずっと私たちを苦しめました。

現在、広島平和記念資料館などで被爆体験を語っています。娘の真里子も広島市の「被爆体験伝承者」となり、母娘で証言活動に取り組んでいます。あの惨状を二度と繰り返してはなりません。核兵器を絶対に使用させてはなりません。私の命の続く限り、語り抜いてまいります。

# 戦争の報道に胸を痛め被爆体験を語ることを決意

## 土本幸枝さん

つちもと・ゆきえ　一九三五年（昭和十年）九月生まれ。八人きょうだいの末っ子として生まれる。国民学校の三年生（九歳）のとき、牛田山の中腹にあった寺（爆心地から三キロ）で被爆。逃れてきた怪我人の介抱をする。十九歳で結婚し、一男一女に恵まれたが、肺線維症や慢性肝炎などで苦しんだ。公園の清掃活動を続け、広島市から表彰される。七十代まで、被爆のことは話せなかった。広島市南区在住。八十一歳。

# 今さらあの苦しみを
# 掘り返して何になるのか

「思い出しとうない！」「言いとうない！」
あのことは「私とは無関係」と決め込み、忘れようと心の底に押し込んでいました。

だけど、ある日「このままでいいの？」「誰にも話さずお墓まで持っていく気？」と自身に語りかける声を聞いたような気がしたのです。

五十代半ば過ぎ、四人目の孫が生まれたあたりから、私の心の中に被爆についてのころのことでした。その男の子が生まれたあたりから、私の心の中に被爆について黙っていることへの「罪の意識」のようなものが、ちょっとだけ出てきました。

息子や娘にさえ話さなかった「あの日のできごと」を、孫ができたことで語り残しておきたくなったのです。

土本幸枝

ところが、いざ話そうと思うと、あのときの嫌な記憶が次々と溢れ出てきます。本で読んだり、誰かから聞いたことではない。実際に私が触って、臭いを嗅いで目の前で体験したことです。その嫌悪感に打ちのめされて「今さら、あのときのことを掘り返してどうするの。私でなくとも、すでに語り部をやっている人はいる。それで十分じゃない」と結局、語ることを拒否してしまうのでした。

そんな葛藤の最中に、ある子ども向け新聞から「被爆証言をお願いします」と声をかけられました。「どうしよう？」と躊躇していたとき、たまたま戦争のニュースがテレビで放送されていたのです。こんなばかげた戦争がまだ続いている。いい加減にしてほしい！怒りと悔しさで、胸がいっぱいに。被爆体験を語る決心がついた瞬間でした。

被爆から六十八年経って初めて、子ども向け新聞で被爆体験を語りました。それが私の平和活動の始まりです。

## 押し寄せる怪我人を大人と一緒に介抱

一九三五年（昭和十年）、雑魚場町（現・中区、現在の国泰寺高等学校の校庭の辺り）。爆心地から一・二キロ地点にあった真言宗のお寺「荒神社」に、八人きょうだいの末っ子として私は生まれました。六歳で母が亡くなり、それでも父や兄姉にかわいがられて、幸せに暮らしていました。

戦争が激しくなると次兄は広島の連隊に入り、その次の兄は満州（現・中国東北部）へ、国民学校高等科だった四兄は学徒動員で宇品の鋳物工場へ勤労奉仕に通うことになりました。

土本幸枝

戦況が厳しくなった一九四五年（昭和二十年）六月、「街の中心部に高射砲の砲台を造るため」と、お寺を中心とした近所の家々に軍から立ち退き命令が出ました。強制建物疎開です。米軍のB29爆撃機を下から撃ち落とすため、ということでした。

いや応なく、何の補償もないまま、私たちは家を捨てて他に移ることになったのです。幸い、わが家は牛田にもう一軒お寺を持っていたので、そちらに引っ越しました。

当時、私は国民学校初等科の三年生でした。

八月五日に平野町（現・中区）の姉の下宿に遊びに行き、夕方に牛田山の中腹にあるお寺に戻りました。翌六日の朝、空襲警報のサイレンが鳴り、私は畑の隅に掘った防空壕へ逃げ込みました。

まもなく、警報が解除になり壕を出たのですが、まだ爆撃機の音がする

のです。飛び去った爆撃機が戻ってきたのかと思いました。見上げると一瞬、爆撃機の尾翼から何かが落とされるのを目撃したような気がしました。とっさに目と耳を塞ぎイモ畑に伏せました。
「ピカッー」という光。
次の瞬間、強烈な爆風と轟音が押し寄せてきました。爆心地から三キロも離れていた畑の端の、タコツボ型防空壕の中にいた父は、衝撃で外へ吹き飛ばされたのです。父は二年後、胃潰瘍で亡くなりました。地面に這いつくばっていた私は無傷でした。

　西の方角の広島市内は真っ黒い煙がかかっていて何も見えません。広島の街は三日間燃え続けて灰になりました。
　原爆投下からどれくらい時間が経ったでしょう。被爆した人たちが戸坂（現・東区）から牛田山を越えて山陰にあるお寺に逃げてきたのです。大

217　土本幸枝

火傷を負って、全身の皮が剝け、真っ赤な肌の人や、顔全体が火傷の水膨れとなって目が腫れて見えなくなった人。体のいたるところから血を流している人、手の施しようのない人たちが次々と押し寄せてきました。

お寺の本堂は周囲の松林のおかげで爆風から守られましたが、隣の住居は爆風で傾いてしまい、畳もめくれ上がってぶよぶよしていました。

そんな状態でしたが、お寺の本堂も住居も開放して、逃げてきた人たちを受け入れました。私も大人たちに交じって被爆者の介抱に当たりましたが、薬なんてありませんから、キュウリの搾り汁やゴマ油を脱脂綿につけて火傷に塗ってあげるぐらいでした。

「火傷の人に水を飲ませると死ぬから絶対ダメ！」と言われているのですが、みんな水をほしがります。脱脂綿に水を含ませて、かさかさに乾いた唇に塗ってあげました。必死で介抱しても、体に紫斑が出た人は必ず、翌朝には亡くなっていました。

忘れられないのは、軍隊の班長さんに背負われてきた若い兵隊さんのことです。爆弾の破片が飛んだのか、頭の右側が十センチぐらい横に、ぱっくりと割れているのです。生きているのが不思議なほどでした。牛田山の山頂には高射砲陣地があって、そこの兵隊さんでした。お寺の中は避難してきた人でいっぱいで、横に寝かせる場所もないので、イモ畑にイモの葉を敷いて寝かせました。
「班長さん〜、班長さん〜」
と、うわ言を言っていた若い兵隊さんの体には、みるみるうじ虫が湧いてきました。箸（はし）でつまんで一匹ずつ取ってあげましたが、とうとう、その日の夕方に亡くなってしまいました。
そのころの私は、あまりの悲惨（ひさん）な状況に「怖（こわ）い」とか「かわいそう」という感情はなくなっていました。

ただ、目の前の人を何とかしてあげなくては、ということだけで動いていたような気がします。
けれど、怪我人は次々と亡くなっていきました。

## 次兄は行方不明
## その家族は三体の骨に

お寺を継ぐはずだった次兄は軍隊に取られ、当日、爆心地近くの部隊に入隊していて、そのまま行方不明に。結婚していて、家族も爆心地近くに住んでいました。後日、姉が見に行ったところ、家は焼け落ち、お風呂場の辺りに三体のお骨が重なっていたそうです。兄嫁とその母と生後八十日の姪のかよ子ちゃんでした。かよ子ちゃんは私にとって初めての姪で、何度か抱っこしてあげたことがありました。そのときの愛らしい顔を思い出

すと、かわいそうでなりませんでした。

また一歳年上の従姉は、爆心地から約二キロの三篠国民学校の朝礼で、グラウンドにいました。全員が大火傷、従姉も顔に大火傷を負いました。戦後、アメリカに招かれ、ケロイド治療を受けました。その話を聞いたときは「まるでモルモットのような扱いだな」と私は思いました。

その後、従姉は結婚し、二人の子どもの母となりましたが、足の踵が火傷で爛れたまま。他の部分はケロイドになって傷口は塞がったのですが、踵だけは七十年間、傷口が塞がらず、靴が履けないので冬でもスリッパを履いています。傷口を再生、修復させないという放射能の影響力は本当なのか、恐ろしいと思います。今でも足の皮膚が割れて赤い肉が剝きだしの状態で、いつも痛がっています。

学徒動員で宇品の工場に行っていた高等科二年の兄は、爆心地を避けて遠回りして帰ってきました。若いお母さんの背中で死んでいる赤ちゃんや、

221　土本幸枝

水を求めて川に飛び込み溺れる人などを目撃。川も道も死体だらけだったと話していました。

爆心地近くの日本銀行広島支店に勤めていた姉は出勤前で、まだ平野町の下宿にいたということです。爆風で崩れた屋根の下敷きになったのですが、たいした怪我ではありませんでした。

下宿が爆心地から一・八キロという近さだったので、一応、似島（現・南区）の救護所に運ばれたのですが、外傷がなかったので戻ってきました。お寺のお手伝いのおばさんは早朝、お使いに行って、広島駅近くの橋の上で被爆。全身、大火傷を負いました。

特に背中、両手、両腕がひどく、両手は握ったままのげんこつ状態。このまま放っておくと手が使えなくなるというので、毎日、両手の指を一本一本剥がすように開かせるのを私も手伝いました。かさぶたが破れ、手のひらは血膿でぐしゃぐしゃになりながらも、おばさんは痛みに耐えていま

した。

## 「元気な子ですよ」と言われ大声を上げて泣いた

　一九五四年(昭和二十九年)、私が十九歳になる数カ月前のことです。原爆で両手を火傷したお寺のお手伝いのおばさんが、木舞業(こまい)(土壁の中の基礎となる竹を編む職人)の男の人を連れて、牛田山のお寺にやって来ました。私のお見合いの相手でした。
　私より八歳年上だというその人を一目見て、真面目(まじめ)な人だと感じました。兄姉たちは「結婚なんてまだ早い!」と反対しましたが、両親はすでにおらず、仕事もない私は彼との結婚を選びました。
　長兄、長女はすでに結婚していました。日本銀行に勤めていた次女の姉

223　土本幸枝

は独身でしたので、妹の私が先に結婚したわけです。
夫は被爆していません。原爆投下の二十日後に滋賀の航空隊から復員してきたからです。夫との間では、私の被爆は話題にもなりませんでした。結婚してしばらくすると、突然、日本人通訳を連れた米兵が、わが家にやって来たのです。私はジープに乗せられて比治山にあったＡＢＣＣ（原爆傷害調査委員会）に連れていかれました。

「二十歳以下の女性全員が検査の対象になっている」との説明でした。私が妊娠していることを告げると、簡単な内診だけで帰されました。妊娠に気づいてから出産までの十カ月間は不安の毎日でした。母が生きていたら相談もできたでしょうが、被爆に無縁の夫にいまさら不安を起こさせるような相談はできません。

そのころ、盛んに「被爆者には奇形児が生まれる」「死産で真っ黒い子

が出てきた」などと噂がたっていました。「そんな子が生まれたらどうしよう？」と思うと、胸が潰れそうでした。

月満ちて、広島市の産院で出産。真っ先に気になったのは、子どもの性別より体の異常の有無です。まだ意識が朦朧としていましたが、医師にそのことを尋ねました。

「元気な男の子で、どこにも異常はありませんよ！」

その言葉でわれに帰り、私は思いっきり声を上げて泣きました。

私は一男一女に恵まれましたが、出産後は生理期間の体調不良で悩まされました。生理期間中は、のたうち回るぐらいの激痛に襲われ、痛みで畳の目が見えなくなるほど。下半身が痺れて、立つことすらできないのです。髪の毛が抜ける、歯茎から出血するといった原爆症特有の症状はなかったのですが、「被爆者認定」を受けました。「肺線維症」といって肺の中に繊維状のものができる病気になったからです。咳が止まらず、四六時中、息

土本幸枝

苦しくて、いつも肩で息をしているありさまでした。
　もう一つは慢性肝炎です。こちらは、地の底に引き込まれるようなだるさがあって、家事さえも長く続けていられないのです。
　その後、肺線維症はなくなりましたが、慢性肝炎は進行して、今は肝硬変に。八年前に胃がんの手術をしましたが治りが悪く、縫った跡がいまだに塞がらず、爛れているのです。そのため湯船に浸かることも、粗いタオルを使うこともできません。被爆の影響は恐ろしいと実感しています。
　そんななか、命あることに感謝し、少しでも社会のため、皆さんのためになれば、と公園の清掃活動を始めました。もう十五年以上、続けており、広島市から二度、表彰していただきました。
　二〇一六年（平成二十八年）五月二十七日、オバマ米大統領が広島を訪問し、歴史的第一歩が印されました。勇気ある決断に感動しました。

その翌日、私は息子や孫とともに平和記念公園を訪れました。三世代で訪れるのは初めてのことです。
「人類のために核兵器のない世界を追求する」とのオバマ大統領の言葉通り、世界中で核兵器をなくす努力がなされることを、願わずにはいられません。

# 「生き残ったことに感謝しようね」
# 母の言葉を胸に平和活動を持続

## 佐藤廣枝 さん

さとう・ひろえ　一九三八年（昭和十三年）七月生まれ。国民学校初等科一年（七歳）のとき、原爆投下二日後、疎開先から母とともに広島市に入り入市被爆。高等科六年の兄を亡くす。初等科六年のときから、あらゆる仕事に就き、必死で家族の生活を守ってきた。四十八歳のときに平和運動に参加。一九九一年（平成三年）、「広島市民平和の集い」を財団法人広島平和文化センターより継承し、現在に至る。二〇〇五年（平成十七年）に「NPO法人HPS国際ボランティア」を設立。「平和を創り上げる」ことを目指して活動を続けている。広島市西区在住。七十八歳。

# 文章を書くためにパソコンを覚え
# 被爆体験を綴った本を出版

二〇〇八年（平成二十年）九月、私はピースボートによる「第一回ヒバクシャ地球一周証言の航海（通称・おりづるプロジェクト）」に参加しました。これは広島と長崎から集まった被爆者が船舶で世界を回り、寄港地で被爆体験を語り、核廃絶を訴えるという意義深いプロジェクトです。約四カ月間の航海ではさまざまな国の人と交流し、戦争の恐ろしさに共感し合ったり、意見を交換したりすることができ、私自身、多くのことを学びました。

なかでも、絵本作家の森本順子さんとの出会いは、私の後の人生を変えたと言っていいほど大きなことでした。森本さんは十三歳のとき広島で被爆。その後、オーストラリアに渡り、自らが広島で体験したことをテーマにした絵本『わたしのヒロシマ』を出版。現在は絵本作家として、また

アーティストとして活躍されています。彼女は学徒動員で亡くなった私の兄と同い年ということもあり、お会いしたときとても親近感を覚えました。

いろいろお話しするなか、森本さんは「話した言葉はその場で消えてしまうけれど文字は残る。あなたが思ったことは、何でも書き留めておきなさい」と言われました。私はそれまで平和活動には、さまざまかかわってきていましたが、小学校にも満足に通えず、勉強もしていないので「読み書き」はコンプレックスを通り越して「トラウマ」でした。ミミズの這ったような字しか書けないし、漢字も知らないのです。

「私は話すだけです」と言ったところ、彼女は「漢字なんか知らなくたって、文字がへたでも、今はパソコンがあるから大丈夫。パソコンを覚えなさい」と言うのです。それでは、とパソコンを始めました。

パソコンで文章を書くようになって、あらためて感じたことは「一人の話をみんなで聞くのもいいけれど、話をしてくれる人を連れてこなくても、

『本』なら、一度に何人もの意見を知ることができる」ということでした。

早速、本を作りました。そして、識者から子どもたちまで多くの人たちの意見を載せました。二〇一三年（平成二十五年）に出版した私の最初の本、『ピカドン　きのこ雲の下で見つけた宝物』です。広島の小・中学校二百六校に配布しました。この本で使った紙は世界中から広島平和記念公園に贈られてくる折り鶴を再生したものです。

二〇一五年（平成二十七年）に出版した『ヒロシマ　ここより永遠に』も、折り鶴の再生紙で作成しました。

私が平和運動にかかわって四年後には、「広島市民の平和の集い」の代表を引き受けることになったのです。その後、「平和公園清掃ボランティア」を立ち上げ、今も続けています。

また、毎年、元日に平和公園に献花台を設け、千人の人が一輪ずつ献花

佐藤廣枝

し、慰霊する「千人一輪献花運動」や「慰霊お餅つき大会」などを開始。

二〇一六年(平成二十八年)は「ヒバクシャによるファッションショー」「子どもたちによる平和集会」などを企画しました。

平和運動は「風化」との闘いです。そのために「ヒロシマの(平和運動の)先人たち」の思いをどう後世に伝えようかと、常に「斬新な企画と執念の持続」が大切と思って取り組んでおります。

## 初めて会った親戚の家にたった一人で二カ月疎開

戦時中、私の父は爆心地から八百メートルの三川町(現・中区、現在の福屋デパートの裏辺り)で、「長木屋」という旅館を営んでいました。

父の義兄(父の姉の夫)が軍隊の上官だったので、当時、この旅館は軍隊

の上官専用になっていました。また、宇品港（現・広島港）から戦地に送られる兵隊たちの宿舎でもありました。家族のほかに、旅館を手伝ってくれる料理人のおばさんや、お膳を運ぶ仲居さん、いつも忙しそうに働いている番頭さんなどもいました。

兄弟は四人で、六歳年上の広島市商・造船工業学校（現・広島市立広島商業高等学校）一年の兄、国民学校一年生になったばかりの私、下に五歳の弟と三歳の妹がいました。当時の一番の思い出は、私と弟、妹の三人が一緒に「七五三」のお祝いをしてもらったことです。私はおかっぱ頭にかわいいリボンをつけ、振り袖を着ました。三人は母に連れられて近くの鶴羽根神社へお参りに。私はちょっぴり澄まし顔、弟と妹は大はしゃぎでした。

一九四五年（昭和二十年）四月、竹屋国民学校（現・中区）に入学した私は、入学時の身体検査をしたきりで広島を離れることになりました。戦火が激

しくなっていたので、入学したときから三年生以上の上級生は引率の先生と一緒に田舎のお寺に「集団疎開」していて、学校にはいませんでした。一、二年生の低学年は、まだ団体行動の「集団疎開」ができないので、田舎に知り合いのある子どもだけが「縁故疎開」をしていました。
　爆心地から二十八キロ離れた浅原（現・廿日市市）の祖父のところに疎開することになりました。六月のことでした。弟や妹は幼な過ぎて縁故疎開もできません。みんなにチヤホヤされ、わがままいっぱいに育った私は、一人で行く「縁故疎開」というものが不安でたまりませんでした。

　母に手を引かれて、しぶしぶ浅原の祖父のところに行きましたが、門の前で、私は母の着物の裾をギュッとつかんで離しませんでした。知らないところで一人ぼっちになるのが怖かったのです。「お前も辛いだろうけど、母さんはもっと辛いの。でも、こうしなければ生きていけないのよ」と言

う母の涙を見て、私はやっと手を離したのでした。
　浅原では、私は祖父の家族と離れた玄関脇の二畳間が与えられました。文机を一つ置いただけの部屋です。初めて一人になり、その部屋で寝た夜はたくさんのカエルの声が怖くて、一晩中、泣いていました。母は浅原に二、三日一緒にいてくれ、転校先の浅原国民学校にも連れて行ってくれました。
　国民学校の正門前で、母は私を見つめ「この門をくぐって学校に入ったら、お前はもう小学生。これからはお父さんやお母さんの代わりを学校の先生がしてくださる。だから、先生のお話は片方の耳だけで聞いてはダメ。両方の耳で聞くと心にもう一つの耳ができる。心の耳で聞いたことは忘れないよ」と語りました。
　そのまま私は浅原に残り、二カ月が経ちました。

# 「絶対生きている」と叫びながら兄を搜す母

八月五日は日曜日でしたが、勤労奉仕で学校から帰ると、何と両親と弟、妹が部屋にいたのです。

兄は造船工業学校の生徒になったばかりで、留守番を買って出たそうです。久しぶりに休みの取れた父が、墓参りを兼ねて私の様子を見に来たのです。弟と相撲をしたり、妹を乗せてお馬さんごっこをしたり、久しぶりの家族水入らずに、三川町のわが家に帰ったような気持ちになりました。

翌六日朝、起きると父はもういませんでしたが、母と弟と妹は「もう一日いてくれる」というので、満ち足りた気持ちで学校に行きました。

朝礼が始まるので、グラウンドに整列していると、晴天の空が「ピカッ」と光りました。先生が大声で「伏せ！」と怒鳴（どな）ると、児童全員が日ごろか

ら訓練していた通り、耳を親指で残り四本の指で目を塞いで、素早くその場に腹ばいになりました。続いて「防空壕に退避！」と号令がかかり、防空壕へ走りました。

しばらくして教室に戻ると、集落ごとに整列して、上級生を先頭に集団下校することになりました。家に帰ると、母は落ち着きなく心配そうな様子。役場から「広島は特殊爆弾で大変なことになった」と連絡があったのです。母は、朝早く帰った父、家に残った兄、「長木屋」の従業員の人たちと連絡がとれず、オロオロするばかり。夕方、父が浅原に戻ってきました。広島に入る途中で「ピカッ」という光と「ドーン」という轟音を聞き、一瞬、空が真っ暗になったと話していました。

父が広島に着いたとき、街は火の海で怪我人や火傷の人たちが逃げまどっていて、着ていた衣類が焼けてみんな全裸に近かったそうです。父は

佐藤廣枝

己斐まで行くと兵隊に止められ、街には入れず、再び浅原に戻ってきたのでした。

翌日、たくさんのおにぎりを作り、裏の竹林から集めたタケノコの皮で包んで、私たちは広島に向かうトラックに乗せてもらいました。トラックの荷台には大勢の人が乗っていました。

兄や旅館で働いていた人たちを捜しに、広島の街に入りました。といっても市内中心部に入れたのは父だけ。私たちは己斐駅近くの草津（現・西区）というところで待っていました。

翌八日、やっと市内に入ることができた私の目に映ったのは、見渡す限りの焼け野原でした。軍用トラックが死体を次々と集めていました。ゲートルを巻いた足首が一本転がっていたのが、今でも鮮明に目に焼きついています。

汗だくになって歩いて行くと、風に飛ばされた火の粉が私の胸に飛び込

んできました。「ジュッ」と音を立てて肌にくっ付き、いくら手で払っても火の粉は肌に食い込んで取れません。泣き叫ぶ私に、母が水筒の水を口に含みプッと吹きかけ、被っていた手拭いを裂いて水に浸し、火傷の傷口に当ててくれました。

そのまま、また兄の行方を捜しに歩きました。私の火傷より、母の頭の中は兄のことでいっぱいなのです。母は「お兄ちゃんは絶対生きている。怪我で口が利けないだけ。母さんの声は聞こえてるはず。ヒデユキ！」と、なかば狂人のようになって叫んでいました。

私の胸の火傷はどんどん痛くなり、とうとう我慢できず泣きだしてしまいました。母が胸の手拭いを取ると火傷の傷口は肋骨が見えるほど深く化膿していました。

母はようやく私の傷のひどさに気づいて「ごめんね！ごめんね！」と泣き出しました。その後は母が毎日、ドクダミ草をすり潰して胸に貼って

くれましたが、火傷の跡は、塞がってケロイドになるまで何カ月もかかりました。

兄を捜しに材木町(現・中区、今の平和記念公園の辺り)まで来ました。父が人づてに、兄たち造船工業学校の生徒が当日、ここに「建物疎開の作業」で来ていたと聞いたからです。行ってみると、辺りに散乱している人骨を発見。百九十五人の学生が、一度に亡くなった場所でした。大きな大人の骨の他に、たくさんの小さな骨も散らばっていました。先生に引率された生徒たちかもしれません。

その骨を見て、初めて母が「お兄ちゃんはもう亡くなったんだね」とぽつり。そして私を抱きしめました。被っていた手拭いを広げると、母は落ちていた人骨を拾って包みました。みんながその場所で手を合わせました。

「廣枝、私たちは生き残った。そのことに感謝しようね。そして生きたく

とも生きることができなかったお兄ちゃんの分まで頑張ろうね。悲しみも苦しみも涙もこの太田川に流していこう。いつまでも心に残すと不平不満になるからね」

母は自身に言い聞かせるように話しました。それ以後、母は愚痴（ぐち）や不満をこぼしたことは一度もありませんでした。

## 家族を守るため学校も行かずガムシャラに働いた

その後、再び親類の家の離れに身を寄せました。農家の生活が始まりました。翌年には、妹が生まれました。妹の世話をしたりオシメを洗ったり、長女の私は忙しい日々を過ごしました。五年生になったころ、大きな台風（キジア台風）に襲われ、鳥小屋も便所もみんな流され、家は柱と屋根だけ

になってしまいました。従妹たちが手伝ってくれた田んぼも、収穫前の稲が泥で埋まり、刈り入れはできなかったのです。
仕方がないので、母と二人で重い炭や薪を背負い、山の斜面を片足ずつ慎重に下りて、麓の村に売りに行ったこともありました。必死になるといろんな知恵が湧くものです。台風の後の復興事業で砂や砕石が必要になり「バケツ一杯、いくら」で、買ってくれることが分かったので、私は砂や砕石を集めてお金に換えたりもしました。
そのころ、父は母の実家のある北海道に行き、ジャガイモやトウモロコシなどの食料調達に駆けずり回っていて、私たちのところにはいませんでした。

私たちは爆心地から遠く離れた浅原にいたので直接の被爆はなかったのですが、二日後に兄を捜しに市内に入ったので、入市被爆。弟は六十五歳

で、がんで亡くなりました。母も、被爆直後から体を悪くして、次第に寝ていることが多くなっていました。

田んぼや畑の農作業から家事まで、私一人の仕事となりました。学校には行かず、昼は台風で荒らされた田んぼの泥を一輪車で運び出し、夜は藁で草履を編みました。ところが、その翌年も台風（ルース台風）がやって来たのです。

もう農業は続けられないと思い、病気の母は市民病院に入院。私たち子ども四人だけの生活が始まったのです。私は長女として、弟や妹を励ましながら働きました。砂浜を掘ってシジミをバケツ一杯採り、飯場に持っていって買ってもらったり、消防署の建て替え工事現場を見つけ、年齢を偽って作業員として働いたりしました。

丸太を一本組んだだけの不安定な足場に上り、丸太にしがみついたまま

腰に下げたバケツの中のセメントを壁の穴に詰め、ゴム手袋で塗り込む「豆塗り作業」は、下を見ると足がすくみ、上を見ると雲が流れるので自分が揺れているように感じて目が回ります。怖いので、壁だけを見続けて仕事をしました。大変な仕事だけに、手間賃は一日二百五十円と破格でした。米一升が八十円の時代です。家族のために、私は二カ所の現場で必死に働きました。

年齢は中学生でしたが、私は学校どころではなかったのです。働かなければ弟妹全員が餓死してしまいます。ありとあらゆる仕事をしました。

その後、見習い看護婦、バスの車掌などを勤めたこともありましたが、中学校すら満足に出ていない私は、望むような仕事に就くことはできませんでした。

結局、自転車に塩鯖を積んで行商に行き、生計を立てたのです。十九歳のときには「糞尿汲み取り」の仕事もしました。

このように、私はガムシャラに働いてきました。広島の裕福な旅館の娘だった私の人生は、たった一発の原爆でメチャクチャにされたのです。

母が亡くなる前に言った「世の中にはお金よりも大切なものがある。この広島に根を張り、欲を捨て、郷土を愛し、人を愛して生きんさい」との言葉がきっかけで、私は平和活動にかかわるようになりました。私が四十八歳のときでした。

長い年月には、転んだり傷ついたりしたこともありましたが、多くの方に支えられ、今日まで来ることができました。

皆さんに感謝しつつ、さらに努力を続けていきたいと思っています。

# 広島を訪れる外国人に英語で被爆体験を伝える

## 小倉桂子 さん

おぐら・けいこ　一九三七年(昭和十二年)八月生まれ。八歳のとき、爆心地から二・四キロの牛田町の自宅近くで被爆した。夫(故・小倉馨さん)は広島平和記念資料館館長を務め、ヒロシマを世界につなぐために尽力した。その遺志を継ぎ、被爆体験の継承に取り組む。一九八四年(昭和五十九年)、「平和のためのヒロシマ通訳者グループ(HIP)」を設立。二〇〇五年(平成十七年)に「広島市長賞」、二〇一三年(平成二十五年)にヒロシマピースセンターより「谷本清平和賞」を受賞。広島市中区在住。七十九歳。

## 「空腹」がきっかけで英語を学び始める

私は被爆者の体験を英語で紹介することや、世界の被爆に関する翻訳などを三十年以上続けてきました。これからも、立ち止まることなく続けていきたいと思っています。「核兵器を使うと、こんなに恐ろしいことになりますよ」と語ることで、世界平和に貢献できると信じているからです。

ところで、私が英語を勉強しようと思ったのは、それほど高尚な理由からではありません。

戦後の食料難時代、「ララ物資」といってアメリカからの救援物資（終戦の翌年設置された日本向け援助物資）が配られたことがありました。父が大きな缶詰を抱えて帰ってくると、お腹を空かした子どもたちは、お腹がいっぱいになるものを想像。生唾を飲み込んで、缶切りで蓋を開ける父の手元を

小倉桂子

じっと見つめました。ところが、缶詰の中身は、なみなみと入ったシロップに浮かぶ赤いサクランボだったのです。ラベルに書かれた「CHERRY（チェリー）」という英語を父は理解できなかったのでした。
空腹を抑えた私は、腹立たしさに震えながら「英語を覚えよう!」と深く、強く決意したのです。それで、子どものころから英語に興味を持ち「アルファベットの歌」をいつも口ずさみ、他人にも「私は英語が得意」と宣言していたほどです。

## 家の中に充満していた血膿と汚物の臭い

原爆投下の一年前に、爆心地近くにあったわが家は二・四キロ離れた牛田町（現・東区）に移転していました。私は六人兄弟の次女で、女学校へ

通っていた長女、旧制中学の長男、国民学校五年生の次兄、そして国民学校二年生の私、下に四歳の弟と二歳の妹がいました。

あの日、長兄は学徒動員で広島駅北側にある東練兵場のイモ畑に勤労奉仕に行っており、次兄は島根県との県境の寺に学童疎開していました。朝、父は私に「何だか嫌な予感がする。きょうは学校を休め！」と言いました。

何事にも几帳面な父は、外出時のゲートル（脚絆）もきちんと巻かれていなければ気が済まないほどでしたが、その日に限って、何度巻き直してもゲートルをちゃんと巻けず、「嫌な予感」を覚えていたそうです。そのおかげで父が街中に出るのが遅れたのです。

姉は布団部屋にいて、私はつまらないので家の北側の道路で一人で遊んでいました。そのとき、突然、目もくらむような閃光に包まれ、次の瞬間、爆風の凄い力で地面に叩きつけられ気を失いました。意識を取り戻すと、辺りは真っ暗で物音一つしません。

249　小倉桂子

意識を失っていたので、「長い時間経って、夜になったのか」と思ったのですが、そうではなく周囲が暗かったのでした。暗闇の中でやっとのことと、かすかに弟の泣き声が……。「あっちが家だ」と私はやっとのことで歩きだしました。

近所の藁葺きの屋根が勢いよく燃え上がっていました。わが家は、父の自慢の総ガラス張りの屋敷だったのですが、夏なので、家中のガラス戸を開けっぱなしにしていたのです。閉め切っていたら家族は大怪我をしていたと思います。それでも、片側に寄せたガラス戸はすべて跡形もなく吹き飛んで、家の中の壁、天井、家具などにビッシリと破片が突き刺さっていました。

硬い柱やコンクリートにまで埋め込んだように刺さっているのです。一体、どれほど強い爆風だったのでしょうか。ガラスの暴風のなか、廊下にいた父は、目の前の大きな松の木に助けられ、どこにも怪我はありません

でした。爆心地に向いていた幹の表面は焼け焦げていました。姉も布団部屋で布団に埋もれていて無事。母も奥の間にいて大事に至りませんでしたが、弟は飛んできた屋根瓦で頭に怪我をしており、妹もガラスの破片で手から血を流していました。

どうすることもできないまま、私たちは茫然としていました。しばらくして、私は近所の様子を見るために外に出ると、黒い雨が降ってきました。少しねっとりした雨でした。そのうちに、東練兵場のイモ畑に行っていた長兄が顔や手に火傷を負いながら、山越えして戻ってきました。
「近所に爆弾が落とされた！」と私が言うと、兄は「ここを狙ったんじゃない。広島中が火の海だ！」と逃げてくる途中で見てきた光景を語りました。山越えの途中で見た大きな雲はアイスクリームを何層も重ねたような雲で、最上部がピンク色をしていたそうです。

半壊した私の家はたちまち負傷した親類、近所の人、知人で溢れ返りました。姉は叔父の背中に刺さったガラスの破片を、泣きながら抜いていました。家の中は血膿、焦げた頭髪、汚物の臭いが充満しています。

てっきり、近所に爆弾が落とされたのだと思っていた私は、兄の話を聞いて、市内を一望できる早稲田神社の高台に行ってみようと、外に出ました。

早稲田神社は東側と西側の坂の上に石段があり、その上に社務所がありました。そこが臨時の救護所に指定されていました。

石段のところまで来ると、東西の坂の下からモゾモゾと蠢く黒い群衆が上がってくるのが見えます。火傷を負って逃げてくる人たちでした。頭髪は焼け焦げ、煤けて黒く汚れた顔は腫れ上がり、瞼は垂れ下がり唇はめくれ上がっています。火傷をした人たちの皮膚は剝けて、指先から垂れ下がっているのです。

幽霊のような、無言の群衆の大部分は軍人と学生でした。その群れは次第に大きくなり、まるでお祭りの人出のように道幅いっぱいに溢れはじめました。中には、傷ついた上官を乗せるためなのか、馬の手綱を引いている人もいました。

逃げてきた学生たちや軍人は坂の上まで来ると、その先の神社の石段を上がる力がないのか、次々とその場にうずくまったり、石段に横になったりと倒れ込み、たちまちもの凄い人数になって周りを埋め尽くしました。

不思議なことに、誰も声を出しません。おびただしい人々が無言で倒れ込む姿は異様でした。見ると、そこには医者らしい人はおらず、石段の上にはバケツを持った軍人が一人で重症者に刷毛でチンク油のようなものを塗っているだけでした。

小倉桂子

## 夢中で水を与えた人が目の前で死んだ

　私には、生涯、忘れられないことがあります。道を歩いているとき、足首を突然、誰かにつかまれたのです。見ると、黒く煤けて血まみれになった人でした。その人は、「水、水をください」と力ない声で必死に頼むのです。その声を聞いて、今まで黙っていた人たちも口々に「水、水、水を」と合唱のように呟きだしたのです。

　私は夢中で走って家に戻り、井戸水をやかんに汲んで、その人たちのところに運びました。私がやかんを持っていくと、われ先にと手を伸ばしてやかんから水を飲みました。嬉しそうに喉を鳴らして飲む人たち。ところが、水を一口飲むやいなや、胃の中のものを「グワッ」と吐き出し、断末魔の叫び声を上げた瞬間、ガクッと首を垂れて絶命した人がいたのです。

私は怖くなってやかんを放り出し、家に逃げ帰りました。後悔と同時に、「このことだけは誰にも話すまい」と心に誓ったのです。
　夜になって父が戻ってくると、「火傷の重症者に水をあげたら死ぬことは分かっているな。お前たちはそんなことはしてないだろうな」と言います。
「はい！」と、とっさに嘘をついたものの、震えるような思いでした。幼い私はそんなことになるなんて知らなかったのです。父が亡くなるまで、家族の誰にもそのときのことが話せず、長い間、悪夢に悩まされました。
　逃げてきた人がわが家に飛び込んできたこともありました。たまたまその場にいた姉に「便所を貸してください！」と言って、そのまま便所に駆け込んだそうです。ザンバラ髪で、頭から流れた血で髪がべっとりと濡れ、目も腫れあがっているその人の姿に、姉は思わず幽霊を見たと思い、

小倉桂子

気を失いかけたそうです。それからしばらくの間、姉は家の便所が使えなかったのです。

父は痩せていて、兵隊検査は「丙種」。戦地に行かない代わりに、町内のまとめ役のようなことをやっていました。わが家には、当時では珍しく自転車と電話があったので、役場から電話で「防火訓練の連絡」が入ると、父は自転車にまたがって町内を連絡して回っていました。原爆投下後も、父は町内の警防団の責任者として、近くの牛田公園で死体を荼毘に付す任務に当たっていました。

「子どもは決して牛田公園に近づいてはいけない」と言われていました。何も話したがらない父に「どうやって死体を焼くの」と私は強引に尋ねました。

公園に穴を掘り、二人がかりで死体を穴に入れ、比較的若い父がいつも

重い頭の方を持ち、年上の人に足の方を持ってもらったそうです。頭を持つと嫌でも死体の顔が目に入ります。カッと見開いたままの死者の目は不気味（きみ）で、なるべく見ないようにしていたと、父は辛（つら）そうに話しました。

一つの穴に十人ぐらいずつ入れて、重油をかけて焼き、焼けた骨は集めてまとめるのです。一言で「死体」といっても遺族にとっては「肉親」です。後で遺族の方から私が聞いた話では、火をかける直前に、重なった死体の中から娘の衣類の一片を奇跡（きせき）的に見つけ出した母親が「娘です！」と声を上げ、周囲の行方不明の子を持つ親から「親孝行な娘さんね。良かったわね」と、うらやましがられたこともあったそうです。

子どもの「遺骨がない」というのは、親にとって耐えられない悲しみです。遺骨が見つからなくても、わが子が建物疎開に行っていて、「死んだ場所」が分かるだけでも幸運な方なのです。少しは気持ちが落ち着きます。

行方不明だと、当初は「どこかで生きているはず」と希望を持つのですが、死亡届も出さずに待っている間に何十年も経ち、結局、割り切れない気持ちのまま諦めることになってしまうのです。

写真で見る原爆投下後の広島の街は、瓦礫だらけで廃墟のようにひっそりと映っていますが、翌日、高台の早稲田神社から見た街は、あちこちから死体を焼く煙が立ち上って、異様な光景でした。特に川沿い、浜辺は何本もの煙が狼煙のようになっていました。夏の盛りですから死体の傷みも早く、溶けてうじ虫が湧くので競うように焼いていました。父は、公園の臨時火葬場で約七百人の遺体を焼いた、と言っていました。

街全体が瓦礫の山になっているので死体を焼く廃材はいくらでもありそうですが、それ以上に荼毘に付す人々が多かったので、後に廃材が不足して困ったようです。ある人はお母さんを荼毘に付そうと、山に行って枯れ木や小枝を集めて焼くのですが、とても枝が足りないので、お母さんの遺

体を生焼けにしたまま、何度も山に枯れ枝を集めに行ったと泣きながら語っていました。

## 夫の遺志を継いで被爆問題に取り組む

昨年、被爆七十年にして初めて兄弟が大阪のホテルに集まり、夜を徹して「あの日」のことを話し合いました。それまでは、法事などで親類が集まることがあっても誰も「あの日」のことは口にしません。それどころか話題が「被爆」になると話を逸らせたり、席を立ったり。というのも、それぞれの伴侶や家族にもまた、多くの悲劇があるので迂闊なことを口に出せないのです。

被爆者の沈黙には、思い出すのが辛いだけではなく、さまざまな事情が

あるのです。

昨年は、すでに両親も亡くなっているし、思い切って戦後に生まれた弟も含め「兄弟七人だけで話そう」ということになったのでした。弟や妹たちはそれほど記憶がないようでしたが、姉や兄たちは堰を切ったように、凄い勢いで話し出しました。七十年間封印してきたものを解き放すかのように。

最後には、姉と兄が「確かにこうだった」「いや、そんなはずはない！」などと言い合いを始めるほどでした。爆心地から二・四キロとはいえ、屋外にいた私が原爆病にもならず済んだのは、遊んでいた場所が家の大きな土蔵の陰だったのが幸いしたのでしょう。

私が「原爆」と本格的に向き合うことになったのは、一九七九年（昭和五十四年）、広島平和記念資料館の館長であった夫が、突然亡くなってから

です。私は四十二歳でした。私たち夫婦の友人で、ホロコーストの大量虐殺を生き抜いた作家・ジャーナリストのロベルト・ユンク氏は、広島の「千羽鶴を折り続けた被爆少女・佐々木禎子さん」を世界に紹介したことでも有名です。

彼は、夫を亡くし無気力になっていた私に連絡をくれました。そして、「核問題の取材で日本に行くので通訳をしてほしい」と言ったのです。私は大学の英文科は卒業したけれど、留学経験があるわけでもなく、まして専門用語が必要な通訳などできないと断りました。

ところが、「肉親の死という悲しみを知り、原爆の恐ろしさを知っているあなたこそが適任なのです」と言われ、半ば強引にユンク氏の通訳をさせられたのです。必死で勉強しました。その経験のなかで、本気で夫の遺志を継いで「原爆・核問題」に取り組もうと私は決意したのです。

小倉桂子

そして、海外から広島を訪れる平和運動家、マスコミ、作家、アーティスト、学者などの通訳やコーディネートを始めました。

その後、ドイツ・ニュルンベルクでの「反核模擬法廷」、ニューヨークでの「第一回核被害者世界大会」に出席し、アメリカ各地の核被害者と交流したり、「世界の首脳・大統領経験者によるOBサミット」では、英語で被爆証言をしたり……。思い出深い仕事は数々あります。

また、ヒロシマの実情を伝える和英対訳「ヒロシマ辞典」（一九八五年〈昭和六十年〉刊）を出版しました。

一九八四年（昭和五十九年）には、広島を訪れる外国人のために、英語で平和記念公園や平和記念資料館を案内できるボランティアガイドを育てようと、「平和のためのヒロシマ通訳者グループ（HIP）」を設立。メンバーとともに通訳やガイドの活動を続けながら、英語で自分自身の被爆体験も

伝えています。
　受け止め方や感じ方は人によってさまざまなので、相手によって話し方を変えるという努力をずっと続けてきました。
　いつも、もっと人々の心に届く方法はないだろうかと日々悩みながら、核兵器の恐ろしさと生命の尊さを多くの人に伝えるために、平和への歩みを決して止めてはいけないと心に決めているのです。

小倉桂子

## むすびにかえて

かねてから池田大作SGI(創価学会インタナショナル)会長は、各国首脳や市民社会の代表が被爆地を訪れ、核廃絶の誓いを新たにすることを提言してきました。

被爆七十一年となる二〇一六年(平成二十八年)、現職の米国大統領として初めてオバマ大統領が広島を訪問。原爆死没者慰霊碑に献花し、核兵器のない世界を追求するスピーチを行いました。被爆者と肩を抱き合う姿が目に焼き付いています。オバマ大統領が「あの日、きのこ雲の下で何が起

きたか」を見て感じたように、一人でも多くの指導者が、この地を訪れることを切に願わずにはいられません。

米シートンホール大学のアンドレア・バルトリ博士は「私たちが悲劇に深く学び、平和と反核の行動を起こせば、その機会を与えてくれた犠牲者の存在に新たな意味が加わる」と語っています。

今、核実験の暗闇が世界を覆うなかで、被爆者が体験した「二度と惨禍を繰り返させてはならない」との叫びこそ、核時代を終わらせ永遠の平和へ向かう行動の原点ではないでしょうか。

広島県創価学会では、一昨年、被爆証言集『男たちのヒロシマ——ついに沈黙は破られた』を広島平和委員会が編纂し、被爆七十年にあたる昨年には、『家族から見た「8・6」』——語り継ぎたい10の証言』を広島青年

平和委員会が編纂しました。そしてこのたび、広島女性平和委員会として被爆証言集『女性たちのヒロシマ──笑顔かがやく未来へ』を刊行することとなりました。

戦争の惨禍でいつも苦しんできたのは女性でした。手にするはずであった幸せも夢も奪い去っていった原爆。家族を失い、自らも火傷に苦しみ、原爆症の不安に襲われ、それでも負けずに生き抜いてきた女性たちの真実の生命の輝きを、このように綴り残せたことは〝ヒロシマの心〟を永遠に語り継ぐうえで計り知れない意義があると確信します。

広島女性平和委員会は一九八二年（昭和五十七年）、創価学会婦人平和委員会による『ヒロシマの心──母の祈り』の出版にあたり、広島編纂グループとして発足しました。その後、名称を広島婦人平和委員会とし、五年後にはジュニア版『ヒロシマ──平和への出発』を編みました。一九九

七年(平成九年)に広島国際会議場で開催した平和主張の集い「ウィメンズプラザ」では、三万四千通を超える応募原稿の中から選ばれた五人の代表による体験主張を通し、平和委員会の活動を広く知っていただくことができました。

二〇〇二年(平成十四年)、名称を現在の広島女性平和委員会と改め、福山女性平和委員会も発足し、平和主張大会や講演会の開催など地道な活動を続けてきました。なかでも、広島での「被爆体験を聞く会」は二〇〇四年(平成十六年)から毎年開催し、本年で十三回目。また、福山女性平和委員会主催の「福山空襲・被爆体験を聞く会」も五回目の開催となりました。体験を直接聞くことは「こんな悲しみを誰にも味わわせてはならない」との、高齢になられた被爆者の思いを引き継ぐ貴重な機会となっています。

池田SGI会長は綴りました。

戦争ほど残酷（ざんこく）なものはない。
戦争ほど悲惨（ひさん）なものはない。

どれほど母たちの涙が流されてきたことか。
どれほど若人（わこうど）の青春（せいしゅん）が引き裂（さ）かれてきたことか。
どれほど子どもたちの笑い声が押しつぶされてきたことか。
歴史を変えよ！　時代を動かせ！　世界を結べ！

　　　（「平和を！　平和を！　そこに幸福が生まれる」詩集『勝利の舞』から）

　母と子、女性たちが心の底から幸せを嚙（か）みしめる笑顔輝く未来を目指（め　ざ）し、「今いるこの場所」から平和のスクラムを広げてまいります。

最後に、本書の出版にあたりご尽力いただいた第三文明社をはじめ、ご協力いただいた皆さま方に深く感謝申し上げます。

二〇一六年十月　「10・27広島県婦人部の日」を記念して

創価学会広島婦人部長　栗原　妙子

else should ever suffer what we did."

President Ikeda of Soka Gakkai International wrote the following poem, which was published in Peace! Peace! That's where happiness is born:

> Nothing is as cruel as war.
> Nothing is as tragic as war.
> How many tears have mothers cried?
> How many of our youth have been cut down in their spring?
> How many children have had their laughter crushed?
> Change history! Move the times! Bring the world together!

Expanding our circle of peace from "where we are now," our goal is a brilliant, smiling future where mothers and children, and all women will feel genuine happiness reaching down to the bottoms of their hearts.

In closing, we express our deep gratitude to the editors at Daisanbunmei-sha and the many others whose cooperation made this book a reality.

To commemorate October 27, Hiroshima Prefecture Women's Division Day

Taeko Kurihara
Director
Soka Gakkai Hiroshima Women's Division

October 2016

Accounts to Pass Forward. This time the Hiroshima Women's Peace Committee published a collection of accounts obtained from women entitled Hiroshima, August 6, 1945 – For a Brilliant, Smiling Future.

Women suffer terribly from the calamity of war. The atomic bomb stole the dreams and happiness they might have had. They lost family members, suffered with burns and scars, were tormented by the fear of A-bomb disease, and yet, they lived with unconquerable will. In these records of the brilliant lives these women led, we firmly believe we are passing on and widely disseminating the "spirit of Hiroshima," an accomplishment of enormous significance.

The Hiroshima Women's Peace Committee started as the Hiroshima Editing Group when the Soka Gakkai Women's Peace Committee published The Spirit of Hiroshima – A Mother's Prayer in 1982. Five years later, we changed our name to Hiroshima Women's Peace Committee and compiled Hiroshima – Departure for Peace. For the peace gathering in Women's Plaza we held an International Conference Center Hiroshima in 1997, we received over 34,000 texts describing war experiences. We selected five storytellers to present their experiences, which drew attention to our activity from the wider peace community in Japan.

The Fukuyama Women's Peace Committee was formed in 2002, and we have worked together steadily to hold peace gatherings and lecture meetings. We have held a hibakusha meeting to hear atomic bomb experiences every year since 2004, so this year was our 13th. In addition, the Fukuyama Women's Peace Committee has held five meetings featuring stories of the Fukuyama air raid and the atomic bombings. Listening in person to an eyewitness is a precious opportunity to receive and pass on the hibakusha message: "No one

# In Closing

President Daisaku Ikeda of Soka Gakkai International has called on the leaders of states and civil society to visit the A-bombed cities and renew their vows to abolish nuclear weapons.

In 2016, the 71st year after the atomic bombing, President Obama visited Hiroshima, the first sitting president of the United States to do so. He offered flowers to the Cenotaph for the A-bomb Victims and made a speech in which he expressed his determination to seek a world free from nuclear weapons. I can still see the scene in which he gently hugged a hibakusha. As President Obama encountered what happened under the mushroom cloud, I wished fervently that many other leaders would visit as well.

Dr. Andrea Bartoli of Seton Hall University in the United States has said, "When we learn the lesson of this tragedy deeply, and initiate peace and antinuclear actions, that will give new significance to the sacrifice of those who gave us this opportunity."

Today, with the darkness of nuclear testing covering over the world, the cry of hibakusha to "Never repeat that tragedy" must become the starting point of action to put an end to the nuclear age and proceed toward lasting peace.

The Hiroshima Prefecture Soka Gakkai Peace Committee published two years ago a collection of A-bomb accounts told by men. The book was called Hiroshima August 6, 1945 – Silence Broken. Last year, the 70th anniversary of the atomic bombing, the Hiroshima Youth Peace Committee published Families Look at August 6, 1945 – Ten

striving to do a good job for him. I determined to take on my husband's mission of engaging with the atomic bombing and nuclear issues.

I began working as interpreter and coordinator for peace activists, media personnel, writers, artists, scholars, etc., who came to Hiroshima.

At an anti-nuclear mock trial in Nuremburg, Germany, I related my A-bomb experience in English. I attended the First Nuclear Victims World Conference in New York and met nuclear victims from around the United States. At a summit for former world leaders I again told my story in English. I have been fortunate to participate in many deeply meaningful events.

In 1985, I published the Hiroshima Handbook, which gives information on the bombing in Japanese and English.

To help foreigners who visit Hiroshima, in 1984, I established Hiroshima Interpreters for Peace (HIP). HIP trains volunteer guides to take visitors around the Peace Memorial Museum and Peace Memorial Park in English. Along with the other members, I guide and interpret for guests. I often tell my own story.

However, I have found that people hold widely varying views and feelings about the atomic bombings. Some have a hard time understanding the truth of what happened. For this reason, I have long tried to adapt the content of my explanations to each individual I speak to.

I'm constantly struggling to find a way to get the message into someone's heart. I have vowed to never stop trying to convey the horror of nuclear weapons and the sanctity of life.

others would change the subject or get up and walk away. This was also because we were married to people whose families had suffered tragedies from the bombing so we wanted to respect their feelings.

Hibakusha stay silent not only because "remembering is painful." Various other factors press us into silence.

Last year, because our parents were dead, we seven children, (a fourth brother was born after the war) made up our minds to talk about it. My younger brothers and sister had only vague memories, but my older sister and older brothers spoke with much emotion, as if a dam had broken to release what had been locked in for 70 years.

They even vied to speak. "This is how it was." "No, it was like this!" Though I had been playing outside and only 2.4 kilometers from the hypocenter, I was lucky to be protected behind a thick dirt wall. I did not suffer physically from the bomb.

It was the sudden death of my husband Kaoru Ogura, former director of the Hiroshima Peace Memorial Museum in 1979, that forced me to directly confront the atomic bombing. I was 42. Our friend Robert Jung, a writer and holocaust survivor, is known for having told the world about Sadako Sasaki, a Hiroshima victim who folded one thousand paper cranes.

When I was sunk in despondency after my husband's death, Jung contacted me. "I'm going to Japan to get material for a story on nuclear issues. I want you to interpret for me." Although I had majored in English literature at college, I had never studied overseas, and I certainly didn't know the specialized terminology of nuclear issues. I turned him down.

"Keiko, you're just right for this! You've experienced the death of loved ones, and you know the horror of the atomic bombing." Half forced, I became an interpreter for Robert Jung. I studied frantically, child died settled their hearts a bit.

When a child's status was "missing", parents would cling to the belief that the child was alive somewhere. They let decades go by without filing a death report. Finally, they would give up, but still lacked a sense of closure.

In photos taken after the bombing, the city appears to be a motionless ruins filled with rubble. However, when I looked down from the Waseda Shrine hill the next day, smoke from cremation fires rose from all around. It was an unearthly scene. Especially from riverbanks and beaches, smoke rose like beacons. Because bodies decomposed and drew flies quickly in the summer heat, the lines of rising smoke almost seemed to race with one another. My father said that the temporary cremation site in the park cremated about 700 corpses.

Because the neighborhood was now piles of rubble and a great amount of wood, it might seem that finding wood for cremation would be easy; in fact, the number of corpses overwhelmed the quantity of waste wood available. In order to cremate his mother, one person climbed a nearby mountain in search of dead trees and fallen limbs; but others had been there first. He wept, telling us that over and over that he had to abandon his mother's partially burned body on the pyre as he climbed the mountain again to scrounge more wood.

## Taking the mantle from my husband

Last year, on the 70th anniversary of the atomic bombing, for the first time, my siblings and I gathered at a hotel in Osaka and talked the night through about what happened "that day." Until then, whenever we had gathered for family memorial services and the like, we had never spoken of it. On the contrary, if someone brought it up, time. When the town office telephoned to order him to notify the neighborhood of a fire-fighting drill, he would hop on his bicycle and ride around telling everyone. After the bombing, as our neighborhood Citizens' Defense Reserve representative, my father helped cremate bodies in Ushita Park.

He told us, "Don't you children come near the park!" He resisted talking about the cremations, but I pressed him anyway. "How do you burn them?"

Speaking with difficulty, he told me that they dug deep holes in the park. It took two people to carry a corpse to a hole. As most young men were off at war, my father, still on the young side of the men available, had to carry the heavier top half of the corpse; someone older would carry the bottom half. Holding the head, he could not avoid seeing the corpse's face. Those with open eyes made him very uncomfortable; he tried not to see their eyes.

After ten corpses had been laid in a hole, they poured heavy oil over them and lit it. Later, they organized the bones so that the remains could be distinguished one from another. To the people cremating them, these were corpses—but to the bereaved, they were family. People who had lost family members came to watch the cremations. A person who witnessed cremations told us that once, just before the fire was lit, a woman amazingly recognized a patch of clothing on a corpse and cried, "That's my daughter!" Another woman who was watching said, "What a loyal daughter you have. How lucky you are!" That woman's child was missing; anyone who knew what became of her child, she envied.

Not having their child's remains was unbearable to parents. Of those who never received their child's remains, those who at least knew where their child died were on the lucky side. Knowing the place the

Hiroshima August 6, 1945

## Someone I gave water to died

One thing I can never forget. As I was climbing the hill, my ankle was suddenly grabbed. I looked down at a black-charred person covered in blood. The person pled, in weak desperation, "Water, please give me water." The silent ones around started to murmur, one after another, as if chanting, "Water, water, water… …"

I ran down the hill and brought back a kettle full of water. Their arms strained for the kettle. They drank, some gulping with happy screams. One, however, upon swallowing a mouthful, threw up the contents of his stomach, and screamed a last scream. The head dropped; the person was dead.

Frightened, I tossed the kettle and ran back to the house. I was sorry for what I had done. At the same time, I vowed never to tell anyone.

When my father came back that night he told us, "You all know not to give water to heavily burned persons. You haven't done anything like that, have you?"

"No!" I blurted, my body trembling. I was too young to know about such a rule. I could not tell anyone in the family what I had done until my father died. For years I had nightmares about it.

At some point, a burn victim rushed into our house, calling to my older sister, "Let me use your bathroom," as she ran into it. Her hair was loose, disheveled, drenched in dripping blood; her eyes were swollen. She appeared ghoulish. My sister almost fainted. For some time afterwards, she avoided our toilet.

My thin father's conscription exam graded him Class C. As he could not be sent to war, his job was to organize our neighborhood. Therefore, we owned a bicycle and a telephone, both unusual at the

was like layers and layers of ice cream, with a top layer of pink.

Our damaged home quickly filled up with injured relatives, neighbors, and friends. My sister wept as she pulled out of our uncle's back one piece of glass after another. Our house filled with the smells of bloody pus, burnt hair, and excrement.

Having heard that our neighborhood was not the only place bombed, I decided to climb the hill beyond Waseda Shrine and see for myself.

Both east and west slopes had stone steps leading to the shrine and beyond to the shrine office, now a rescue station.

When I reached the steps and looked down, fumbling its way up the west and east steps was a squirming, writhing black mass of burnt people seeking shelter. Hair was singed. Sooty, dirty faces were swollen large. Eyelids drooped, lips turned up. Burnt skin was peeling off, hanging from the fingertips.

Most people in this ghostly, speechless procession were soldiers and students in singed uniforms. The crowd grew larger and larger. In time, the shrine path was as packed as if it were a festival. I even saw someone pulling a horse on a rope, as if preparing to hoist up an injured officer.

Once people reached the top of the hill, lacking the strength for the stone steps to the shrine, they squatted or fell down on the steps. Soon a huge number of people covered every inch of space.

Strangely, no one spoke. Something very eery about an enormous crowd of people falling over in silence. I saw no one who looked like a doctor. There was a soldier on the stone steps carrying a bucket of zinc oxide oil and a brush to apply it to the badly burned.

and it was nighttime. But that turned out not to be so. Straining to hear in the darkness, I barely picked up the cries of my little brother; that told me which way our house was. So my house must be that way. The darkness lifted enough to let me get to my house.

I saw a straw-roofed house in the neighborhood swiftly going up in flames. Our house was my father's pride—a stately structure with many sliding glass doors forming its walls. Because it was summer, all the glass doors were open. Had they been closed, the family would have been wounded, maybe killed, by flying glass. Even stacked to the sides as they were, every glass door splintered beyond recognition, losing its shape as it blew in, glass piercing every wall, ceiling, and piece of furniture.

Glass even pierced hard wooden pillars and concrete. What kind of blast was capable of that? Though he was in the house, my father on the veranda was sheltered by a large pine between him and the explosion, so he suffered little injury. The side of the tree facing the hypocenter was charred black.

My sister in the closet was buried in futons and also escaped injury. My mother was in an inner room, safe from flying glass. My brother, however, was hit in the head by flying roof tiles. My little sister's arm was pierced by glass shards and bled profusely.

We could do nothing but sit in a daze. In a while, I went outside to see what had happened to the neighbors and was hit by black, slightly viscous rain. About that time, my brother who had been working in the sweet potato fields at the Drill Ground crossed the hill to get home. His face and arms were burned.

I cried, "They bombed our neighborhood." Having seen much more than we, he replied, "Not just us. Hiroshima's a sea of flames!"

Moreover, he described the big cloud he had seen from the hill. It

Trying to repress my hunger, trembling with fury and powerful determination, I decided to learn English. This is how I developed an interest in English as a child. I used to hum the alphabet song. I even bragged to others, "My English is very good."

## Our house stank of pus and filth

One year before the atomic bombing, my father moved us from our home near the hypocenter to Ushita-machi (now, Higashi-ku): 2.4 kilometers north. I was the second daughter of six children. My older sister attended Girls High School. My oldest brother was in middle school (under the old system) and the next oldest brother was a fifth grader in elementary school. Then came me, eight years old, followed by a four-year-old brother and two-year-old sister.

That day, my oldest brother was mobilized to work in the sweet potato fields planted on the Eastern Drill Ground north of Hiroshima Station. The next oldest brother had been evacuated with his class to a temple at the border between Hiroshima and Shimane prefectures. In the morning, my father said, "I have a bad feeling about today. Stay home from school!" My father was the fastidious type who would never go out without his gaiters neatly wound around his calves. That day only, try as he might, he could not wind them properly, which gave him a sense of foreboding. It also meant he was late getting out of the house.

My older sister was in the futon closet. I had gotten bored and gone out of the house to play by myself in the road on the north side. I was enveloped in a blinding flash. The next instant, the blast slammed me against the ground and knocked me out. When I came to, all was dark and completely silent.

Because I had been unconscious, I wondered if hours had passed

Hiroshima August 6, 1945

# I tell my story in English to visitors in Hiroshima

**Keiko Ogura**
Born in August 1937. Exposed at eight years old near her home in Ushita-machi, 2.4 kilometers from the hypocenter. Inheriting the mission of her husband, the late Kaoru Ogura (former director of the Hiroshima Peace Memorial Museum), who endeavored to connect Hiroshima with the world, strives to pass on A-bomb experiences. In 1984, founded Hiroshima Interpreters for Peace (HIP). Awards: the Hiroshima Mayor's Prize in 2005; the Hiroshima UNESCO Activism Prize in 2009; the Hiroshima Peace Center's Kiyoshi Tanimoto Peace Prize in 2013. Lives in Naka-ku, Hiroshima City, Seventy-nine years old.

## Hunger impelled me to learn English

For more than 30 years, I have told the stories of hibakusha in English—in speech and in writing. I will continue as long as I am able. I believe that I can contribute to world peace by saying, "This kind of horror is what using nuclear weapons will bring."

But when I started learning English, it was not for such a noble reason.

During the shortages following World War II, the United States sent food and clothing under the name "LARA Relief Materials." When my father came home one day carrying a large can of food, we hungry children thought its contents would surely fill us up. Salivating, we stared at our father's hands working on the lid with an old-style can opener. But when he got the lid off, it was brimming with red cherries floating in syrup. For my father could not read the word "CHERRIES" printed on the label.

I'm grateful to all those people and am resolved to continue working for peace.

work as a laborer.

I climbed the unstable log scaffolding where, clinging to a log, I stuffed into cracks cement from a bucket I hung from my waist, smoothing it with my hand in a rubber glove. Up in the scaffolding, if I looked down, my legs seemed to weaken. When I looked up and saw clouds running through the sky, I felt I was swaying and got dizzy. It was so frightening, I kept my eyes on the wall. This work was so dangerous that my daily wage was an exceptional 250 yen. We could buy ten cups of rice for 80 yen, and that could feed my family for a few days. I worked desperately at two construction sites.

When I should have been going to junior high, I still had no time for school. If I were not earning money, my siblings would starve. I did every kind of work I could find.

I worked as an assistant nurse, a bus conductor and many other jobs, but I never did graduate even from junior high school. That made it impossible to get and keep a decent job.

Ultimately, I made a living carrying salted mackerel on a bicycle and selling it on the streets. Finally, when I was 19, my father came home. Together we found employment emptying non-flush toilets. I have worked like crazy. My leisurely life as the daughter of a prosperous ryokan owner in Hiroshima was completely destroyed by that atomic bomb.

When I was 48, something my mother told me before she died drove me to peace activity.

She said, "There are things more precious than money in this world. I hope you'll take root in Hiroshima, abandon greed, love your hometown, and care for your people."

Through these long years, I have fallen and been hurt many times, but I have survived thanks to support from many people.

our cousins helped plant was filled with mud, with the rice buried under that mud. We lost the entire harvest.

To get money, my mother and I carried heavy charcoal and firewood on our backs down the mountain. We had to pick our way carefully, step by step, then walk to the village to sell them. I was so desperate I did everything I could. I learned that the municipal government was buying sand and crushed stone to restore typhoon damage, so I collected and sold sand and rocks by the bucket.

Meanwhile, my father had gone to Hokkaido where my mother's parents lived. He was running around finding food, like Hokkaido's famous potatoes and corn. But he was not with us.

At the time of the explosion, we were in Asahara, far from the hypocenter, so we were not directly irradiated. However, we entered the city after two days of the explosion to look for my older brother, so we were exposed to residual radiation. My younger brother passed away at 65 due to cancer. Mother's health was so seriously harmed by radiation, she gradually spent more and more time in bed.

This left me with all the work, from farming to housework. I didn't go to school. During the day, I carried mud in a cart from paddy fields ruined by the typhoon. At night, I wove straw sandals. Then, the next year, we were hit by Typhoon Ruth.

I realized I couldn't keep farming. Though only in the sixth grade, I took my family back to Hiroshima City. My mother was soon hospitalized at the Municipal Hospital, which meant we four children were living alone, without parents. As the oldest child, I worked to make a living and support my brother and sisters. I went to a shallow river to dig buckets of freshwater clams. I brought them to a construction worker's camp and sold them. There, I heard about a construction job rebuilding a fire station. I lied about my age and got

We kept looking for my brother. We went to Zaimoku-cho (now, Naka-ku, an area that is now part of Peace Memorial Park). My father had heard that students from my brother's shipbuilding school had been working there demolishing buildings for a fire lane. We arrived and found human bones scattered all around. We stood in a place where 195 students were all killed instantly. There were some big adult bones surrounded by many smaller bones, probably students with their teachers.

Seeing those bones, my mother said, "Hideyuki is dead." She held me tight. She took the towel from her hair, opened it, picked up some bones from the ground, put them in the towel and wrapped them carefully. We all put our hands together in prayer.

She spoke to me, but as if she were talking to herself, "Hiroe, we survived. We must be grateful for this. We should do our best and live all we can for Hideyuki, who couldn't live for himself. Let's let our sorrow, grief and tears flow down this Ota River. If we don't let them go, they'll cause continual misery."

After that, she never complained or talked about being unhappy or blamed anyone or anything.

## Working like crazy to help my family

We took refuge in my grandfather's house in Asahara. This time, we got to live in a small, separate house on their property. We began working as farmers. The next year my mother gave birth to my sister. As an older child, I was soon busy taking care of my new baby sister, washing her diapers, etc. In 1950 when I was a fifth grader, a huge typhoon named Kezia hit Western Japan. Our henhouse, outhouse, and other farm structures were washed away. Our house was left standing, but was only a skeleton of pillars and roof. The paddy field

We were going to look for my brother and the workers at our ryokan. However, only my father was allowed to go to central Hiroshima. The rest of us had to wait in Kusatsu (now, Nishi-ku), a neighborhood near Koi Station.

The next day, the eighth, I finally was able to get to downtown Hiroshima. I could not believe the scene that met my eyes. Hiroshima was a burnt plain, as far as I could see. A military truck was gathering corpses, one after the next. The image of a gaiter-covered leg rolling along the ground is burned into my memory.

As I walked forward drenched in sweat, an ember blown by the wind hit me in the chest. It stuck onto my skin, where it sizzled and burned. It was stuck on my skin and wouldn't let go, no matter how hard I tried to knock it away. I screamed and cried. My mother took a mouthful of water from a water bottle and sprayed it on my chest. She took a towel from her hair, tore it, soaked it in water and applied it to my burn.

After that simple first-aid, we started walking again to find my brother. Much more than my burn, my mother was thinking about my brother. She screamed crazily, "He must be alive! He just can't speak because he's injured! He has to hear me calling him, Hideyuki! Hideyuki!"

The burn on my chest got more painful every day. Finally, I couldn't bear it anymore and started to cry. My mother took off the towel she used as a bandage and found the wound open so deep she could see down to my rib bone.

For the first time, she realized how bad my burn was. She began to weep. "I'm sorry. I'm so sorry!" She ground up some *dokudami* leaves and put paste on my chest every day. Still, it took several months to close, and it formed a keloid scar.

I woke up the next morning, the sixth, to find my father had already left, but Mother said she and my brother and sister would stay one more day. I went to school feeling completely happy.

I stood with the other students in a row in the school ground waiting for morning assembly. I saw a flash in the clear blue sky. A teacher yelled, "Get down!" We had all been carefully trained, so we immediately fell to the ground, putting our thumbs in our ears and covering our eyes with the other four fingers. Then came an order to "Take cover in the air-raid shelter!"

Later, back in the classroom, we were told to arrange ourselves by neighborhood, then we walked home in groups led by older students. When I got home, my mother looked restless and worried. She had gotten a notice from the town office saying, "Hiroshima was destroyed by a new kind of bomb!" She could do nothing but walk around fretting because she couldn't reach her husband, who had left for Hiroshima early that morning. She couldn't reach her son either, nor any employees of her ryokan. That evening, Father came back to Asahara. That morning he had seen an enormous flash and heard an earth-splitting boom on his way to Hiroshima. Then, the sky went pitch black.

He told us that by the time he arrived, Hiroshima was a sea of fire. Burned, injured people were running this way and that. Their clothes burned off, most of them were nearly naked. As he came to Koi, the west end of Hiroshima City, he was stopped by soldiers who told him he couldn't go further into the city. He came back to Asahara.

The next day, we made rice balls, wrapped them in the skin of bamboo shoots we got from the bamboo grove behind the house, then boarded a truck bound for Hiroshima. The bed of the truck was full of people.

the tears in her eyes.

In Asahara, I was given a two-tatami mat room beside the entrance, separated from his family. I had nothing but a writing desk in my room. That night I was alone for the first time in my life. I had to sleep by myself in that scary room. I was terrified by what sounded like millions of frogs croaking just outside my window. I wept all night. My mother stayed in Asahara for a few days to help me adjust. She took me to Asahara Elementary School, where I would be going.

My mother looked at me with great intensity in front of the school gate and said, "When you pass through this gate and enter into this school, you're an elementary school student. Your teachers are your parents here. So you just can't listen to them with one ear. You will listen with both ears and also the third ear in your mind. You'll never forget things you hear with your third ear." Then, I was in Asahara alone. Two months passed.

## Mother kept screaming, "He has to be alive!"

August 5 was Sunday, but I had to go to school for labor service. When I came back, I was surprised and delighted to see my parents, my little brother and my sister in my room. My older brother had just become a technical junior high school mainly for shipbuilding students and didn't want to miss school, so he said, "I'll watch the house. Please go see Hiroe." My father was able to take a few days off for the first time in a long while, so he brought everyone but my brother to visit the family grave and see how I was doing. I wrestled sumo with my brother. I got down on all fours and let my sister get on my back, while I crawled around like a horse. I had a wonderful few hours with my family for the first time in two months. I was so happy I felt as if I was home in Mikawa-cho.

their best kimono to visit the local shrine and pray for sound growth. This festival takes place in November. My best memory of this festival was when I was seven. My five-year-old brother, three-year-old sister, and I were all celebrated together that year. I put a pretty ribbon in my bobbed hair and wore a colorful long-sleeve kimono. Mother took the three of us to visit Tsuruhane Shrine, which was near our house. I tried to look prim and proper while my brother and sister were just jumping with excitement.

I entered Takeya Elementary School (now, Naka-ku) in April 1945, but only went to school for the required pre-school physical exam. Suddenly, I had to leave Hiroshima. Because so many cities were being bombed, we kids in third to sixth grades were evacuated to temples in the countryside with teachers and classmates. First and second graders were considered too young to live in a group so evacuation in class units was not deemed feasible. The younger children could only seek safety through friends or relatives in the countryside.

My father's parents lived in Asahara (now, Hatsukaichi City), 28 kilometers west of the hypocenter. My parents decided I was old enough to evacuate and sent me to Asahara. That was June. My little brother and sister were considered too young to be without their parents. In my family, I had always been indulged by everyone around me and grew up doing nearly everything I wanted to do. I was quite frightened by the prospect of moving to my grandparents' house all by myself.

My mother had to pull me by the hand to Grandfather's place. She let me go when we got there, but I grabbed her kimono sleeve and refused to let go at the front gate. I was afraid to be left alone in this strange place. My mother said "I know this is hard for you. It's hard for me, too. We have to do it to make sure you survive." I let go when I saw

I agreed to be the lead organizer for the Hiroshima Citizens' Peace Gathering. Later I formed a Peace Park Volunteer Cleaning Unit to clean and rake up fallen leaves from the many trees on the roads and grounds in Peace Park. I am still doing that today.

I also started a campaign called Flowers for a Thousand People. We set up a flower stand in Peace Park on New Year's Day to enable visitors to Peace Park to offer flowers to the cenotaph.

Peace activity is a battle against fading interest. To keep it from dying altogether, I continually look for new ways to pass on the philosophy of the Hiroshima's Pioneers of Peace movement. Through this work I emphasize innovative program planning and enduring commitment. In 2016, I organized a Hibakusha Fashion Show and a Children's Peace Gathering.

## Lonely evacuation to unknown relative's house

My father ran a ryokan (Japanese inn) Nagakiya in Mikawa-cho (now, Naka-ku), 800 meters from the hypocenter. His brother-in-law (older sister's husband) was a high ranking officer in the Army, so my father's ryokan was designated for use by senior officers. Our ryokan was also a guesthouse for officers being sent to the front from Ujina Port (now, Hiroshima Port). Besides family members, we had employees, including ladies who cooked high quality Japanese food, waitresses who carried meals to customers on small tables, and a head clerk who was always busily working on something.

I was the second of four siblings. My older brother (six years older than me) was a first-year student at a technical junior high school mainly for shipbuilding. I was in the first grade, and I had a five-year-old brother and three-year-old sister. One of our favorite festivals was Shichi-go-san (seven-five-three). Children of those ages would put on to work outside on building demolition and was killed by the bomb, I felt instant closeness the moment we met.

We talked of many things, and she said, "The words you speak vanish with the conversation, but if you put your words on paper, they remain. You should put down your thoughts, whatever comes to your mind." I had been involved in various peace activities, but I had never even completed elementary school. I missed my chance to study proper reading and writing. My feeling about my writing ability went far beyond mere inferiority complex. It was trauma. The characters I wrote looked like the tracks of an earthworm. I could barely read or write kanji (Chinese characters) at all.

I said, "All I can do is talk." She replied, "Even if you don't know kanji, even if you can't write legible hiragana, we have computers now. Learn the computer." So I began learn it.

As I started to write I realized, "It's Okay for people to hear my story, but if I publish a book, I can give the reader a chance to encounter many different views from different people, and all without organizing a conference."

I compiled a book from children to elderly knowledgeable people. That first book, published in 2013, was called *Pikadon – A Treasure I Found under the Mushroom Cloud*. "Pikadon" means flash-boom. Atomic bomb survivors called the atomic bomb pikadon. I distributed my book to 206 elementary and junior high schools in Hiroshima City. The paper used for that book was made by recycling paper cranes sent from all over the world to Hiroshima Peace Memorial Park.

In 2015, we published of messages whose contributors ranged another book on paper made from recycled cranes. It was called *70 Years since the Bombing of Hiroshima – Messages from Here to Forever*.

I had gotten involved in peace activity in 1986 when I was 48. In 1990

# "We must be grateful we survived" Mother's words compelled me to work for peace

**Hiroe Sato**
Born July 1938. When the atomic bomb was dropped on Hiroshima, she was seven. Two days later, she and her family were exposed to radiation on entering the city. Her older brother was killed. Hiroe began working in the sixth grade, desperately helping to support the family. Joined a peace circle at 48. Asked by the Hiroshima Peace Culture Foundation in 1991 to organize the Hiroshima Citizens Peace Gathering, continued doing so for 14 years. Founded HPS International Volunteers in 2005. Keeps active for peace. Lives in Nishi-ku, Hiroshima City, 78 years old.

## Learned to use a computer
## Published A-bomb books

In September 2008, I joined the First Global Voyage for a Nuclear-Free World: Peace Boat Hibakusha Project. This remarkable project organized by Peace Boat took hibakusha from Hiroshima and Nagasaki by ship around the world telling their stories and calling for the abolition of nuclear weapons at each port of call. During the nearly four-month voyage, I met people from many countries, exchanged views, discussed how horrifying war is, and learned a great deal.

My greatest encounter was with Junko Morimoto. I can say that meeting changed my life. Junko Morimoto is an artist and illustrator. She was exposed to the atomic bombing in Hiroshima when she was 13. She later moved to Australia and published a picture book entitled *My Hiroshima*, which depicted her A-bomb experience. Maybe because she is the same age as my older brother, who was mobilized

grandchild. It was the first time three generations of our family visited there together.

"Let us now find the courage, together, to spread peace, and pursue a world without nuclear weapons." He left this message in the A-bomb Museum, and I hope everyone on this planet will heed his words and strive to create a world free from nuclear weapons.

the doctor.

"You have a perfectly normal, healthy baby boy!"

That words brought me back to myself. I sobbed out loud with joy and relief.

I was fortunate to be given a son, then a daughter, but after each childbirth, I suffered poor health during my periods. I would suffer such severe pain I was writhing on the floor. The lower half of my body went numb, and I couldn't stand up. I never had the symptoms of atomic bomb disease, such as hair loss or bleeding from gums, but I was certified an A-bomb survivor because I contracted "pulmonary fibrosis," a disease in which fibers proliferate in the lungs. I couldn't stop coughing. I had difficulty breathing, and I used my shoulder to help me breathe.

Another A-bomb disease was chronic hepatitis. I felt extreme fatigue, as if I had been drawn into the bowels of the earth. I could barely do the necessary housework.

Later, the pulmonary fibrosis cleared up, but the chronic hepatitis progressed to hepatic cirrhosis. I had surgery for gastric cancer eight years ago, and the incision took a very long time to heal. The opening was stitched together, but never really closed. It is still festering. I can't soak in the bath or use rough towels. I know in my own body the horrifying effects of radiation.

Still, I am glad to have lived this long. I wanted to serve my community, so I started cleaning the parks in my neighborhood. I've doing it now for more than 15 years, and I have received awards twice from the City of Hiroshima.

On May 27, 2016, President Obama visited Hiroshima, marking a new stage in our history. I was moved by his bravery.

The next day, I visited Peace Memorial Park with my son and

bomb, came to the temple on Ushitayama with a man. He was a craftsman who built the bamboo framing for mud walls, and she brought him to see if he and I might get along as partners.

I immediately felt he was a decent gentleman. He was eight years older. My older brothers and sisters were all opposed saying, "It's too early for you!" But my parents were already gone, and I had no job, so I chose to marry him.

My oldest brother and sister were already married. My second oldest sister was single and had a job at the Bank of Japan.

My husband was not an A-bomb survivor. He was discharged from an Air Force unit in Shiga Prefecture, returning 20 days after the atomic bombing. My exposure was not an issue for him.

After we had been married some time, a U.S. soldier accompanied by an interpreter suddenly visited our house. I got a ride in a jeep to the Atomic Bomb Casualty Commission (ABCC) on Hijiyama Hill.

I was told that all women twenty or younger were subject to examination. When I told them I was pregnant, I was allowed to leave after a simple internal exam.

During the ten months I was pregnant, I was continually anxious. If my mother were alive, I could have shared my concern with her, but I couldn't tell my husband. He had said he didn't worry about me being a survivor, so I couldn't make him worry at this point.

Around that time, threatening rumors were everywhere. "A-bomb survivors give birth to deformed babies." "Her baby was born black and dead." I felt like my mind was being crushed. "What if I have a baby like that?"

The time came. I gave birth to my baby in a hospital in Hiroshima City. What I wanted to know first was not if it was a boy or girl but whether it was normal or not. I was still barely conscious but I asked painful.

My brother was a second-year student in elemenntary high school but was mobilized to work in a factory in Ujina. He came home taking a long route to avoid the hypocenter area. He told us he saw a dead baby on its young mother's back. He saw people jumping into the river seeking water and drowning. He said the rivers and streets were full of corpses.

My older sister was working for the Bank of Japan Hiroshima-Branch near the hypocenter. She was in her room in Hirano-machi getting ready to go to work. She was trapped under the roof when it collapsed in the blast, but had no major injury.

Her room was 1.8 kilometers from the hypocenter, which is considered close, so she was taken to the relief station on Ninoshima Island (now, Minami-ku), but she came back on her own because she had no injury.

Our housekeeper at the temple went out shopping early in the morning. She was exposed to the bomb on a bridge near Hiroshima Station and got severe burns all over her body.

The worst burns were on her back, hands and arms. Her hands were fused into permanent fists. If she let her hands stay that way, she wouldn't be able to use them, so every day, she had to open her hands by pulling and stretching her fingers one by one away from her palms. I helped her sometimes and saw the way the scabs were torn apart. Her palms were covered with bloody pus, and she endured quite a lot of pain.

## Sobbed out loud when I heard "healthy baby"

It happened a few months before I turned 19 years old in 1954.

Our temple housekeeper, whose hands were burned by the atomic me.

However, most of the injured victims died one after the next.

## Second oldest brother still missing
## His family reduced to ashes

My second oldest brother, who was expected to inherit the temple, was drafted by the Army. He was stationed near the hypocenter on August 6, and has been missing ever since. He was married and lived with his family near the hypocenter. My older sister went to the ruins of house. It was burned to the ground, and three skeletons were piled on top of each other near the bath. They were his mother-in-law, his wife, and their daughter, Kayoko, who was eighty days old. Kayoko was my first niece. I had held her several times. Recalling her sweet face in my arms, I felt so sorry for her.

A cousin who was a year older than me was out on the grounds for morning assembly in Misasa Elementary School, about 2 kilometers from the hypocenter.

All the students suffered serious burns. My cousin was badly burned on her face. She was invited to the U.S. after the war. She received many painful surgeries to get rid of her keloid scars. Hearing about her treatment I thought, "They treat those girls like guinea pigs."

Later, though, she got married and had two children. The burns on her heels ulcerated and never healed. The burns on other parts formed keloid scars over closed wounds, but the burns on her heels have refused to close for 70 years. She still can't wear shoes so she wears slippers, even in winter.

Radiation has the terrifying power to keep injured tissue from reproducing or healing. Even now the skin on her heels is cracked open, exposing red flesh. She complains that they are constantly

Others whose faces were blistered became blind as their eyes swelled shut. Some were simply covered in blood.

Our temple's main hall was protected from the blast by a pine grove, but our residence standing near it was tilted by the blast. Tatami mats were turned over and strewn randomly.

Although our temple grounds were damaged, we opened the main hall and residence to accept the fleeing victims. I worked with the adults to help take care of them. We had no medicine, so all I could do was to apply cucumber juice or sesame oil to the burns with cotton.

We were told we should never give water to people with bad burns because they would die if we did. But all of them desperately wanted water, so I soaked cotton in water and wiped their dry, rough lips. No matter how I tried to do my best for them, those with purple spots on their body died by the next morning.

I can never forget a young soldier who came on the back of the leader of his troop. The right side of his head was split open about ten centimeters wide. Something must have hit him during the blast. It was unbelievable that he was still alive. On top of Ushitayama was an antiaircraft battery. He had been stationed there.

The temple was already filled with badly injured people. We had no space to lay the soldier down. We arranged potato leaves out in the potato field and laid him there.

"Captain, Captain…," he called.

Maggots bred quickly all over his body as he called deliriously for his leader. I picked them off one by one with chopsticks, but he died that evening.

I lost all emotion. I didn't feel frightened. I couldn't feel sorry for him. The situation was so extreme, I became numb.

I simply acted out of necessity, trying to help the person in front of

our houses and move to other locations. Fortunately, my family had another temple in Ushita, so we moved there.

I was a third grader.

On August 5, I visited my older sister, who rented a room in Hirano-machi (now, Naka-ku). That evening I returned to the temple, which was about halfway up Ushitayama, a small mountain north of the city. The following morning, August 6, an air-raid warning sounded, so I took refuge in a shelter near the corner of a garden.

Soon, the warning was cleared. I left the shelter, but I could still hear the sound of a plane. I wondered if the plane had left and come back.

I looked up and saw something drop from the tail of the bomber. I instantly pressed my eyes and ears as I had been trained to do, and threw myself into the potato field.

A bright flash was quickly followed by an intense blast and roar.

My father was in an octopus trap shelter at the end of a field, three kilometers from the hypocenter. He was blown right out of the shelter by the shockwave. He died of a gastric ulcer two years later. I was down on all fours but had no injury.

I looked west toward Hiroshima but could see nothing but black smoke. Hiroshima burned for three days. The whole city was reduced to ashes.

I didn't know exactly how long it was after the bomb exploded, but crowds of victims began arriving to take refuge in the temple behind the hill. They climbed over Ushitayama through Hesaka (now, Higashi-ku), the next town. Many who were impossible to treat swarmed ceaselessly into our temple. Some suffered such serious burns that their skin peeled off to show the bright red flesh below.

memories? Plenty of other survivors are telling their stories. Let that be enough."

In the midst of my struggle, some young reporters for a children's newspaper made a request. "Please give us your atomic bomb eyewitness testimony." I hesitated. "What should I do?" Just then, I happened to see a TV news program about war.

"Such foolishness is still going on. This is disgusting!"

My heart was filled with anger and frustration. It was at that instant that I made up my mind to talk about my A-bomb experience.

I told my story for the first time 68 years after the atomic bombing for a children's newspaper. That was the beginning of my peace activity.

## Caring for the injured surging in

I was born in a temple in Zakoba-machi (now, Naka-ku), 1.2 kilometers from the hypocenter. It was 1935, and I was born the last of eight siblings. My mother passed away when I was six, but my father and siblings loved me, so my childhood was happy.

When the war got intense, my second oldest brother joined a regiment in Hiroshima. The next oldest went to Manchuria, and the fourth oldest, who was only a junior high student, was mobilized to work at a foundry in Ujina.

By June 1945 the war was going badly for Japan. The Army issued an order to temples and certain private homes in the neighborhood. We had to move out to let the Army build a battery of antiaircraft guns in the center of downtown Hiroshima. It was forced evacuation. They said it was to shoot down U.S. B-29s from the ground.

Like it or not, without any compensation, we had to abandon

Hiroshima August 6, 1945

# I speak from experience —
# War is absurd

**Yukie Tsuchimoto**
Born September 1935, the youngest of eight siblings. Exposed to the atomic bomb in a temple on Ushitayama, a small mountain 3 kilometers from the hypocenter, Though only nine, she helped care for the injured who took refuge in the temple. Despite suffering the effects of radiation, she cleaned parks for many years, receiving commendations from the city of Hiroshima. Was unable to speak about her A-bomb experience until she was 70. Lives in Minami-ku, Hiroshima City, Eighty-one years old.

## Why would we repeat that suffering?

"I don't want to remember it!" "I don't want to talk about it!"

I made myself believe, "It has nothing to do with me." I pushed it to the bottom of my heart. All I wanted was to forget.

Then one day, I felt I heard a voice asking, "Is this right? You're going to take it to your grave without telling anybody?"

In my late fifties, around the time my fourth grandchild was born, I began to feel guilty about not telling my A-bomb experience, and this sense of guilt gradually grew stronger. I had never told even my son and daughter about "that day," but suddenly, because of my grandchildren, I wanted to share my story and leave my memories for the future.

However, the first time I made myself talk, those hateful memories sprang up full force in my mind. These were not experiences I read in a book or heard somewhere. They were things I had touched, smelled, or seen with my own senses. I was overwhelmed by strong emotions and ended up unable to speak. "What am I doing digging up those bad veterinarian, I think.

Later, my mother never, ever spoke about her eye. Whenever I remember her, I am keenly aware that the atomic bomb scars not only bodies but leaves wounds that no one can heal deep in the heart.

A year after the war ended, I was working in the Assistance Bureau in Otake-City, and it was there I met my husband. Our first child we named Hironori. He was a cute little baby with pure white skin. People in our neighborhood came to see him and share our joy. He was our greatest source of hope.

But 18 days after his birth, this baby that had been nursing happily and healthily just two hours earlier suddenly began writhing in pain and died. From his chest down onto his abdomen the baby was covered with the purpura (spots of death) that I had earlier seen on my own arms. His diagnosis — A-bomb disease. Though the war was over, the atomic bomb was still causing us to suffer terribly.

I still tell my story in the Peace Memorial Museum and elsewhere. My daughter Mariko has become an A-bomb Legacy Successor. Such tragedy must never be repeated. Nuclear weapons must never, ever be used. As long as I have life, I will continue to speak out.

I heard that the Army Hospital pharmacy, with it's doctors and medicines, was now working out of Hesaka Elementary School (now, Naka-ku). We put mother on a cart attached to the bike and I took her to Hesaka. It took three hours. However, once we got there, a soldier told us, "Just few moments ago, the doctor and the nurse vomited blood and died." Since I had come a long way, he went on, "The veterinarian who took care of military horses is still alive."

All I wanted was to help my mother, so I decided to have him look at her. Finally, he put her down on a straw mat in the classroom and said, "I'm going to operate on her."

At that, three soldiers came and sat astride her to keep her from struggling. The vet took a scalpel and stood by my mother's head. When my mother saw that, she said, "I don't need this surgery. Stop this now!"

My mother, who was head nurse, looked at the vet as if she understood what kind of operation it would be. The vet said, "Deep in your socket, the nerves of the eyes are connected to each other. If we don't do anything, the rot will spread to your other eye and blind you. We have to take your right eye out now and disinfect the wound!"

There was no anesthetic or any sort of painkiller.

I desperately explained to Mother, "If he doesn't cut off your right eye, you won't be able to see at all!" The operation began.

I was unable to watch; I left. Through the closed door, I heard my mother's screams, wails, and sounds of struggle.

Her right eye was cut off without anesthetic. The horrible shrieks continued for more than an hour. I couldn't bear it. I crouched in the hall, shivering, and praying continually. "Save her. Please save Mother!" If he had been a general internist, he probably wouldn't have attempted the operation. He was able to do it because he was a

"Chee-chan…"

One of those rounded bandaged bodies in front of me seemed to have called my name.

Mr. Takabayashi said, "If she called your name, she must be your mother. Let's look for her gold teeth." He unwound the bandage to get a look at her mouth.

And there they were, her gold teeth.

"It's Mother! For sure!"

To make sure, I pulled out the bent leg of the rounded body in front of me. Then, I saw what remained of her white nurse's uniform. When I pulled on the skirt of that uniform, hundreds of maggots fell out. They had entered her wounds and were eating her down to the bone. I began to cry.

Mr. Takabayashi took a tomato out of his pocket and tried to have Mother eat it. She had eaten nothing for six days. When the tomato went into her mouth, she moved it slowly. I spent that night next to Mother plucking out flies, one by one. They were huge, they bit down into her flesh and resisted my pull. When I put my strength into my fingers to pull, they would come off with their mouths full of my mother's skin.

The next morning, Mr. Takabayashi got a cart and came to get us. We took Mother home in that cart. Her right side was burned black, her left full of glass fragments. The women of the neighborhood were waiting outside. They lifted her out of the cart, brought her into the house, and laid her in her room. Then they took off her bandages.

As they did, I heard one of them shout in shock.

Surprised, I looked at her face and saw that her right eye had popped out of its socket. Glass shards stuck into her face all over. Her nose was broken so I could see the bone.

It was all she could do to keep breathing.

When I got to the open area in front of the hospital, a big crowd was gathered. There were already three large piles of bodies prepared for cremation. I searched through them for my mother. At that point, I felt so much pain I couldn't stand it, so I went home.

In the evening of the fifth day, I started feeling very bad. I was dizzy. When I put my hand to my head, big bunches of my hair would come out.

I noticed on both arms purple spots the size of eggs, three or four of them. "Is this how I'm going to die?" I was suddenly wracked by fear.

In the morning of the sixth day, Mr. Takabayashi, a neighbor farmer, said he would help me search. Though I was wobbly, I went with him to Funairi (now, Naka-ku) area.

A person standing in the ruins of Funairi Hospital said, "The injured were taken to Eba Elementary School." We went to look there. So many corpses lay in the halls, we could hardly walk. The classrooms were full of burn victims and bodies that stank so much, I could hardly breathe. In the heat, the burns and the bodies were rotting. White maggots were all over them. People were piled on each other, their faces destroyed, their bones visible.

Calling my mother's name, I went around looking into the faces of the dead, turning their faces this way and that to make sure she was not among them.

I went to all the classrooms, but my mother was nowhere. As I entered the last classroom, on some desks pulled together, some people were lying in fetal position, their faces and bodies wrapped in bandages. They looked like dead bodies hardened with bandages.

Next to Mr. Takabayashi, I faced those desks and called my mother's name.

alive can't see or hear. They are just waiting for death."

I didn't want to believe that my mother was dead, but since I had come all this way to find her, I started looking at the bodies on the bank to see if she was one of them. I knew I would recognize her three gold teeth. I used two wood sticks to pry open the mouths of the corpses, but the lips swollen up to five centimeters made it surprisingly hard to open their mouths. Their faces were no longer human. Still, feeling neither fear or repulsion, I desperately looked into the mouths of forty to fifty dead people.

But I didn't find my mother.

## When I finally found my mother, she was barely breathing

I remembered that my aunt (Mother's brother's household) and my cousin in the fourth grade lived near Takajo-machi (now, Naka-ku), so I decided to go and look there. Because it was near the hypocenter, all the houses had burned to the ground leaving hardly a trace. I found my aunt's name written in charcoal on a water cistern, so I started digging in that area with my shoes. The roof tiles and stones I dug up were still hot.

Turning things over here and there, I found a part of some clothing I had given my cousin. Then, I found the skeletons of an adult and a child facing each other. The bones were burned clean. They must have burned quickly.

Strong emotions assailed me, but when I calmed down, I took a few bones from each of them, wrapped them in my handkerchief, and took them home.

The next day I went out again to look for my mother. This time, I went to the Red Cross Hospital. On the way, I saw two or three huge rats gnawing at corpses tumbled down near the river.

there on her body. And it turned out that she was Mihoko Kagawa, one of the girls I was to swim with on the beach at Tsutsumigaura.

At the appointed time, she had gotten onto a streetcar heading for Koi Station. Just before arriving, the bomb exploded as she stood in the car holding onto the strap. When she came to, she was in the river. She crawled out and fled to my house. Otsuka-san, the other friend who was to meet us for swimming, escaped with light injuries—Mihoko, though, was later to go missing.

I went back to my house, fearful for my mother who was working at the Army Hospital. The next morning, the city was still burning, so I wet my air-raid hood, put it on my head, and went searching for her, carrying a water bottle. My mother had not been home for a week. She was staying over at the hospital, working night and day for soldiers sent back from overseas.

When I got to the Aioi Bridge near the Army Hospital, I looked at the river. It was still full of corpses the rising tide had brought in. They were piled right down to the bottom of the river, so many, I could hardly see the water. Bodies that had spent the night in the water were terribly bloated, their faces swollen round like rubber balls. The transformed appearance looked nothing like human.

My mother could be one of the bodies. At that thought, I turned to the river and called, "Mother, Mother!" over and over. On the other side of the river, I saw three men stripped down to loincloths pulling floating bodies out of the water onto the bank. All three were hygiene soldiers from the hospital. They were saying, "We're the only three who survived, we're sorry."

I went over to the three men and said, "I'm looking for my mother."

One of them said, "Almost no one from the hospital is still alive. A few hundred lived until this morning, but most spouted blood from their mouths, noses, and ears and died. The few dozen who are still away, the structure tilting. All the houses in the neighborhood were in the same condition. I wanted to get to it but I was trembling all over and couldn't stand. I touched my head casually and felt sticky blood running down.

In the sky, a completely black cloud or smoke or something was roiling up and spreading out. It was weird and unnerving. Injured people covered in blood were everywhere. A man's back was full of glass shards. Old nails on a wooden chip protruded from a woman's split abdomen.

Looking out to the road, I saw crowds of people coming up the slope with burns, their hair singed, standing on end, themselves covered with soot and ash. Their skin was peeling and red, hanging like strips of kelp from their shoulders, down their arms and from their fingertips. They were shouting, "Help! It's so hot! My throat hurts! Water, please!"

People came out of their houses. Shocked by the gruesome sight, they spoke to the strangers. "Hang on. Don't die! Where did you come from?" Some people tried to get under the eaves of our houses to get out of the sun. They collapsed and fell over dead one after the next. Many were burned so deep into their throats that they couldn't make a sound.

After a little while, it darkened like the end of day just before a completely black rain came pouring down. When those drops hit arms and legs, they made a round stain as if a black bean had stuck there.

Suddenly, out of the crowd, a woman rose unsteadily to her feet and began shouting, "Chee-chan."

"Hey, you're calling my name. Who are you?" I asked. She was burnt black all over. Her hair stood on end. Her cheek was gashed and blood was oozing out. Blood was also coming from holes here and

Nishi-ku), which had become a military factory. I used a big file to smooth out the bumpy surface of the part.

The kaiten were single-seated torpedoes. Young soldiers of 14 or 15 who had just graduated from higher elementary school would get intensive training for three months, then were expected to steer the torpedoes into an enemy ship. In other words, they were kamikaze in the sea.

On August 5, I was on the night shift. Just before dawn we were told, "Women's Corps members only, go home and get some rest." I left the factory. The summer night sky made the whole war seem like a false rumor. It was completely blue, and we could still see stars shining.

We hadn't had a day off in two or three months, so my fellow volunteers Mihoko Kagawa and Kazuko Otsuka and I agreed to rest a little, then go to the beach at Tsutsumigaura.

The beach at Tsutsumigaura had been strafed once, so swimming was prohibited, but we had been swimmers for our school. I was a distance swimmer and could swim for hours on end. This was my specialty, so I was pining to swim again.

We had said we would get together at Koi Station at 8:15 am. After hurrying through the wash and other housework, I was in our entrance getting ready to leave. I stopped and took out a pocket mirror to once again check my braids, of which I was proud.

It was that instant. A flash of lightening and then, a tremendous roar. I lost consciousness. My home in Koiue-machi was three kilometers from the hypocenter. When I came to, I was lying in a sweet potato field thirty meters from my house.

"What am I doing here?"

Looking at my house, I saw the roof tiles and windows all blown happened.

When she first started wearing a false eye, whenever she was about to put it in, I would look the other way, get up from my seat, or find some way to avoid seeing. I sort of felt sorry for her.

At first, Mother was also worried about her false eye. When we were taking a family picture, she would casually turn her head to the side that would hide the false eye. When we went to see our friends, or when she went to the doctor, she would always take her granddaughter Mariko with her. Mariko's job was to be a lookout on the right, Mother's blind side. The false eye was not exactly round. It was a bit sunken in the back. It is very hard to make a false eye exactly the same shape as an eye. She had it remade many times.

In the socket, the scalpel had cleanly cut away her nerve. Red scar tissue clumped up in the hole, like the gum where you put in a false tooth.

Once I tried to get her to tell me about "that time." She pressed her lips together and stayed quiet a long time. Finally she said only, "I don't want to talk about it!"

She left this world when she was 62. In the end, I was never able to hear about "Mother's right eye."

## Called by a friend covered in blood

In August 1945, I lived with my mother (then, 42), who was head of nursing at the Army Hospital in Koiue-machi (now, Nishi-ku). I had just graduated from Yamanaka Girls High School (now, Hiroshima University). In those days, when you graduated from a girls' school, you were obligated to serve in the Army or Navy. I joined the Women's Volunteer Corps and was assigned to make parts for kamikaze submarines (kaiten) at the Toyo Canning Plant in Tenma-cho (now,

Hiroshima August 6, 1945

# Mother's eyeball cut out without anesthetic—her screams still ring in my ears

**Chisako Takeoka**
Born February 1928. At 17, a recent graduate of a girls high school, exposed to the atomic bomb in the entrance to her house three kilometers from the hypocenter (in Koiue-machi). Her mother, head of nursing at the Army Hospital, was injured so badly her eyeballs popped out. Mother survived, but eventually died without ever speaking about what happened to her eyes. Chisako testified in 1982 at the dialogue meeting of the UN Special Session on Disarmament in New York, and in 2001 at a Russian university. She is an official A-bomb storyteller at the Hiroshima Peace Memorial Museum, working with her daughter, who has been designated an A-bomb Legacy Successor by the city. Eighty-eight years old; lives in Asaminami-ku, Hiroshima City.

### "I don't want to talk about it!"

I often saw my mother's false right eye lying near her pillow. At first glance, it looked like a piece of candy.

So soon after the war, a false eye case was unaffordable. Before sleeping, she would put cotton in a small paper candy box, take out her eye, and put it in the box. When she couldn't find just the right used candy box, she would put it on a small plate and leave it by her pillow.

The false eye would get dirty, white with mucous. Mother would wash it carefully with water. However, as she got used to it, when she didn't have water, she would turn her back, stick it quickly in her mouth, clean it with her tongue, and poke it back in as if nothing had

I had no A-bomb symptoms like bleeding from the gums or losing hair. Neither did I develop any serious illnesses. I thought, "I'll never be affected by my atomic bomb exposure." So when I got pregnant with my first daughter, I had no fear and delivered her with no problem.

About thirty years after the war, I ran into an old friend from the girls school. She worked for the prefectural government office and was in charge of organizing documents related to the atomic bombing. She said, "That day, I just passed Hiroshima Station in a train, but I got an A-bomb Health Book." She went on to suggest, "You were near the hypocenter, so you're eligible. You should apply for a Health Book."

To do that, I needed to have someone testify that I was in Hiroshima at that time. I looked for Head Nurse Taniguchi at the Hiroshiama Red Cross Hospital. She was old, but in good health. She stated that I was in the hospital, so I got an A-bomb Health Book.

After receiving the Health Book I developed colon cancer, followed by gallbladder cancer. The gallbladder was removed. I have no idea if my illnesses were effects of the atomic bombing, but I can't eliminate my fear or my feeling that the bombing caused them.

I pray for genuine peace on earth and that we never produce any more hibakusha.

November 4. My father went with me. There, for the first time, I learned that many of my classmates had died. I was so shocked I prayed sincerely for their peaceful repose.

## Lived without fear but developed cancer at 80

I settled down in my parents' house in Mihara and started studying flower arrangement and tea ceremony. One day a girl a bit older than I suggested, "I know a good person for you. Would you like to meet him?" He was two years older. He had trained as an elite special submarine navigator and was assigned to be a "human torpedo." Just before he made his one-way sortie, the war ended. His attack was cancelled, and he survived. He came back to Mihara the year after the war ended.

My family owned a saltpan and was relatively wealthy, so the go-between lost confidence and told the young man, "Her family is rich. They might reject you. I know another good one who's the daughter of a cigarette store owner. Shall I introduce you to her?" But the boy was highly competitive and was offended by her second suggestion. He simply said, "I don't need a cigarette store girl. I'll have that saltpan girl." And we got married.

My husband was not a survivor. I was in the Red Cross Hospital, 1.5 kilometers from the hypocenter, but I was in the well-shielded kitchen, so I was not sure if I could properly call myself "exposed." I generally felt that A-bomb effects were things that happened to others.

Since I felt that way, I shared with my husband the things I had seen in Hiroshima immediately after the bombing. He was appalled, of course, but he, like me, assumed that experience had nothing to do with us.

Mukainada Station, which took a long time.

I heard that a few days earlier, a unit from Akatsuki Corps in Osaka had come to Hiroshima. They were lining up in front of Gokoku Shrine the morning the bomb exploded. Hundreds of them were killed. In Mukainada Station, I wondered how they had prepared such a huge number of plain wood coffins. I saw hundreds of white coffins loaded on a freight train. Each coffin carried a unit code and name.

When I showed my handwritten Disaster Certificate to the station staff, he said, "If you don't mind riding with coffins,…" I sat leaning back against a mountain of coffins. Swaying on that freight train, I just waited to arrive at my home town. When I got off at Mihara Station, people were surprised and gathered around me. I had gotten off a freight train, which should not have been carrying any passengers. They threw many questions all at once. "You came from Hiroshima?" "What happened there?" I escaped those people and hurried home. Arriving at home, my mother was amazed. Her eyes grew round and burst into tears. "I heard Hiroshima was totally destroyed. I'm so happy you made it home!" My father had regretted sending me to the Red Cross Hospital. He sobbed, "I'm sorry, I'm so sorry."

Hiroshima Red Cross Hospital started treating atomic bomb survivors immediately after the bombing. But many doctors and nurses had been killed, so they were badly understaffed. I received several telegrams asking me to go back to the hospital.

Because I had seen such painful scenes, I had no desire at all to go back. Every time a telegram came to my house, I reacted slowly and tried to postpone making up my mind. I think my father went to the hospital and apologized for me.

"You should go at least once, if only to greet them!" My father finally told me, so I went to the hospital three months later, on

Meanwhile, fires ignited and blazed up.

Some already charred victims had no idea which way to go so they ran aimlessly this way and that. Soldiers were shouting, "Go to the Army Air Field!" I didn't know which way the Army Air Field was, but I followed the crowds.

The ground was hot. The rubber soles of my shoes immediately melted and fell off. I found one geta (wooden clog) and a military boot on the street so I wore them. I went from place to place looking for safety from the fire, then waited for daybreak.

The next morning I went back to the Red Cross Hospital, but the Annex where I lived had vanished.

Fire had also broken out in Yamanaka Girls High School (now, Hiroshima University), next door. The whole school was gutted by fire during the night. I went inside the burnt ruins of the gymnasium. One of my friends from Nursing School was sitting feebly on a balance beam. Glass fragments filled her face. Lines of dried blood covered it.

The windows in the dormitory were all shattered, and many students were seriously injured by flying glass. The glass windows in the kitchen were protected by wire netting so I was spared glass fragments.

When I saw a charred mother die while nursing her baby in front of the hospital, I was suddenly terrified. I thought I should go home to Mihara.

No matter where I tried to cross, the bridge had burned down. I kept walking and looking for a bridge. I went forward for a while, then, at a desk placed out near the road, a soldier was issuing Disaster Certificates. I told him, "I want to go home to Mihara." He hardly looked at me as he wrote, "Disaster Certificate" and handed me a paper about the size of a credit card. I carried the paper as I walked to

immediate evacuation!"

I was washing plates, but the instant I heard the boom I dove into the space between two rice-cookers standing next to each other. A beam from the ceiling fell down and my classmate, who was working with me, was trapped under it and died.

The lights in the building went out, so it was pitch black inside. In fact, no light was coming in the window either. It was dark as night outside. Buildings crumbled so we couldn't tell what building was what.

I desperately screamed, "Dad, mom, help me!"

Soon I realized there was no way my parents were around. Thinking, "God must be here," I started screaming, "God! Help me!"

The sky outside was wrapped in black mist, but at times, from slits in the mist, beams of white light thrust in. My mouth was so dry from fear, I couldn't say a thing. Then I thought, "I'll be in trouble if I stay in here!" I cried out loud, again and again. Fortunately, someone outside removed some rubble. I was freed. Watching my step carefully, I quickly climbed out of the building.

When I got out, the black mist gradually cleared out of one meter around my feet. Very slowly, the mist or smoke lifted. Like a black curtain rolling up, the area around me grew light again.

I looked around and was shocked. I saw people fallen over with blood covering their faces. Others were groaning with arms or legs torn right off. The clothes had completed burned off one victim, leaving only a belt. A mother held a baby whose skin seemed to be melting off. One with skin peeled off was so burned I couldn't tell if I was looking at its face or the back of its head. Such misery spread before my eyes. Dead bodies were scattered everywhere.

was two years of education after graduating from a girls school; or Course B, which was four years of education after graduating from higher elementary school.

Half the third floor of the Red Cross Hospital was a women's dormitory with over 30 residents lived. More than a dozen of us couldn't be accommodated there, so we were in two rooms of a one-story house near the hospital called the Annex. As a first-year student, I was assigned to a room in the Annex.

Dormitory residents ate meals in a dining room attached to the Annex. Next to the dining room was a kitchen where female cooks prepared meals assisted by a few residents, who were assigned cooking duties by turns a week at a time. At 6:00 a.m. we stalted putting tableware and big kettles of tea on the tables.

## Escaped through a crowd of corpses

The morning of August 6, 1945, I was on kitchen duty. After finishing breakfast, which started at 7, residents returned to their rooms. I was washing utensils with Hiraoka-san, the other resident on kitchen duty. Suddenly, we saw a brilliant flash. It seemed to me the light was not that big, but the violent, roaring boom that followed made me think, "Our dorm's been hit by a bomb!" About a week earlier, a B-29 had flown over and scattered a massive quantity of handbills. Some of the bills landed in a heap in front of our dormitory.

Head nurse Taniguchi came out with a bucket shouting, "Don't touch them! Don't read them!" She was collecting the bills in her bucket, but they were everywhere, so we could read them without picking one up. On a bill the size of a postcard, an illustration of a plant with a chimney carried Japanese text that said, "We're not fighting citizens. We're going to drop a bomb soon. We demand your

# Saw flash and heard roar at Red Cross Hospital, 1.5 kilometers from the hypocenter

**Sachiko Yamaguchi**
Born April 1933. At the time of the bombing, 12 years-old a first-year student at Hiroshima Red Cross Nursing School(now, Japan Red Cross Hiroshima Nursing University). Was in the school kitchen, 1.5 kilometers from the hypocenter, but had no injury. Went back to her house in Mihara, got married. No appearance of A-bomb symptoms, never thought herself an A-bomb survivor. Her friend told her she was eligible for an A-bomb Health Book, so she applied. Developed gall bladder cancer, then colon cancer after age 80. Eighty-three years old; lives in Mihara City, Hiroshima Prefecture.

## Going to Red Cross Nursing School to be an army nurse

I was the third of three sisters born to parents who managed a saltpan in Mihara, a city in the eastern part of Hiroshima Prefecture. I was the tomboy. Every day when I came back from the school, I would climb a big hemp palm standing next to the saltpan because I loved to watch the town from atop that tree.

It seems my father was thinking, "We can't send a soldier from my family because my children are all girls. I wish we could at least make one of them an army nurse. Then we'd be serving the country." Because I was so physically active, he sent me to the Hiroshima Red Cross Nursing School on the grounds of the Hiroshima Red Cross Hospital in Hiroshima City to become an army nurse. I went right after I graduated from a girls school.

In those days, the Red Cross Nursing School had Course A, which

were, "I'm dying because I helped my country, so don't cry."

By the day the war ended, August 15, all of the twenty students taken in at the rescue station had died. From Osaka came an officer and a non-commissioned officer to take over from the dead commander.

On August 18, a dissolution ceremony was held at the destroyed headquarters. The non-commissioned officer dismissed us five students and sent us home to our parents with a simple "Thanks for your hard work."

We parted with, "See you at school second semester!" but as soon as I got home, I came down with high fever, diarrhea, and weariness profound enough to drag me to the depths of the earth. These radiation effects kept me at home for two years.

Nonetheless, in my heart I vowed to pray the rest of my life for the repose of my dead classmates who fulfilled their responsibilities until the last moment and to give witness that they lived! I summon my courage to continue to testify on their behalf.

embankment and fallen in the water.

At dusk, medic rescue teams came from Yamaguchi and Okayama and carried 20 injured students and 30 injured soldiers to the temporary rescue station set up in the preparatory school.

We stayed with the injured students to help out. They all cried, "Water! Give me water!" The medics initially told us, "Burn victims die if you give them water, so don't!" When they saw the injured dying off rapidly regardless, they must have decided to offer water to those who had no chance. They told us quietly, "Give them one sip at a time." I filled a kettle with water and doled it out.

An officer was sitting down, his face blue, a piece of wooden pole thrust 20 centimeters into his back. The flesh around the skull of another soldier with an open hole in his brain quivered with each breath. Some people's eyeballs had melted because they had peered at the airplanes in the sky. Abdomens were split, intestines were spilling out. The rescue station was filled with people in frightful condition.

At the end of the day, Furuike-san, Miyagawa-san, and Morita-san returned. Rejoicing to reunite with members of our team, they, Itamura-san, and I went to the Communications Room to get a little sleep. From the rescue station sounded the cries of young soldiers. "Mother!" In our exhaustion, even their piteous screams could not keep us awake.

The next morning, we went to the rescue station to help. Only one day after the bombing, white maggots were breeding in the burns on the bodies of students and soldiers.

Mothers appeared searching for their mobilized children. One cradled her severely wounded daughter and called her name ceaselessly. When the mother's tears fell on the face of her mortally wounded daughter, she awakened enough to smile. Her last words

Hiroshima August 6, 1945

Surrounded by flames, Itamura-san and I prepared to die.

## Helping at a shelter for the injured

Though it was daytime, it was as dark as dusk. As we stumbled around, pitch-black rain began to fall in large muddy drops that quickly became a torrent. We stayed in the pond, fully drenched.

In 40 minutes, the rain stopped so suddenly, it seemed it had never been. But it had stopped the fires. Ignorant that it was a deadly downpour full of air-bore radiation, we gave thanks for the rain. Many who were rained on fell ill with A-bomb disease.

We walked behind the destroyed castle tower to search for our friends and found three students sitting on stones. Usually, we could read each other's names on the nametags we wore, but these students' clothes were so tattered, we couldn't see tags. The face of one had swollen to twice its size and shut her eyes. Another's neck was broken, turned backwards. She was barely conscious.

We recognized the one in the middle—it was Hamaoka-san. Her right elbow joint was ripped apart, showing her bone and tissue. Her hanging arm looked ready to fall off any second. She was desperate for water, but there was no water anywhere.

"We'll come back for you later, so wait here," we said, and then, "Where are the others?" Listlessly, Hamaoka-san pointed, "Over there." In that direction lay the Army's Joto Bridge. On the other side of the moat was the Military Preparatory School.

I stood and headed that way. When I crossed the Joto Bridge, I heard the sound of a body hitting water. "Hamaoka-san?" Murmuring a prayer, I hurried back. There she was, floating on her stomach in the moat. In her intense thirst, she must have leaned down from the talking to the Shikoku Military District Headquarters, which had called to provide information.

"Are the lines open?"

I went around the room picking up strewn telephone receivers. The first two or three were dead. But I kept trying and finally, the one connected to the Fukuyama Regiment was live.

"Hiroshima is annihilated!"

I shouted into the phone.

"You said "annihilated?"

"Yes sir. It's annihilated."

"What do you mean, "annihilated"?

I was at a loss until I remembered the words of the injured soldier.

"We've been hit by a new kind of bomb, sir."

Then came the sound of wood crackling. Flames were approaching the bunker. We dashed outside and saw a soldier trapped under Building 1, writhing to get free.

We ran over to him, but the thick pillars overlaying each other on him were too heavy. Two of us could do nothing, but janitor Matsui came up. The three of us wedged a thick pole under the pillars and used it as a lever to raise them, little by little, until the soldier was able to crawl out.

No time to rejoice. The flames were upon us.

We ran to the open area in front of Imperial Headquarters where the day shift students would have gathered for the morning assembly prior to shift change. No students there.

The flames were so powerful, the air was so dry, that my hair was on the verge of catching fire. Our faces were crimson from the heat. Our clothes were so hot, we instinctively jumped into the pond in front of the ruined headquarters. But even though we covered ourselves head to toe in muddy water, it dried immediately.

I got as far as "Yellow alert for Hiroshima, Yamaguchi—." Suddenly, a white flash furiously pierced my eyes.

"An accident!" I thought, as I lost consciousness. After perhaps four or five minutes, I gradually regained consciousness within an ash-colored fog.

Desks were toppled, chairs were broken, and I had been thrown three meters. The switchboard lay on top of me.

I saw no one else in the room. Squinting through plumes of ash and dust, I could make out Itamura-san in the corner of the room, pressing on her eyes and ears. With only a minor cut on her eyelids, she seemed to be okay.

Comprehending nothing, we went outside. The first things we saw were remnants of the three buildings that had stood on the premises. Building 1, the Headquarters; Building 2, Officers Quarters; and Building 3, the auditorium—all had been pushed over and smashed. The ruins of the castle tower formed mountains of lumber and mud walls. There were no flames, as we would see had we been hit by incendiary bombs.

Still uncomprehending, I scrambled alone up the embankment. The Chugoku Newspaper Building and the Fukuya Department Store were the only tall buildings in the city; the rest were one-story wooden homes; now every neighborhood was transformed into rubble. But as yet, no fires. I could see Ujina Port just before me, though it was 4 kilometers away. I could even see Ninoshima Island, nine kilometers away. No buildings blocked my view. Below the embankment, an injured soldier groaned and shouted, "We were hit by a new bomb!"

When I came back to the communications room, Itamura-san was on the telephone saying, "That's completely impossible!" She was

with military facilities were spared. Because bombers were leaving us alone, starting at the end of July, the long night shift was divided into early night shift and late night shift, each group composed of 15 students.

## An injured soldier shouted, "New bomb!"

On August 5, I was assigned to the early night shift. At 5:00 pm, we took over from the day shift and worked until 1 a.m. In the middle of the night, we received the report "Enemy aircraft sighted over Bungo Channel, heading north." I sent out an alert, then a warning, to NHK and the various military factories. As they received these notices, they turned on sirens to warn the people and military personnel.

Around 11:00 p.m., a large formation of 100-to-120 B29s attacked Nishinomiya in Hyogo, then Imabari in Ehime; Ube in Yamaguchi was bombed at 4:00 a.m. "To your posts!" sounded the order.

The late night shift students were awakened. I did not go off shift at 1 a.m., but worked the night through without a wink of sleep.

At dawn, things finally quieted down; I hurried back to the dorm, poured tea on a bowl of rice, mixed it, returned to the bunker, and waited for the day shift to arrive.

When the hour passed 8:00 and my replacement still had not arrived, I was getting impatient when suddenly, this report: "Three B29s over Hiroshima, from the east." But neither alert nor warning had emerged from the Strategic Command.

At 8:13, finally a buzzer told us that a memo was slipping through the window at the bottom of the door. It said, "Yellow alert." Turning to the switchboard, I simultaneously inserted several cords to call the personnel at military factories. I knew the routine and felt no particular tension.

was 5 p.m. to 8 a.m. and the third shift worked Sundays after the night shift. Girls who worked the night shift had to attend the 7:30 morning assembly in the open area in front of Imperial Headquarters. Then they did schoolwork at the nearby dormitory until the afternoon, when they slept in order to get up and work again at 5:00 p.m.

The Strategic Command comprised four rooms. In the room next to the entrance, 25 people sat with receivers on their ears to pick up information from 20-plus monitoring posts covering the Chugoku region. If they picked up a report of enemy planes spotted in a certain area, they would hit a key that would turn on the designated flashing light over a map on the wall of the innermost office.

The second office was for soldiers in the Communications Unit. In the third room, four dispatchers (students) faced the wall in two rows and delivered orders from the Strategic Command to various military stations and bases by telephone. On the opposite side of that room was a switchboard. When the Strategic Command issued an order, cords had to be inserted into jacks connecting direct lines to NHK, the prefectural office, military plants, etc. Warnings had to be sent simultaneously. Operating the switchboard was my job.

On the bottom of the door was a little window. When an order was issued, a buzzer would sound as a memo passed through the window. The four dispatchers and I would notify the army bases and military plants on direct telephone lines. We had code words for "yellow alert" and "air-raid warning," and gave a number first to indicate the time of the alert or warning.

The innermost room was behind a very thick wooden door that could not be opened. The commanders and officers allowed in that room used a special door on the opposite side.

When air raids began regularly demolishing other cities, I wondered why "military city Hiroshima" and its castle grounds dense girl used to sit here... That one sat over there." When I mentioned a particular girl, her face would come up to me.

Somehow I was able to finish and get back to my house, but my distress from that one experience caused my platelets to decrease in number, and my thrombocytopenia erupted again. My doctor ordered peace and quiet, and I had to lie low for two years.

When my symptoms improved at age 63, I began giving my testimony again. For by then, I had understood that I had lived that long because I had a mission: to tell the story accurately for my friends who had died in that place.

I began to receive requests to speak at schools and other institutions as well. Even now, though, I only speak inside the ruined bunker whose square, low-ceilinged rooms of sooty, bare concrete have been cleared of transmission equipment, chairs, desks, even doors. Nothing remains but humid air lingering throughout. The students who have to listen to me in those rooms probably feel uncomfortable. But when I speak there, I sense my dead classmates speaking with me.

At the time, I was in my third year at Hijiyama Girls School, mobilized to the Chugoku Military District Communications Headquarters. In the side of the embankment bordering the moat surrounding Hiroshima Castle a semi-underground bunker was invisible to the air. It was the Strategic Command for relaying orders throughout the Chugoku region.

On April 7, 50 students of Hijiyama Girls High School had been appointed to the Student Communications Squad working in the Strategic Command, off limits to all but selected military personnel.

After another 40 students were added to the 50, tasks were allocated among 90 students in three shifts. Thirty students worked each shift. The day shift went from 8 a.m. to 5 p.m.; the night shift

Hiroshima August 6, 1945

# First to report the atomic bombing over short-wave radio

**Yoshie Oka**

Born January 1931. In her third year at Hijiyama Girls High School (now, Hijiyama Girls Secondary School), mobilized to serve in the underground communications command of the Chugoku Military District Headquarters. Working as member of Student Communications Squad (0.7 kilometers from the hypocenter) when bomb was dropped. From the demolished bunker, reported the bombing to the Fukuyama Regiment. For the sake of perished classmates, continues to tell her story. Eighty-five years old, lives in Naka-ku, Hiroshima City.

## Giving testimony with my departed classmates

In September 1991, when I was 60, I first related my experience in the atomic bombing.

For many years I had steadily refused requests to "give your testimony." If even recollecting the experience was painful, how could I possibly bear to put words to it?

"Please talk to my students! They're the same age as you when it happened!" It was this plea by a teacher of third-year students in a public junior high school in Tokyo that moved my heart.

But I made it conditional: "Only if I can do it at the place where my lost classmates fought the war with me." I meant the ruins of the Chugoku Military District Communications bunker that remained on the grounds of Hiroshima Castle.

When the time came and I tried to speak in that room steeped in painful memories, recalling my dead friends left me at times speechless. Eventually, I was weeping. As I spoke, I pointed. "That

In September 1988, when I was working at the Peace Culture Foundation, I underwent surgery for breast cancer. During my five months of sick leave, my doctor told me that three polyps found in my stomach "will need continuous monitoring." In truth, I live with the constant fear of developing another cancer.

Even so, I continue to tell my story, to appeal for nuclear abolition, and to try to convince people of the folly of war. I will go on fighting to overcome fear and make my appeal.

war and call for the abolition of nuclear weapons, we will make the same mistakes. I decided to spend my life working to free the world of these weapons.

After eight years working at the orphanage for blind A-bomb victims, I got a temporary job at City Hall issuing A-bomb Health Books to survivors. I had enrolled in Girls Commercial School because I wanted to work at a bank, but the bombing took that possibility away.

Because I didn't want to be thought ignorant, I began to study. With the permission of City Hall staff, I began auditing classes at Hiroshima University. Particularly interested in English, I bought textbooks and studied on my own.

I later got a job at the Hiroshima Peace Culture Foundation, in the section that writes protest letters sent to governments of countries when they conduct a nuclear test. I was assigned to translate those letters into English, so my independent English studies served me well.

I worked at the Peace Culture Foundation for 27 years and retired in 1993. Afterwards, I traveled overseas almost every year to share my A-bomb experience.

Because I wanted people to learn about the atomic bombings and the nuclear issues and spread the message for nuclear abolition and lasting peace to the world, in 1996 I established the Association to Communicate the Heart of Hiroshima. Most members are young university students and teachers.

We invited educators from American public schools to visit classes in public high schools in Hiroshima. We provided opportunities for Japanese and American teachers to exchange views on peace and how to teach history. We eventually put up a website and used the Internet to have conversations with people in other countries.

invited to Osaka for cosmetic surgery. Reverend Kiyoshi Tanimoto of Nagarekawa Christian Church had launched a movement to provide more than 80 young female bomb victims reconstructive surgery. I was 20.

I was chosen to receive surgery in Osaka. Because my injuries were relatively light, I was in the last group to go to Osaka. Over seven months, I underwent 12 operations.

When incisions around my eyes allowed the lids to close properly, I felt a joy I can't describe. Until then, my unclosable eyes would ceaselessly collect dust and dirt that formed painful lumps as they rolled around my eyeballs.

Flesh from my thighs transplanted to my bent elbows and fingers finally freed them to move normally. I was overwhelmed with gratitude. I remembered my mother's advice: "Always be good to others. It will come back to you."

I gave up on marrying and vowed to "live for others."

Around that time, my benefactor Reverend Tanimoto opened an orphanage for children who had lost their sight in the bombing. I was invited to work there. The orphanage opened with three children but quickly grew to 30. I felt very sorry for children whose sight had suddenly been stolen by the bombing. They couldn't even button their shirts. To go to the bathroom, they had to grab our shoulders or our hands. One child told me he had lost his sight because he looked at the bomb. "The heat ray ran to my eyes. I never saw anything again."

Helping the children gave me a reason to live. I worked hard as a nurse for children who could not see.

And my thinking about the bombing deepened. I understood that it is people who create wars and atomic bombs. That unless people abhor windows. I passed my own Hiroshima Girls Commercial School. When I got to Oko Elementary School, painful burns and the heat finally made me lie down near my old school. I collapsed under the eaves of a house on the road. My Aunt Hamamura found me there, carried me home on her back, and then to a rescue station on the hill nearby.

For four days, I ran a fever near 40 degrees, suffered diarrhea, and bled from the gums. I lost half my hair. Often I lost consciousness and hovered near death.

My family daily carried me by stretcher to the rescue station at Oko School for treatment. Burns covered my face, arms, hands, legs, even my feet.

The doctors warned that staying in bed with my legs straight would cause my burned scarred knees to heal without the ability to bend. They forcibly bent my knee joints, which tore off the scabs and sent the blood spurting. The pain was so horrible, I wanted to scream. "Just kill me!"

## A nurse to blind orphans

After the war, food was scarce in Hiroshima. I tried to help my family make ends meet by sitting on the floor performing tasks with my deformed hands. I prepared vegetables grown on the hill in back of our house, removing the vines from sweet potatoes. I sewed buttons on clothing.

"You're too weak." and "Your face is covered with keloids." These initial reasons for denying me a job were soon followed by, "radiation exposure might make you sick." Other rumors withered all talk of marriage: "She'll give birth to handicapped children."

Targeted by such prejudice, I was living without hope when I was

In the river, which was smothered in something like black smoke or mist, a great many raised their voices together, as in an incantation. This resounded in my ears like the roar of the sea.

The raging heat of my body drove me into the river, just like the others I saw. "Aren't you Matsubara-san?" I looked at the person who had called out, but severe burns had swollen her jaw and neck into each other, so altering my classmate Mit-chan that only her voice told me who she was. The river was full of people like Mit-chan and me, people burned beyond recognition.

At this point, reason returned. I understood that the bomb had not just targeted me, but everyone. About that time, flames were leaping from the way we had just come, chasing us. Mit-chan and I got out of the river on the opposite side, crawled up the bank, and found a road.

People staggered around like sleepwalkers. Torn streetcar cables had tumbled onto the road along with collapsed electric poles. People's heads were plunged into fire cisterns, where they must have died seeking a drink. People immobilized by injury slumped over here and there.

When we got to Kojin Bridge, Mit-chan gazed at me, her eyes flooding with tears. "This is it for me. Go on by yourself!" She collapsed on the ground.

I wanted to carry her on my back to a rescue station, but I was so exhausted, I was on the verge of falling down myself. I left in remorseful silence. Three days later, her parents found her and took her home, but she died soon after. Even now, when I think about Mit-chan, I feel my heart will break.

I made it through the Danbara shopping area, picking my way over the road strewn with shards of glass from shattered shop doors and barely make out the wings of a B-29. I was looking carefully at the plane when, seemingly from the tail appeared an enormous orange and bluish-white flash. I dove to the ground as a huge roar sounded all around me. I thought I had been targeted.

I don't know how much time passed, but when I came to and looked around, the world was darkened by clouds of dirt and dust. I could see nothing. Where were Funaoka-san, who had been near me, and other members of my team? Had they been thrown elsewhere?

From the ground up, the air gradually cleared. I looked at my body and was astonished. Having been told that white clothing would stand out to the enemy pilots, we had dyed dusky purple my white top and monpe work pants. The heat ray had virtually burned this dark cloth cleanly off. Only rags of fabric over my chest and bottom remained. My white canvas shoes remained on my feet, but burns had swollen my insteps—they were about to burst out. The unbearable pain forced me to take off my shoes. From then on, I was shoeless.

Checking my body more closely, I saw that both hands, arms, and legs and face were terribly burned. The swollen red skin peeled off, glossy like cellophane, leaving blood-red flesh beneath. The skin of my fingers and arms hung like rags and was turning yellow as blood seeped through it.

Maybe because I had sheltered my face from the flash with my right hand, it was especially burned. Terrified, I began to run away in the dark, stubbing my feet on rubble, falling down. The way in front cleared enough that I made it to the bridge.

A crowd of the injured huddled at the foot of the bridge. Most were nearly naked because the heat ray had burned off their clothes. Blood flowed from charred black skin. Some corpses were burned completely black, with only white teeth distinguishable from the rest.

Whenever I cried over my misfortune, she wept by my side. "You'd have been better off dying."

Only later did I learn that while I hovered at death's doorstep, my mother took her kimonos to the countryside to pay for my treatment. When I learned that she had sold her precious kimonos, I vowed, "I'll never cry in front of Mother again!"

When my seven months of treatment at home ended, I returned to school. Of my roughly 250 classmates, fewer than 50 had come back.

## "Go on!" Her eyes welling with tears, my friend told me to flee

That day, we first-year students at Hiroshima Girls Commercial School (now, Hiroshima Shogyo) had gone to clean up debris from building demolition at Tsurumi-cho (now, Naka-ku), 1.5 kilometers from the hypocenter. About 500 first- and second-year students and eleven teachers had gathered at our meeting place at the foot of Hijiyama Bridge. It was a refreshing morning under a clear, cloudless sky.

When we arrived at our task site in Tsurumi-cho, I slid off my shoulders the backpack that held my lunch box and first-aid kit and left them in the work shed. One after another, the groups ordered to join the demolition force at Tsurumi-cho arrived on the scene—mobilized students in the lower grades of junior high schools and girls schools from various districts, along with volunteer corps from companies.

Our school divided into teams of four to pick up broken roof tiles, fragments of wood, nails, etc. and drop these into wire containers or baskets. We called, "Yo-sha! Yo-sha!" as we grasped and heaved.

Just then, my friend Funaoka-san shouted, "I hear B-29s!"

The earlier yellow alert had been canceled so I thought she must be wrong, but I looked up anyway. In front of a white contrail I could

Hiroshima August 6, 1945

# My mission found through despair, I join with the youth to appeal for abolition.

**Miyoko Matsubara**

Born August 1932. Exposed at 12 years of age at Tsurumi-cho (now, Naka-ku), 1.5 kilometers from the hypocenter. Deep burns on face, arms, and legs left her unable to close her eyes or bend her elbows. At 20, received reconstructive surgery in Osaka.. After retiring from the Hiroshima Peace Culture Foundation, established the Association for Communicating the Heart of Hiroshima and devoted herself to the movement to abolish nuclear weapons. Eighty-four years old; lives in Minami-ku, Hiroshima City.

## Shocked at my face in the mirror

When I first secretly saw my face in a mirror, I couldn't speak. Even in the dusky light, I could not believe that what I saw—it was a demon's face, swollen, red and covered with stiffly twisted skin. The skin around my eyes was tight, like an overripe tomato. I had no eyebrows.

"Is that . . . me?" Despair overwhelmed me. Tears flowed without end.

Though my whole body had suffered deep burns, others had rescued and somehow gotten me home that same day. As I recovered, I worried increasingly about my face and begged my mother to bring me a mirror. She refused, and the deep burns prevented me from walking. But one day, I crawled to the mirror stand.

"If you'd given me better treatment, I wouldn't have ended up like this!" With no other place to vent my rage and grief, I would lash out at my mother.

"If only it had happened to me, not you!" she grieved.

I'm a Peace Volunteer who guides people through the Hiroshima Peace Memorial Museum and tells them about the A-bomb disaster. I joined the Hiroshima World Peace Mission, a project to "send pilgrims out to speak about the bombing to the world." As a member of the team, in February 2005, I traveled to Pakistan and India to tell my story.

At the end of one event in India, I left the building and was shocked to see a ragged girl of 12 or 13 standing with a baby in her arms—surely, her child. Near a fancy military facility, I saw barefoot orphan girls scrounging through trash for food. When I saw the same scene in Pakistan, they looked like orphans I remembered from Hiroshima.

I never want to see children suffering like that again. Children are a treasure of the Earth.

I spoke at schools in India as well and urged, "Be friends with children in Pakistan, your neighbor country." I heard retorts like, "No!" or "They're enemies!" The two countries have a complex history, but I was astonished to learn that instead of "Let's make friends," children are taught, "Beware, they're our enemies!"

In that moment, I understood that we must have thorough, global peace education if our children are to have a bright future.

Hiroshima August 6, 1945

My mother died in 1950. After she was cremated, we picked out some of her bones from the ashes, as is the custom. But the radiation had left my mother's bones so fragile that my chopsticks would break them, not grasp them. I noticed glittering spots on her skull. When I looked closer, they were pieces of glass still embedded in the bone. After the war, my father was overcome with remorse for having subjected his students to militaristic education. "I'm so sorry for what I did." When he encountered somebody he had known as a teacher, he would make an apology. And after my mother died, he turned into an empty shell.

What launched my peace activities was something I found after my mother died. Sorting through her things, I came across a three-page letter from my sister Mieko. She had written it to our cousin Makoto, who was at the naval pilot training school. "It's starting to feel like late fall at home . . . When you come home as a hero, you'll feel like a stranger. So many houses have been taken down and sweet potatoes are growing on the Eastern Drill Ground. It isn't the old Hiroshima anymore."

Mieko, the 12-year-old first-year student at First Prefectural Girls School, was a gentle soul. She and I used to perform traditional Japanese dance for patients at the Army Hospital, accompanied by a record playing on a phonograph. Our family had an organ, which was unusual before the war. Mieko would play for my brothers and me when we sang nursery rhymes and other songs.

Because we never found any trace of her, that letter became my keepsake. The first time I read it, rage against the atomic bomb welled from the bottom of my heart. I decided to tell people about the horror of that bomb so her death would not be in vain.

crying, "Mother! Mother!" "A-bomb orphans" like these are said to have numbered more than 6,500 in Hiroshima. For at least five years, orphans who survived the bombing fought a different kind of war.

Though they wandered the city trying to find something to put in their empty stomachs, there was virtually nothing there for them. Yakuza (gang) members would feed them, but as payment, they might put pistols in their hands and order them to steal or kill on their behalf. Even 12-and 13-year-old orphan girls sold their bodies to survive.

The Makurazaki Typhoon that attacked Hiroshima a month after the bombing flooded the rivers and swept away many orphans who were sleeping under bridges. One cold winter's night, dozens of orphans were found clustered under a bridge on the Enko River. They had frozen to death, clinging to each other.

In April, a new school year began. I went to see what had happened to my school, Onaga Elementary; it had burned down. Not knowing where else to go, I headed for the familiar Tenmangu Shrine. On New Year's day in previous years, I had gone there to see the first calligraphies. This shrine was also where we students would go to pray for good grades on our tests. As I sat down on the stone steps to the shrine, classmates began to appear, one by one.

"You're alive!" we exclaimed joyfully to each other. Eventually we numbered about ten.

Even three years after the war, when we'd wade into a river, we'd step on human bones. The cleanup crews had not been able to thoroughly clean the river bottoms. Bones remained there for years.

Because so many children had disappeared without a sign, whenever someone picked up a belt buckle or metal button from a school uniform, people would crowd around asking, "Is that my child's?" "Is that my grandchild's?"

When the freight train neared Mukainada staition, a blaring yellow alert siren brought it to a screeching halt. I had no strength to get off and run for cover. The ride to Nishi-Takaya took an hour.

At Grandmother's house, we learned that my father's youngest sister and his oldest sister's family of three were dead. Thereafter, until her death, Grandmother would place her hands together in front of the Buddhist family alter and cry, "It's cruel. So cruel. If only there had been no *pikadon* (flash and boom)."

About three months later, my parents finally moved from our house in Onaga to Nishi-Takaya. This ended their miserable search for my sister. One day, I saw my mother's kimono in the metal washtub so I thought I would wash it. I poured water vigorously into the tub and watched it turn bright red. That was when I learned that my mother had been pregnant and had a miscarriage.

In those days, "human bone powder" was considered a good treatment for burns. In the absence of proper medicine, people crushed the bones of corpses and sold this as medicine. We sprinkled this on my little brothers' burns.

The site where my father and his students had been working on building demolition was the east side of Hijiyama Hill. Because they worked in the hill's shadow, they escaped the flash. My father was helping the injured in the Danbara commercial area. It took him three days to make it back to our house.

## Children around the world must be taught the importance of peace

After the war, children who had returned from their evacuation site in Miyoshi(now, Miyoshi City) walked around the burnt ruins,

I saw the charred corpse of a child around four years old. Only the eyeballs were clearly distinguishable from the blackened body, as they had popped from their sockets.

Soldiers were burning countless bodies. Hundreds of corpses lay in every direction. Those who carried the bodies and those who poured heavy oil on them worked in silence. The whole scene was unreal. Among the bodies were some who still breathed. Now and then, too exhausted to shut my ears, I listened, stupefied, to their final screams.

Because we were in too much pain to move, we lay down on the fields of the Eastern Drill Ground and spent the night among corpses. For three days and three nights we listened to the city of Hiroshima burn. The shocking scenes enveloped in the bright red of fires permanently spoiled the sight of sunsets for me.

The next morning, all the wooden bridges that had spanned the seven rivers of Hiroshima had burned and fallen into the water.

After leaving the Eastern Drill Ground and returning to our broken house we found strangers taking shelter in it. The second day, my grandmother (father's mother) came to us; it was decided that we would take refuge at her house in Nishi-Takaya (now, Higashi Hiroshima City).

But mother said, "Mieko might come home, so I'll stay here!" Leaving her there, my brothers, Grandmother, and I boarded a freight train bound for Nishi-Takaya. The freight train was full of corpses. We had no idea where they were going.

Around that time, I started to feel ill. My gums bled, filling my mouth with blood. The smell of corpses made me nauseous and weak. I could no longer stand up. I lay on the floor groaning, "I can't move, I can't move." I was later diagnosed with radiation-induced aplastic anemia.

three-year-old was seriously burned on the back, arms, and legs. He was screaming. His undershirt and shorts were burnt to rags. Burns peeled his skin from the neck to the left arm. These burns later turned into keloid scars. Even in summer, he wore long-sleeved shirts with high collars to hide them.

Neighbor houses tilting over heaps of rubble seemed ready to collapse. As it was breakfast time, people had been cooking with flames. Soon, here and there, houses began to burn. In time, flames enveloped the entire area. The most piteous sight was a child whose mother was trapped under her fallen house as flames approached. He was screaming, "My mother! Save my mother!" But nothing could be done.

The fires spread over a wide area. I can still hear the heart-wrenching screams of a little girl trapped under a pillar as she burned to death.

As we ran away, we encountered people whose clothes were mostly burned off, their skin hanging in strips. People who could not move because their eyeballs were popped out. "Please give me water! Water!" moaned people burned so deeply that we could not tell their gender. Eventually they all stopped moving.

Because the city was in flames, people in our neighborhood fled to the safety of the Eastern Drill Ground. I ran with my blood-soaked mother and my little brothers. I must have breathed in radiation, because I could barely breathe. I vomited repeatedly.

The Eastern Drill Ground was a horrible sight—people near death whose faces were split open like pomegranates and covered in blood; people whose ripped arms exposed white bones; corpses with intestines spilling out. Wandering among the corpses and injured people were countless children, crying and looking for their parents.

Tokyo, Osaka, and other major cities. Every time B29s flew overhead, I was frightened. All the strong males had been sent to war, so women and girls practiced fighting fires with bucket relays. We also practiced thrusting with bamboo spears.

When the war turned against Japan, children between six and nine years old were evacuated with their teachers by truck to temples in the countryside. At the same time, older children between ten and thirteen were forced to help take down buildings to prevent fires from spreading during air raids.

## From radiation exposure to aplastic anemia

I was eight, a third grader at Onaga Elementary School.

My father was a teacher at Matsuyama Commercial School (now, Setouchi High School). Our house stood three doors from his school. Early that morning, my father was out supervising students in building demolition. With both father and Mieko were off taking down houses, eating breakfast at home at Onaga (now, Higashi-ku) were mother, me, and my little brothers, age five and three.

Just after 8:00, we heard the drone of airplanes, but because the earlier yellow alert had been cleared, my brothers shouted, "Japanese planes!" and ran outside to wave at them. In a clear blue sky, wings glinted in the sun.

Just then, a huge flash. A tremendous shock wave followed. When I came to, I had been thrown onto the dirt in the yard.

The walls of our house crumbled. Pillars bent. Bleeding from pieces of glass piercing her head, my frantic mother came outside. I was sure that an incendiary bomb had fallen right on our house.

Our house was 2.8 kilometers from the hypocenter. My five-year-old brother had been under the eaves and was uninjured, but the no avail.

When there was nowhere left to look, they daily made the rounds to pray at the seven temples and shrines clustered around the foot of Futabayama Hill.

I have no memory of my little brothers or me speaking with our parents during that time. They were so desperately focused on my sister that we were not in their field of vision.

We didn't even have a good photograph of my sister to remember her by. Because Japan was at war, we did not take family photos. Years later, when a relative gave my parents a photo of her at seven years old, taken the day she started learning Japanese dance, they gazed adoringly at her image.

If only they could have found something of my sister's in the burnt ruins of Dohashi—anything at all would have helped give them closure.

Having found nothing of her at the site, they went on year after year feeling, "Mieko might be hospitalized somewhere." "One day, she might just appear!" Perpetually hoping that she lived, my parents died without ever reporting her death to the municipality. I grieve for my parents and my sister.

Ever since I could remember, it was war, war, war all the time. Every day, we went to the streets to send off soldiers to the front, waving flags and shouting to cheer them. "Banzai! Banzai!"

Every day I went to school wearing a cushioned air-raid kerchief, baggy monpe work pants and a top my mother made out of a kimono. At school, every time an air-raid warning sounded, we hurried to the shelter. We learned hand-flag signals in the playground and other war exercises. I can't remember sitting at our desks having a real lesson about anything. The radio announced the aerial bombardment of

# That my sister's death be not in vain, I tell my story

**Emiko Okada**
Born January 1937. At eight years old, exposed to the bombing at home, Onaga (now, Higashi-ku), about 2.8 kilometers from the hypocenter. Suffered pernicious anemia. Her 12-year-old sister never returned from her building demolition task. Because no remains or anything she had that day were ever found, both parents died thinking their daughter might still be alive. Her sister's death motivated Emiko to become a peace activist. She has told her story in India and Pakistan. Seventy-nine years old; lives in Higashi-ku, Hiroshima City.

## My parents believed that my sister was alive

My 12-year-old sister went off that morning calling cheerfully, "See you later!" She went to help take down buildings for a fire lane. She never came home. She went to the Dohashi (now, Naka-ku)area, only 800 meters from the hypocenter.

For the next three months, my parents searched the burnt ruins and rescue stations. They often trudged to the ruins of her building demolition site, but never found anything that looked like hers, much less her remains.

When they heard that some students from First Girls School (First Hiroshima Prefectural Girls High School, now, Hiroshima Minami High School) had made it to Koi Elementary School, they rushed there, propelled by hope's faint glimmer. At Koi Elementary, they heard, "On the way, some girls tumbled into the Tenma River." That sent them to the Tenma River to scour the area for days.

When they learned that many injured people had been ferried to Ninoshima Island now, Minami-ku, they took a boat to the island—to

Hiroshima August 6, 1945

My father was a carpenter. He went to his work in Mitaki (now, Nishi-ku) every day. On August 6, he had a stomachache and stayed home, 1.5 kilometers from the hypocenter. He was killed by the bomb.

My mother was working at the Mitsubishi Plant in Eba (now, naka-ku), more than four kilometers from the hypocenter. She was safe.

She immediately started walking around the city looking for my father, my sister and me. She walked all over, became exhausted, entered and fell in asleep in a school building that was still standing. It was Honkawa Elementary School, not far from the hypocenter.

The next day when she woke up, she was astonished. The school was full of huge piles of dead bodies.

Every time I talk about the events of August 6, my heart feels a pain, as if another piece of glass hidden in my body was coming to surface.

something, so she sold fruit, laying it out on a wooden door. She couldn't get any rice, but sometimes she could make and sell side dishes. Some time later, she started her restaurant again.

Since I had lived with my husband only one week after our marriage, we knew nothing about each other.

One thing I learned after living with him a while was that he didn't like work. Jobs were very hard to find, even for military veterans, but he didn't even try. He spent his days doing nothing but playing around.

No matter how busy we were in the restaurant, he never showed the slightest will to help. He must have thougt since he was a child that he didn't have to help in the busy restaurant.

When we started selling snow cones from a night stall during a neighborhood event, he thought that was fun so he helped a time or two. But soon he stopped, saying, "I'm tired!" Those were the only times I saw him working.

Our first daughter was born the next year, then a second daughter three years later. Both deliveries were relatively easy. I had no concern about the atomic bombing. The restaurant was always busy, and I had to take care of a bedridden invalid. I had no time to worry about anything else. That brother-in-law passed away in October 1948.

My husband frequently had affairs with women and was often away from home. One day he said, "Would you change her dress?" After I changed the dress on our second daughter, he took her to another woman's house. I endured it all thinking, "I will bear all this for the sake of our daughters. Maybe he'll change someday." But after seven years of a bad marriage, I divorced him.

My two daughters were adopted by my in-laws, and I returned to my parents' house in 1952.

there with me, but I do remember a man in his mid-30's with a fist-sized hole in his chest. He looked like he was dying.

A glass fragment two centimeters across was buried in the back of my right knee. Because the blast blew from that side, the glass was buried mostly in my right side. More than a month had passed, so the glass was covered by my flesh.

The pain I felt when those pieces were taken out was so bad I can't help shivering even now as I recall it. The doctor cut my leg and removed the glass without anesthesia.

On the day I went to Itsukaichi, my mother-in-law started going to Hiroshima to look for her husband, who had been involved in building demolition. She even went out to Ninoshima Island (now, Minami-ku), and there she learned the bad news. He had been taken there and had died on the island. Because she was busy with the search, then struggled with grief, the treatment for the glass in my leg didn't start until one month later. During that time, I was busy limping around taking care of my brother-in-law.

My father-in-law's mother lived in Hiroshima with his sister. She died shielding her grandchild. She was found holding the child tight to her chest. Both were completely charred. It seems they were burned alive.

## My husband returned from the front with no will to work

The war ended. My husband came back from the front a month later.

Near the end of spring 1947, my mother-in-law started selling food in front of a streetcar stop in Ujina. She had managed a restaurant in Senda-machi, but when the war turned against Japan, she had nothing to sell, so she suspended her business. We couldn't eat unless we did hypocenter) the bleeding was so bad I was losing consciousness. I recovered my senses just before falling off the bridge. I made it across only because someone helped me.

"I have to get down below the bank! I'll be targeted and shot by an enemy plane!" I fought my way down to the river and hid behind a boat moored in the river. An old woman crouched by the boat holding tightly her dead grandchild. Her shoulders shivered as she cried, "How can I apologize to my son?" I saw a boy of 14 or 15 crying. I approached him and saw his mother dead by his side. She had no injury at all and was still beautiful.

I have only hazy memories of that time. I don't remember if I talked to anyone or not. I think I might have talked to a worker from the factory nearby. I think he told me, "A truck that was supposed to go to our plant in Itsukaichi is waiting in Koi. I can give you a ride to Itsukaichi. You want to come with me to Koi (now, Nishi-ku)?" I must have told him my mother-in-law was in Itsukaichi.

We walked toward Koi. I got lightheaded on the way, then sick. I clearly remember shouting, "Leave me here!" I have no memory of how I got to Koi or what kind of vehicle I rode in. Somehow I managed to get a ride in that truck. I got to stay that night in his plant.

The next morning, I headed for my mother-in-law's evacuation site. I was walking on the riverbank filled with anxiety thinking, "Is she okay? Will I find her all right?" Unexpectedly, I ran right into her. I clung to her without thinking and sobbed out loud.

One month later, my mother-in-law put me on a cart and took me to a hospital in Hatsukaichi to get the glass fragments removed. The hospital was packed with survivors. I don't remember exactly who was

Hiroshima August 6, 1945

## Thrown into the backyard filled with glass fragments

In 1945, I was 20 and a marriage was arranged. My husband was my age and was drafted. A week after the wedding, he joined his regiment in Iwakuni City, Yamaguchi Prefecture. I still moved in with his busy household, but that was nothing unusual in those days.

My father-in-law worked for a fire station and was busy demolishing buildings for a fire lane. He had a bedridden son (my husband's older brother) who was mentally disabled. Someone threw a snake onto his chest when he was in junior high. Because he was so timid, he started to cry hysterically and never really recovered.

My biggest task was to attend to my brother-in-law's personal needs, so when an air-raid warning sounded, I took refuge in the shelter carrying him on my back. The war got more intense, and my mother-in-law was evacuated to Itsukaichi (now, Saeki-ku) with her son. That was one month before the war ended.

On August 6, I was at my in-laws' house behind Red Cross Hospital in Senda-machi. My father-in-law went out to Kako-machi (now, naka-ku) for building demolition early in the morning. I finished breakfast and was putting on monpe work pants to go out into our field.

I didn't see the flash. I didn't hear any roar. I just experienced a huge blast. When I came to, I found myself in nothing but my underwear. While changing clothes, I had been thrown into the backyard. I was barefoot.

Glass shards were piercing my whole body, and my white chemise was covered in blood. With no idea what had happened, I thought, "I have to get out of here." I climbed up the bank on bare feet with blood gushing from my right leg.

As I crossed Minami Ohashi Bridge(1.75 kilometers from the

yesterday.

I also suffered from anemia. Soon after the war ended, I worked in a restaurant managed by my mother-in-law. During my periods, my anemia would get worse. I was struggling. When I needed to get something from upstairs, I would try to climb the stairs, but I would get dizzy. Sometimes I barely made it up. I would stagger and almost fall down the stairs.

Later, when I divorced my husband, I had to find a job. I had a hard time. After a long search, my friend introduced me to the Central Wholesale Market. I got a job there.

The Public Health Office dispatched a medical examination car once a year, and all market employees could get health examinations.

Every time, I had to go back for another exam due to anemia. I always had to go to the another hospital. It became a part of my routine.

At my workplace, we would receive an order, then we had to quickly make packages by gathering certain products and putting them in a bag by a deadline. I was working with colleagues, and they knew I was weak, so they took good care of me, saying, "Don't work too hard." However, I was a carpenter's daughter, and I grew up watching my father's finish his projects one by one in a spirit of togetherness with his fellow workers. I never allowed myself to rest.

I continued when I was so tired I could barely keep standing. I wanted nothing more than to lie down, but I used all my strength to endure. Now I think that struggle actually made me stronger.

# Worked desperately despite severe anemia

**Nobuko Suzuki**
Born February 1925. Exposed to the atomic bombing when she was 20 in her husband's house in Senda-machi(now,Naka-ku), 1.7 kilometers from hypocenter. Glass fragments remained in her body for decades; some she had to have removed. After the war, suffered serious anemia, helped in restaurant run by her mother-in-law. After getting divorced, she worked hard in a job it took a long time to find. Remarried in 1956. Lives in Sakata, Hatsukaichi City; 91 years old.

## Glass fragments emerging after 33 years

I wonder why glass fragments buried deep in my body suddenly came to the surface. They moved around my body and suddenly, they popped out from some unexpected place. One touched a nerve. It made the area prickle, and when I touched it, I felt a strange, hard lump under my skin.

It didn't bother me much at first, but the prickly feeling got stronger. At the hospital the doctor cut the skin over the lump, and there was a glass fragment about five millimeters across. I don't remember exactly, but I think I underwent this same process at least four or five times.

The first piece was taken out in 1978. It came from the outside of my left knee.

"Keeping it in your leg for 33 years, it should have turned into a diamond, but it seems to still be glass. It won't do you any good." The doctor and I laughed.

For me, the 33 years since that day were both forever and like

## Moving to a new house, our exposure was secret

My family moved on July 31, 1948, from Kamiichi to a new house in Nobori-cho, a neighborhood in Hiroshima City. I entered Nobori-machi Elementary School, and started in the second semester of third grade. After moving to Nobori-cho, my mother never went back to Kabe. Nor did she ever mention the atomic bomb. Our neighbors in Nobori-cho knew only that we had evacuated and come back, so we didn't talk about the bomb.

Even when someone raised a topic related to the bomb, she never took part in the conversation. Only once when a neighbor with an A-bomb Health Book said, "It's helpful. I can get free medical treatment." She muttered with a sigh, "But I have daughters." She was probably aware that she had "secondary exposure" from nursing radioactive survivors in Kabe.

She lived the rest of her life insisting we had nothing to do with Kabe or the atomic bomb. Her approach was so consistent and so frightening, we never mentioned Kabe in front of her. Mother weighed only 35 kilograms. She was so thin she had to get blood transfusions quite often. Even those transfusions, she insisted, had nothing to do with the atomic bombing. Thanks to her attitude, I felt no anxiety when I married at 30, nor when our daughter was born eight years later.

Maybe Mother knew that fear is the greatest cruelty.

In Kamiichi survivors were also accepted at the Obayashi Hospital and a temple. Once, a victim drove a three-wheeler truck into town, stopped in front of general store in Kamiichi and shouted, "Give us things to wear, anything, even rags!" In that truck were people whose clothes were so burned they were practically naked.

In addition to survivors, we saw many dead people. Bodies filling a large cart were carried to a sandbar in the river. Because the river was too deep, the cart couldn't reach the sandbar, so the men carrying them grabbed the corpses with fire hooks and threw them up onto the sandbar like fish. I guess they could do that because the corpses were children and fairly small women.

I heard from others that a few of the "corpses" were still breathing. They groaned or writhed when hooked. Even now when I see a sandbar or fire hook, that sight comes back to my mind and I'm horrified. The corpses on the sandbar were lined up, covered in heavy oil and cremated. When wind blew the smell toward us, I couldn't eat. Of those who took refuge in our house, five died, some were taken to hospitals, and the rest had light injuries. Those who could went to stay with relatives. All were gone in less than a week.

On August 21, my father was discharged from the regiment he had served in Kyushu. He immediately went to see what had happened to his workshop in Honkawa-cho. His craftsmen had been all killed. They were still lying on top of one another. Two weeks had passed, so they were decomposing badly.

He walked around near the hypocenter for several days searching for his brothers and their families. He was the first of five brothers. He was exposed to a lot of radiation and died at 56.

taking refuge in our house. All were women or children, no men. My mother was extremely busy caring for them—distributing wet towels or helping to take off their burned clothes. And throughout, she was carrying my sister on her back. I was near the survivors, too, helping my mother.

Around the time that younger brother with purple spots died, his older brother showed up. He had serious burns all over his body. Even his face was wrapped in bandages, leaving holes for his eyes, nose and mouth. I was frightened of him, but he survived.

Soon after the bandaged brother came, his older sister arrived. She had walked through first-aid stations all over the city looking for her two brothers. She told my mother, "You shouldn't be here. I heard it's not good to breathe the air where the injured are housed." She had heard about "contaminated air" at the relief stations.

Immediately, my mother rented three empty houses in the neighborhood and moved some families there. My sister and I moved into a room in a big house we rented from the farmer next door. We slept there.

That older sister who told us about the contaminated air developed purple spots and died the following day. Another person we helped was a middle-aged lady who died leaving her children behind.

We ran into that bandaged brother again later. I didn't recognize him, but he talked to my mother. The bandage was off so we could see his face. His earlobes had melted. They were just two holes opened on the sides of his head. One side of his nose was also melted, leaving just a hole. His face was red with keloid scars. I got sick just looking at his face.

He told us he survived because maggots bred in his wounds. They ate radioactive substances along with the bloody pus.

she saw a bright, instantaneous flash, she thought I was playing with mirrors again. She warned, "Don't play with mirrors, Kazuko!" Kamiichi suffered hardly any damage from the bombing. Our houses were not tilted. Our windows were not broken. Basically, no one noticed.

Therefore, my family expected not to be affected. We had moved to Kabe on March 29 on the last shipping wagon. However, as I mentioned, my mother took good care of others. Many neighbors from Senda-machi visited us after we moved, saying, "How's life out here?" Because she had maintained these relationships, residents of Senda-machi who were exposed to the bombing came to our evacuation site.

They came one after the next, relying on my mother for help. Because we nursed those people, my mother, my little sister and I (another sister was born after the war) appear to have had secondary exposure. I was six then.

**Nursing survivors**

The first visitor after the atomic bombing was the younger of two brothers, sons of a teacher at a dressmaking school. He came that afternoon on a "refuge wagon" bound for Kabe. He entered our house quite cheerfully calling, "I'm home!"

He was full of energy. He went right away to the river behind our house to catch fish. But that night he came down with a high fever. He started groaning, "I'm tired! It hurts!" He groaned all the next day and was cold the following morning. Purple spots had appeared on his face, arms and all over. He had looked so healthy. He had no burns or serious injuries, but he died in three days. It was quite shocking.

By that time, a dozen neighbors exposed in Senda-machi were

When her bile duct was blocked, I boiled down bile that was drawn from her with a needle. I made bile pills, wrapping them in mashed sweet potato to make them easier to take. We had to return bile to her body. If it stopped flowing through her digestive organs, her life would be in danger. But boiling down that bile smelled so bad I could hardly stand it.

## Evacuated to Kabe, 15 kilometers from the hypocenter

My father worked with paulownia wood, processing it for geta (clogs) and chests of drawers. At one point, he employed more than 60 craftsmen. His workshop was in Honkawa-cho(now, Naka-ku), and our residence was in Senda-machi(now, Naka-ku), but my mother, my sister and I were evacuated to Kamiichi, which was in Kabe, north of Hiroshima.

We planned to go back to the house in Senda-machi on August 5 to get some things we needed. We went to the station to find the train completely full, even the aisles and entrances. We gave up, thinking we couldn't board a train like that with an eight-month-old baby. If we had ridden that train, we would have been killed by the bomb.

My mother always took care of others. She was leader of our neighborhood association until right before she gave birth to my sister. Despite her big belly, she went around the neighborhood calling, "Yellow alert!" We had fire pounders at our house. They were like mops to be soaked in water for use in extinguishing fires ignited by an incendiary bomb. My mother kept the fire pounders for the whole neighborhood association and maintained them ready to use.

Kamiichi was more than 15 kilometers from the hypocenter. My mother told me I often used to play with mirrors. That day, when

Hiroshima August 6, 1945

The first occasion came four years after the bombing. I was a fourth grader. Suddenly, my sheets turned yellow. I had a liver disorder that lasted several days. Serious jaundice turned not only my skin and the whites of my eyes yellow, it caused yellow sweat that got on my sheets. When my menstruation started, I suffered terrible pain. I was forced to take whole days off from school and work.

When I started working for a company, all of a sudden I got a high fever, nearly 40°C. I had great difficulty even standing. When I lay down, I recovered in a few hours, as if nothing had happened. I often experienced this symptom and believed I had some sort of abnormal constitution. After 70, I developed uterine and ovary hypertrophy. My womb and ovaries were removed. At 72, I developed bladder cancer and underwent another operation.

My younger sister was eight months old at the time of the bombing. A few days after the bombing, she got a cold. Her condition worsened rapidly, and she was carried to the hospital in a coma. Her legs swelled to three times their size, and the doctor had to incise them to squeeze out the bloody pus. My mother said that her pus filled a bucket. She was hospitalized for more than a month. She escaped death, but was always weak. When she entered elementary school, my mother begged her teacher, "My daughter is doing well to be alive. Please don't give her much homework."

I believe her condition is related to being carried on our mother's back for several days while her mother was nursing A-bomb survivors.

My mother contracted both stomach cancer and bile duct cancer. She was hospitalized more than two years before dying at 72. Treating her bile duct cancer was extremely expensive. If only she had had an A-bomb Health Book, her treatment would have been free of charge. But she had never had been willing to apply.

# Mother refused the A-bomb Survivor Health Book to protect her daughters from being *hibakusha*

**Kazuko Kamidoi**
Born June 1939. Six at the time of the atomic bombing. Previously evacuated to Kabe (now, Asakita-ku), more than 15 kilometers from the hypocenter. Having nursed A-bomb survivors with her mother, she received secondary exposure. She and her mother suffered liver disorders, cancers, and other health problems. Father walked around the hypocenter looking for his brothers and died from radiation exposure. Lives in Saeki-ku, Hiroshima City; 77 years old.

## Poor health might be radiation

"I'll never make my three daughters hibakusha!" My mother firmly rejected the idea of applying for an A-bomb health book. Extensive publicity for the new A-bomb Health Books said, "Survivors can get medical treatment for free." But my mother never listened. She had heard too many people say, "Her husband's family found out she was in the bombing and sent her back." Or "The match was broken off because she was hibakusha." We all heard this kind of thing here and there.

But because of my mother's attitude, my sister and I thought, "We have nothing to do with the atomic bombing." I contracted various diseases, but always assumed they were unrelated to radiation exposure. I got pregnant and gave birth to a child with no fear of radiation effects. I lived with this attitude for more than 70 years. But when I think back, I have had many occasions to wonder, "Is this an effect of secondary exposure?"

I was invited to join a volunteer group when I was 57. "If I had been dead, I couldn't have done anything. Because I'm alive and in good shape, I want to be useful to others." With this attitude, I accepted the invitation. I visited a nursing home for the elderly twice a month as a member of the volunteer group. I helped them with meals, cleaning their rooms and changing their sheets.

In 2004, when the group had been working more than 20 years, we received a commendation from the neighboring city of Fukuyama. I kept up my volunteer work as long as I could, but around the time I turned 80, it became too difficult. I just didn't have the physical strength, so I retired.

Now, I tell my A-bomb experience as a member of the Fukuyama City Atomic Bomb Survivors' Association. That way, I express my sincere desire to build a peaceful society free from nuclear weapons. We must stop all war because wars inflict too much suffering on too many. I hope I can pass on my experience and this conviction to young people.

a midwife. I felt relaxed and comfortable. I birthed a healthy baby girl. I was so relieved, thinking, "I was exposed, but it seems I wasn't affected."

Then, I got pregnant again and gave birth to a second girl. Again, we had a midwife come to our home, but soon after the midwife left, the baby's condition changed suddenly. She had a convulsion and died on her seventeenth day. I have no words to describe my surprise and sorrow. I was wracked with fear. "I wonder if this is because of my exposure?"

My husband had never said anything about my exposure. He probably knew I was a survivor, but I thought maybe he didn't see it as a problem because he was impaired as well.

My father often spoke to me about my husband, probably wanting to comfort me after we got married. "He could possibly be a big success." But sometimes, later, he followed that in a lowered voice with, "Or, he will be a complete loser, one or the other."

As my father guessed, my husband failed at everything he tried, and each time we asked for my father's help. He became addicted to alcohol, and my married life became nothing but trouble. We divorced by agreement when I was 31. I took our 8-year-old daughter with me.

A few years later, my urine suddenly turned dark brown. It continued for weeks so I went to the hospital for a checkup. I was told, "It might be a thyroid disorder." Whatever it was, that atomic bomb messed up my life.

Later, my father gave me the funds to open a coffee shop called Romance. It was right in front of Onomichi Station, and I ran it for 20 years. I caused my father all kinds of hardship all my life. I feel sorry for him, but I am more than grateful to him.

father started looking for a chance to introduce me to a prospective husband. I was only 19, but it's natural that he wanted me to get married if possible.

My marriage was arranged for exactly one month before my twentieth birthday. My husband was the younger brother of my brother-in-law and six years older than me. His eyesight was quite poor so he hadn't been drafted. He had gone to southeast Asia as a civilian employee of the army and returned to Onomichi.

Rumors were going around that "A-bomb survivors will die young" or "Survivors will have deformed babies." I believe my father was a bit desperate. He just wanted someone to marry his daughter.

Because it was a time of severe shortages, we didn't have an extravagant wedding, but we did take wedding pictures at a nearby photo studio wearing formal kimono.

I attended the Coming-of-Age Ceremony about three months after my wedding. The ceremony was held in the auditorium of Tsuchido Elementary School in Onomichi. The scar on my face was hardly noticeable, but I still had a bright red scar on my neck, so I went to the ceremony wearing a high collar blouse. I met classmates from high school for the first time in a long time. I was afraid they would find out about my exposure in Hiroshima, so I left as soon as I could. Later, I went through the whole summer with long-sleeve dresses.

My father prepared a house for us. I tried to pretend that what happened in Hiroshima was just a bad dream. I concentrated on housework, on being a wife, and lived with no serious trouble. But when I got pregnant two years later, I felt terrible anxiety.

I had nobody to talk to about this fear, so I encouraged myself saying, "If I give birth to a deformed baby, so be it!" I was ready to accept my fate. I gave birth not in a big hospital but at home with

I had barely managed to get home to Minari now, Onomichi-City a little after 9:00 in the morning on August 7. The first thing I did was drink water. I still remember that delicious cold water.

Seeing my terrible burns, my mother and younger brother were upset. "It's horrible! Looks painful!" Unlike conventional burns, the burns from the A-bomb heat ray were both deep and wide, with foul-smelling pus oozing out. The smell attracted flies, so I was always in a mosquito net my mother hung for me.

The next day, I went to a clinic in Onomichi, but the doctor had no idea how to treat burns caused by an atomic bomb. I just got a standard burn ointment. My mother heard from a neighbor that cucumber was good for removing heat. Every day she grated cucumber and applied it to my burns. At the time of the bombing, I was wearing a gym shirt and monpe work pants. Mysteriously, my clothes didn't burn at all, and all my burns were on my right side. Burned were my arms, face, neck and shoulder where they were not covered by my gym shirt. I got keloid scars that remained a long time on my shoulder and arms.

## My second daughter died after 17 days

One of the reasons I went to Hiroshima Women's Higher School of Education was a suggestion from my brother-in-law. My father never expressed regret openly, but I am sure he thought, "I should never have let Ritsuko go to Hiroshima." Thinking "I never want to go to Hiroshima again!" I stayed in Onomichi.

At first, my father thought it would be impossible for me to marry. When I was able to go out by myself, he said "You better learn some skill." He had me go to a dressmaking school in Onomichi.

After a year and a half, when the scar on my face faded away, my

Hiroshima August 6, 1945

The Station was crowded with people waiting for a train that was not sure to come. People were talking. "What kind of air raid was that?" The number of survivors taking refuge in the station increased. Finally, when it was completely dark, a train came into the station. The train had its lights off to avoid being seen by an enemy plane. That completely dark train filled immediately full. With a desperate effort, we got on the train and left Hiroshima at last. But the train stopped at Hongo, three stations before Onomichi. We went to an inn in front of Hongo Station, explained that we were injured because a bomb dropped on Hiroshima, and they let us stay the night.

I used the inn's telephone to tell my parents I was alive. My mother answered the phone. I didn't know the word "atomic bomb" so I said, "I got injured by a bomb, but I can walk, so I'll go home by the first train tomorrow morning."

The friends I was with said, "Finally, we can stretch our arms and legs!" They lay down, but I couldn't. Lying caused too much pain. I leaned against a chair and waited for daybreak.

The next morning, I got on the first train feeling impatient. The train filled up at Hongo Station with people going to work or school. Daily life was still happening there, and the tragic sights I had seen in Hiroshima seemed unreal. With my hair disheveled, my face burned, and my arm hanging in a sling, I felt ashamed. I hid myself in a corner of the car.

Finally, the train arrived at Onomichi Station. As soon as I saw my father, who had come to the station to meet me, I started to run. I shouted "Daddy!" I clung to him and sobbed.

My father said, "You made it! You made it!" He was stunned to see me with such thick oil on my burns. All he could say was, "Mother is waiting. Let's hurry home!"

The situation on the street was more tragic. A person whose face was bloody all over was gasping for breath. A mother half-naked was hysterically screaming her child's name. A child covered with serious burns wandered around crying for his mother. A person with skin completely peeled off was groaning, "I'm hot! Hot!"

Dead bodies lay scattered like logs. Their hair singed and bristled, their faces and bodies covered in ash and black soot, they were indistinguishable even as male or female.

We found a first aid station set up by the Army and entered. It was already full of seriously injured victims. Then, I saw thousands of corpses loaded on a big truck. I wondered where they had come from.

In the scorching summer heat, I waited for my turn to receive treatment, enduring the terrible stench that made me nauseous and intense pain. I felt as if the flesh had been ripped away from the upper right part of my body. Finally, my turn came. They applied a thick layer of oil on my arms, neck and face, then hung my right arm in a triangular sling.

We received some dry bread and sugar candy as we left. I put the sweet sugar candy in my mouth and gained some strength. I headed straight for Kaitaichi Station with my classmates. Several places on my body that had been hit by falling debris in the school started to hurt. Every time I breathed I felt pain in my ribs. My neck was swollen, and I had hard time to holding my head up.

But I was afraid of being left behind by my friends. I did my best to keep up. My friends were all full of fear, so nobody said anything. We kept walking, speechless in the heat. It was morning when we left school and went to the first-aid station. By the time we arrived at Kaitaichi Station, it was twilight.

their heads, bent their knees and crouched in the approved posture. Everyone was silent.

When the alert was cleared, smiles came back to faces, and we all streamed back to school. I went up to my classroom on the second floor where I waited for the teacher.

Shortly before the start of our first class, at 8:15, a brief, powerful light like a camera flash filled the room. With no time to think what happened, I lost consciousness. Our school was 1.6 kilometers from the hypocenter. When I came to, I was trapped under the fallen school building and hot. The area was dark. I couldn't see much. A big beam leaned heavily on my back. I called the name of the classmate who had been sitting next to me, but got no answer. My entire body was in pain, maybe because of burns. The right side of my body was hot and spongy.

I gathered all my strength and tried to move, thinking, "I have to get out of here!" I slipped through a hole and saw a dim light over my head. I climbed up and popped out onto the roof.

The Hiroshima I saw from that roof was an empty field. All the tall buildings were gone. Hiroshima had vanished, leaving hardly a trace. The window beside my desk had been open, so I was not pierced with broken glass, like some, but my right side, or window side, was burned.

One of my teachers stood firmly in the rubble like a demon. With a fierce look he shouted, "Get away quick! Run east!" Smoke was already rising from the collapsed building. I ran to the east with several classmates who had also crawled out from under the debris. They had burns and other injuries, some severe. Glass fragments pierced their faces, arms and legs. Blood oozed out here and there, but we had no time to treat such injuries. We pressed both on large wounds, then desperately ran away from the school.

so they ran out of school teachers, who had traditionally been all male. I was desperate to get into that Women's Higher School of Education. However, I would have to live in a dormitory, so I needed extra money beyond the school expenses. It was not easy economically. However, my father offered to pay all the expenses because he wanted me to follow my dream. My father managed a company that produced and sold straw ropes and mats. He was successful, so my family was relatively wealthy. Also, my brother-in-law was a teacher and suggested that I become a teacher. These men supported my effort to go to that school. I was the only one from Onomichi attending Hiroshima Women's Higher School of Education. I had never been to Hiroshima City, so my father accompanied me to the entrance ceremony and handled all the procedures, including getting me into a dormitory. My life in the dormitory got underway.

The school was so new that some of the buildings were not yet completed. Our school temporarily rented rooms. Because of building problems, I entered school in June instead of April. I remember lessons in the classroom explaining "the proper attitude of a female student preparing to be a teacher." Just as I was taking this first step toward my dream, a single atomic bomb cruelly shattered that dream.

## Trapped unconscious under the school building

That morning, cicadas started singing very early, telling us the day would be hot. I was preparing to go to school when the dreaded siren issued a yellow alert. I quickly put on my air-raid hood, grabbed my emergency bag containing medicine, daily necessities, a flashlight and a few other things, put it over my shoulder and headed for the air-raid shelter in the playground.

In the shelter, my classmates pulled air-raid hoods tight over

Hiroshima August 6, 1945

# Grateful for my life, I live to be useful to others.

**Ritsuko Seidai**
Born November 1927. Exposed at 17 to the atomic bombing at Hiroshima Women's Higher School of Education(now, Hiroshima University), 1.6 kilometers from the hypocenter. Seriously burned, received treatment in Onomichi City. Studied at a dressmaking school and got married. Second daughter died after 17 days. Divorced at 31, raised her daughter by running a coffee shop. Received commendation from Fukuyama City for her long contribution as a volunteer in a nursing home. Lives in Fukuyama City; eighty-nine years old.

**My dream of becoming a PE teacher was blown away by the atomic bomb**

"I should never have gone to Hiroshima!"

I was tormented by regret for a long time. Dreaming of becoming a teacher, I went from Onomichi, a city in the eastern part of Hiroshima Prefecture, to the Women's Higher School of Education in Hiroshima City. I returned home two months later in tatters.

I was the middle of three siblings. I had an older sister and a brother five years younger. I was so physically active, my family called me a tomboy. My dream since childhood was to be a physical education teacher.

The Women's Higher School of Education in Hiroshima was established to train female teachers, and it opened the year I graduated from Onomichi Girls High School (now, Onomichi-Higashi High School). This school was necessary because all the men were off at war

In 2011, I visited 13 countries and told my story at 14 venues for university and academic institutions. I was a MOFA non-nuclear special ambassador on the Peace Boat's Global Peace Voyage. On March 13, I gave my testimony at UN Headquarters in Geneva, Switzerland.

"We can never repeat this horrific history. For the sake of peace, I will tell my story, however much it pains me to recall it." Clinging fast to this conviction helped me share my story. However, just after speaking at UN Headquarters, I collapsed. In fact, I had been worried for some time about my legs giving way. When I returned home, I went to the Kure National Medical Center and was found to have a brain tumor. I underwent frontal lobe brain surgery. Fortunately, I recovered, but it is clear that no part of my body escaped damage by the A-bomb. I can't bear the thought of others going through this.

A dozen or so years ago, my granddaughter's composition won the grand prize in a prefectural competition. The title was *The Atomic Bombing of Hiroshima*. She wrote, "I'm grateful to my grandmother, who did everything she could to survive." I am so thankful that even my granddaughter's generation is inheriting the A-bomb stories we strive to leave behind.

It pains us to talk about experiences we wish not to remember. But my mission is to "pass my story to the future," so I continue to talk to students who come to Hiroshima. For 30 years, I have served as president of the Kure Hibakusha Association.

after marriage, and strong people can get weaker. These things happen—marriage is a gamble." She gave in. "All right then! But don't tell anyone she's a survivor, you hear?"

Two years after I became a member of the Yamanaka family, I became pregnant with our first daughter. Because I still had a hole in my lungs from tuberculosis, the doctor said, "Your body will give out completely if you have this baby." My husband agreed. "Your health is more important than any baby. Let's let it go." I appreciated his concern, but I felt I had been given this chance for a reason. I dearly wanted this baby. I had already shown symptoms of thrombocytopenia (failure of the blood to clot) so the doctor warned, "This means you can't have a Caesarian section." When my labor started, I was so weak I quickly tired and fell asleep. Undergoing childbirth while unconscious is very dangerous. The fetus can get stuck in the birth canal and die.

It took three days and three nights, but I gave birth to a baby girl of 2000 grams (4.4 pounds). When she emerged, she looked like Hotei, (a Buddhist deity with a long, thin head). She looked so adorable, I was head over heels in love. When we demand too much, we pay a big price. After she was born, I felt so ill, I was bedridden much of the time. My husband and his mother took great care of me and our baby.

In time, I became the mother of three daughters. Seventy years have passed since the atomic bombing. All three of my daughters regained their health, married, and had children. I am grandmother to seven.

I will never forget commemorating the end of World War II at Nippon Budokan Hall on August 15, 1995. That year, representing the bereaved families of the Hiroshima hibakusha, I was given the opportunity to offer flowers at the ceremony. After the ceremony, I was deeply touched when Empress Michiko honored me with kind words.

such things! Why, we reject them!"

After that, we changed the official location of my exposure to the bomb from Sumiyoshi Shrine (about 1.3 kilometers from the hypocenter) to our home in Eba (about 3 kilometers away).

Because my father ran a contract company for Mitsubishi Shipbuilding, my mother asked him to look for a suitable candidate among the employees. One day, she called me at work to announce that my father was critically ill. Shocked, I hurried home. I arrived breathless at the front door, announced, "I'm home!" and opened the door to see a young man, a stranger. I quickly grasped that Mother had invited him there as a prospective suitor.

I protested, "I'm already seeing someone! And I'm not well from TB yet!"

He replied, "I can wait until you change your mind."

Still longing for the boy I had been forced to let go, I kept trying to chase him away, going so far as to bring out an X-ray of my lungs.

But as the young man later told me, he had already decided to marry me the moment he heard me call out, "I'm home!" His subsequent single-minded pursuit finally touched by heart. At the age of 23, I married him. I became a wife.

But first, I burned in the cook stove all the love letters from my university boyfriend. When we returned from our honeymoon, I heard he had tried to commit suicide. That was too sad an ending.

It was very hard for hibakusha to marry people of normal health. Although my husband had quickly been attracted to me, much later he told me what he and his mother went through. When he told her I was a hibakusha, she had responded, "Her poor health will plague you your whole life." He countered, "Weak people can become stronger his dreams for a tourism-oriented Japan. But then I was diagnosed with tuberculosis and entered the hospital again.

He loved to read. He would visit my bedside toting books that inspired him by Nietzsche, Ishikawa, and other writers. We talked for hours in my hospital room.

In time, he proposed to me like this: "If I pass the exam, I'll work for the Foreign Ministry. Let's live together in Tokyo." Then, this: "I want you to attend my graduation ceremony wearing a kimono."

At the ceremony, I met his mother, who arrived from Fukuoka. Then I visited their Fukuoka home a number of times. These were the best times I had ever had. But one day, his mother took me aside and said, "Promise not to tell my son what I am about to say to you. I simply cannot accept you, a survivor of Hiroshima, as a bride in our family."

I was dumbfounded. Shock turned everything black for me, but I did my best to retain my composure. I politely turned down the money she offered me as compensation and promised to relinquish the relationship without giving her away.

If I throw myself into the Bungo Channel, my body will float out to sea and never be found... Riding the boat back to Hiroshima, I could think of nothing but dying, right then. When shall I jump off? When shall I jump off? I was still struggling frantically with myself when the boat landed in Hiroshima.

I called him on the telephone. "I have TB. I don't know what will become of me, so I can't marry you." Over and over he pressed me, "Why did you suddenly change your mind?" But I could not cause him to resent his mother. I remained silent.

After that, his father wrote me a long letter apologizing for breaking off the relationship. When I told my mother why his family had broken off the marriage talks, she was furious. "Anyone who would say

After the bombing, I fell ill, first with severe diarrhea. Then my hair fell out, until I became completely bald. My brothers all lost their hair as well, so I didn't stand out so much. When people asked what happened to my hair, I answered, "The pikadon ate it," to make them laugh.

Some who survived without obvious injury and were quite healthy the day the bomb fell came down the next morning with purple spots like small adzuki beans all over their bodies—and died. Some suddenly bled from the ears, nose, gums—and died. We saw this over and over again.

I, too, was suffering maladies peculiar to A-bomb exposure: diarrhea, fever, bleeding from the gums, nosebleeds. Moreover, when the explosion blew apart the nearby factory, I had been pierced by countless pieces of glass. The larger ones were extracted at Eba Army Hospital, but after the war, sometimes red lumps would appear and suppurate painfully on my back and arms.

When my family cut into these with a razor blade, chocolate-colored pieces of glass pushed through the skin. This went on until about 1977.

## Lost dreams of youth, then meeting my husband

My post-bombing ills led to many hospitalizations at the Mizuno Hospital at Togiya-cho(now, Naka-ku), but treatments gradually restored my health. At 18, I got a job at Fukuya Department Store. Around that time, an upperclassman at my high school introduced me to a student at Hiroshima University. He was two years older than I.

It was just eight years after the war. A fresh breeze wafting in the air foretold the dawn of a new age. He fascinated me as he talked about

calling their children.

The morning of the 7th, soldiers came in trucks to pass out rice balls. We ate them and drank water from broken pipes that spilled it ceaselessly. *Where is our father, our relatives, everyone who matters to us?* However desperate we were, we could do nothing but simply wait.

So when our uncle (our father's brother) hired a boat and came looking for us, it was a sudden ray in the darkness. "When we heard that a new type of bomb had been dropped on Hiroshima, we started out right away, but the roads were closed so we couldn't make it to Eba. We rented this boat." So saying, our uncle helped us into the boat. As we traveled from Honkawa River to the open sea, we thumped continually against floating corpses; the collisions slowed our progress, rocked us, and upset me.

When we arrived at my uncle's house, my father appeared. He worked at the Ordnance Supply Depot and had been exposed inside a streetcar riding to the Akatsuki Corps headquarters. Worried about us, he had started back to Eba, but when he crossed the Sumiyoshi Bridge, he stopped to help soldiers pulling corpses from the river with hooked poles.

Years later, my father lost his eyesight as cancer spread through his body. I still remember the diapers my mother made for my father out of old cotton kimonos. They were dyed by massive amounts of bloody pus, as though his intestines had melted. In the laundry room of the hospital where my father lay, families of patients in the same condition as my father washed diapers dyed bright red and hung them up. As they scrubbed, they all sighed with the same question on their minds. What will happen now?

Every day, many patients died, one after another. Barely ten years later, my father died. He was 53.

off the burning embers, I careened headlong down the riverbank. I ran for my life. When I made it to the wall around the Yoshijima Prison, I finally felt safe. Once again, a thick wall stood between me and the flames.

Suddenly, a shout. "Hey, anyone trying to get back to Eba?" I looked out to the river and recognized the man who had shouting from rescue boat that had come down from Eba. I boarded the boat, crying with relief at a familiar face.

The other people in the boat were old men and women, their faces burned black, their hair standing on end. But when I looked more closely, I realized, "These people are young." I realized at that moment that I, too, might appear to be an old woman.

When I finally got to our house in Eba, it had collapsed. No one was around. As I searched the area, I ran into a woman from the neighborhood. "Your mother might have gone to the air-raid shelter at Kaihoji Temple," she suggested. I hurried there, but found no one. I continued to walk around until I found my mother and four younger brothers in a nearby air-raid shelter.

My youngest brother was a nursing infant only three months old. Although my mother was burned from her back up to her neck, she was frantically protecting her children.

That night, soldiers came to the shelter and said, "You're in danger here—go to the hill over there." Our family was too exhausted to move. The other three or four families huddling there were in the same condition. In the silence I could read deep despair and resignation. Let's just die together right here.

Fires burning through the night turned it as light as day. Till dawn we heard the clatter of carts and hand carts, cries and groans of the injured, desperate wails of children calling their parents, and parents

Hiroshima August 6, 1945

air-raid warning, and the passengers were told to get off the bus.

When the warning was canceled, I began walking to the clinic.

After crossing the Sumiyoshi Bridge and arriving at Sumiyoshi Shrine, the strap broke on one of my geta clogs. I sat down in the shade of a factory nearby and prepared to repair my strap. A man came out of the building and said, "It's hot out here. Come inside and do it." He handed me a length of hemp to replace the broken strap.

I crouched down to replace the strap—and was bathed in a flash as bright as if the sun fell onto the Earth. Smashed against the ground with a force that stole my breath, I lost consciousness.

I was about 1.3 kilometers from the hypocenter. Shielded by the wall of the building, I was miraculously spared serious burns. When I came to, I was buried under a pile of rubble. "Help! Help!" I screamed. Through cracks in the debris, I saw army boots with tattered gaiters wrapped around them, then an apron on a person who was shouting, "Where are you? Where are you?" He removed debris until he could extend an arm to me.

When I grabbed the man's hand, the skin slipped right off. He immediately turned his palm to face mine so that we could pull against each other's cupped fingers. He pulled me out.

I could see flames arising from the rubble here and there, but fortunately, not yet next to me. I got out as quickly as I could. The scene that met my eyes was not of this world. The morning light was replaced by a murky dusk through which people were fleeing right and left in complete confusion—hair frizzed wildly on heads; half-naked bodies under clothing burnt into tatters.

I have to get home. As I tried to figure out which direction would take me to Eba, ferocious flames bore down on me. They traveled with such speed, I feared they would swallow me. Weeping and brushing they all overcame their diseases. But before we could breathe a sigh of relief, I was found to have thyroid cancer in 2005. The thyroid is a butterfly-shaped gland below the Adams apple. The entire right side of mine was removed, and most of the left. The tissue and bronchial tubes in the front of my neck were also cut out.

That surgery cost me my voice. Throughout the 40-day hospitalization, I had to write down whatever I wished to say.

Each time I overcame a disease caused by the bombing, a new one loomed before me. My heart weakened so much I thought it would give out. Even so, I exhorted myself: Lie down and let this defeat me? I will not! I learned to shout in order to force sound out, and gradually, my voice returned.

## The ferocious flash and blast knocked me unconscious

On August 4, 1945, I was an 11-year-old sixth grader in Eba Elementary School. My fourth-grade brother and I left our evacuation site on Kurahashi Island to return to our house in the Eba now, Naka-ku District of Hiroshima. We were to stay for two nights and three days.

For some days, I was waking up with so much mucus on my eyes it took a while to open my eyelids. My parents decided I should be seen at the Miyake Ophthalmology Clinic near the prefectural office. We arrived at our house in the early evening of the 4th. The plan was for me to be treated on the 5th and 6th and return that evening to Kurahashi Island.

Early on the 6th, I boarded a bus at the Eba Bus Stop for the 20 minute ride to the Miyake Ophthalmology Clinic. When the bus passed the Ikken Teahouse, a yellow alert sounded. It was later upgraded to an

Hiroshima August 6, 1945

The first time my fear proved justified was my oldest daughter's cancer. Later, the effects of my exposure appeared in the two younger ones as well.     My middle daughter complained, "Whenever I go out in the sun, I get sick." We took her to the Red Cross Hospital, where the diagnosis was aplastic anemia. Our youngest, then 19 and in her second year at university, complained of stomach pain. She was examined at the Atomic Bomb Hospital and diagnosed with ovarian cancer. Two years later, she developed thyroid gland cancer.

Each time my children fell ill, I was terribly distressed. In my heart I begged, "Forgive me!" and pressed my palms together in prayer. I felt a certain resignation when disease attacked me, but when my children took sick, I wanted only to change places with them.

That was impossible, but for a mother, nothing could be more miserable. "May my daughters conquer disease and find happiness." That is all I wanted.

In 1962, when I was first diagnosed with A-bomb disease, I was a busy mother of three young girls. I was troubled by cuts that did not stop bleeding. If my finger got cut, to stop the bleeding, I would have to wind a rubber band below the cut so tightly that the finger would turn purple. The diagnosis that time was thrombocytopenia. In 1970 I underwent surgery for A-bomb cataracts. Despite my fragile health, my husband and I worked together as best we could to raise our daughters.

In 1974, when our oldest was in high school, I was diagnosed with ischemic cardiac disease. I tired easily and often had to lie down. When I walked, my legs would shake. When I stood by a river, or when a car passed nearby, I felt I was almost pulled into the flow.

Two years later, our oldest daughter fell ill. Then the middle one, then the youngest. Fortunately, all the surgeries were successful, and

# Scarred in body and spirit, I want to spare others.

**Emiko Yamanaka**
Born March 1934. At 11 years old, while in 6th grade at Eba Elementary School, she was exposed on her way to an eye doctor at Sumiyoshi Shrine, about 1.3 kilometers from the hypocenter. Combating thrombocytopenia, cataracts, thyroid gland cancer, brain tumors, and other maladies, she married and raised three daughters. All suffered cancers due to their mother's exposure, but survived. In March 2011, as a MOFA special disarmament ambassador on the Peace Boat's Global Voyage for a Nuclear-Free World, visited 13 countries and told her story at 14 universities and academic institutions. Eighty-two years old; lives in Yoshiura Kure City, Hiroshima Prefecture.

## Cancers in all three daughters

In 1976, my oldest daughter, who had just started college, suddenly developed a dark mole-like stain under her left eye. Soon, a similar one appeared under her nose. My mother-in-law said, "Poor thing, and such a pretty face too. Let's go to the hospital and have these removed." She took her to an orthopedic hospital in the area.

The growth was removed. It appeared to be a tiny mole about two millimeters in diameter, but as they cut, they found it had extended a root a centimeter deep into her flesh. It was skin cancer.

My father had become bedridden and died of multiple cancers. I struggled with several A-bomb illnesses: thrombocytopenia, cataracts, and ischemic cardiac disease. All three of my daughters, though frail, were able to go to college. But fear had always stalked me. "What will happen to my girls?"

appreciation makes me glad I was allowed to live this long.

In 2010, as a representative of Japan Confederation of A-bomb and H-bomb Sufferers Organizations I went to UN Headquarters in New York to attend the NPT (Nuclear Non-Proliferation Treaty) Review Conference. It's rude to say so, but I had no interest in that conference. I have no faith in leaders who continue to claim we need nuclear weapons. But if we speak to the next generation, they may grow up and join with each other to get rid of these weapons. Children are the wellspring of peace. In England, too, local supporters gave me a chance to talk to schoolchildren.

In August 2015, I underwent surgery for liver cancer. I don't know how long my health will allow me to continue this work, but for as long as I can, I will talk to the world, especially to the children.

survivors understood that we'd not be able to marry people with normal bodies, the number of survivors marrying survivors increased. However, cruel things were said even about this choice: "These couples will definitely have deformed children," and worse.

The rumors were so hurtful that when my husband's company proposed a transfer to Osaka, we easily agreed. However, perhaps because of his exposure, my husband tired easily. After we moved to Osaka, I would get phone calls from train station personnel. "Your husband is resting here at the station because he doesn't feel well. Please come and take him home." He underwent examinations that found nothing.

I often got colds, but would recover if I drank cold medicine. Because we were not in Hiroshima, we were not abreast of what was discovered about "A-bomb disease." We didn't worry much about it, which, in a way, was a good thing.

Later, my husband founded a subcontractor that made trademarks for electrical products in Osaka. We kept going by encouraging each other. I led a satisfying life, obtaining a teacher's license, studying clothing design, and helping design fashion shows. We moved from Osaka to Tokyo and did not return to Hiroshima until our mid-fifties.

That was when we learned that people were continuing to die of A-bomb disease. While my keloids had decreased in size, my fears of A-bomb disease actually grew.

Nonetheless, through referrals by friends, I began to tell my story to students who came to Hiroshima on school visits. More than 20 years have passed since I began this. At first, ten minutes into the story I would start crying and have to stop. But the somber eyes of the students fixed on me strengthened me to go on. Some would later send me letters. They do so even now. Reading their frank words of

Some girls came back to school blind. One girl whose face was disfigured by burn scars collapsed at school from anemia. Her deformed mouth wouldn't open, so we had a hard time helping her breathe. Another girl whose fingers were fused together was unable even to hold a pencil. It was painful to see her show us her fingers as if it were funny. School life for most of us was miserable.

## We survived by encouraging each other

One day, a young man and his mother came to our house and asked if he could marry me. Across the street from our house was a factory that made bank safes and gate doors. An employee a year older than I had seen me commuting on the Ujina Line. When his mother first learned that I was an A-bomb survivor, she opposed his intent to propose. "She probably won't be able to help farm our fields." Later, she relented, and came with him to make the proposal to my parents. He, too was a survivor, having been exposed.

My father's first response was, "I can't allow my only daughter to be taken far from us!" In the end, he gave in. "I'm grateful that you will take her as a bride." When we married, I was 19 and he was 20. Because we had both been exposed to the bombing, we promised to support and help each other.

In those days, ugly rumors abounded about survivors marrying each other. If a family were approached by the family of a young woman who'd been in the bombing, they were likely to reject the offer firmly. "Absolutely not! Who knows what kind of child she'd give birth to?" The question was no longer whether one had keloids or not. Now, people simply wanted to stay clear of any one who was exposed. This change in attitude followed the news that the new bomb dropped on Hiroshima was an atomic bomb whose radiation left effects. When

it contained would have rotted your body from the inside. It was also good that you vomited soon after the bombing in the grove of Toshogu Shrine."

But my nephews and nieces who returned from their evacuation sites would screw up their noses and complain, "Set-chan's room smells so bad, I can't go in there." The lymphatic fluid that oozed out with the pus emitted a powerful stench.

Over and over, the scabs on my burns would come off. In the end, the thin skin would swell up into an ugly, red rubbery mass. Two or three months later, reddish thin, keloidal skin would finally form and the bleeding would stop. What I was left with were keloids under my left arm running all the way to my fingertips. On my right, they ran on the outside, from the elbow to the top of the arm. My left thigh was left with a bright red keloid that climbed up onto my buttocks. Because I had been bending over to weed, I was burned from the back side, but for some reason my upper back escaped the flash. Even so, a third of my body was burnt—if any more of my skin had been lost to burns, I would not have survived.

Around October, I was able to return to school, where I learned about the cruel deaths of my friends. I thought my heart would break. By about the end of our third year of high school, the students who had keloid burn scars on their faces stopped coming to school.

"You're lucky, Set-chan, you don't have keloids on your face." Every time one of them said that, I felt somehow accused, wounded. What could I say? They say, "A girl's hair determines her life." When burn scars on the heads of girls left them with a bald spot, or when all their hair fell out, what they endured I can't imagine. Girls who went through this gradually fell silent and withdrew.

made a decision. "I'm going to leave this house to Setsuko instead of her brothers off at war. No matter what, I won't let her die!" I had four brothers who were each five years apart. All were soldiers who made it home after the war.

Lacking proper medicine and equipment but using knowledge he had gained as a medic in the Sino-Japanese and Russo-Japanese wars, father faithfully applied cooking oil to my burns, sprinkled them with baby powder, and wrapped them in gauze so that the bandages would not adhere to the burns. Even so, when the gauze was removed, unbearable pain shot through the top of my head. Removing the gauze slowly did nothing to reduce the pain. My father would hold me down and tear it off all at once. Blood flew everywhere. I screamed and lost consciousness.

Afterwards, oil was reapplied, baby powder sprinkled, and gauze wound around my arms and leg. This was repeated until we ran out of oil and baby powder. In the end he was painting cucumber juice on my burns.

It was a fierce battle with no assurance of success. Evidently my mother prayed, "I'm going crazy with this. Please allow our daughter to die." The ordeal must have been even worse for my father.

Day after day, my parents argued about whether he should do this treatment, but he insisted that there was no other effective way to heal my burns. Mother's hands turned purple and swelled from washing my bandages, gauze, and clothing. Awful substances were oozing out of me.

In later years, we decided that the daily blood-letting that accompanied the gauze changing had helped me. A doctor said, "If your blood hadn't been constantly purged, the contaminated pus one to report to about the students waiting on the hill.

## Mother prayed, "Just let her die"

Suddenly eager to see my mother, I headed to my house ten minutes from the school. At almost 4:00 pm, the street was empty and quiet. As I tottered into our neighborhood dragging my left leg behind me, I was suddenly surrounded by neighbor ladies whose faces were red with blood.

At this distance—3.7 kilometers—from the hypocenter, the blast had thrown many houses down. Flying glass had pierced faces and bodies, covering them in blood. Mothers whose children had been outside working on building demolition were fearful and waiting for them out on the street. When they saw me they shouted with joy as one and ran to me. One cried, "If Set-chan made it back, my daughter must be all right too!" Just then, surely from relief, I passed out.

When I came to, I was in my house. The roof had been blown off, so I was looking up at the stars. My mother's face, covered in dried blood, was peering down at me and frightening. The neighbors used scissors to cut off the clothing that stuck to my body. Dipping cloths in disinfectant thinned in a bucket, they carefully wiped off mud from the lotus field, blood, and pus.

They brought precious rationed cooking oil and applied it to my whole body. In a room strewn with glass and other objects thrown by the blast, they cleared off a section exactly large enough for me, rolled out a straw mat, and laid me on it.

The next day, I came down with a fever near 40 degrees that lasted a week. The doctor gave up on me. "I don't know how she's still alive!" At that time my father, who had been sure I would die, apparently they just kept going as if they couldn't be bothered. One of us fell off when she could no longer walk. Another split off to go in a different direction. We were scattering.

When we passed the Clothing Depot and neared our school, we saw a flooded paddy growing lotus roots. The fresh green leaves made us feel we had suddenly entered heaven. We all waded into the paddy. The cool water soothed our hot bodies. Of course the water must have been muddy, but we drank to our heart's content.

We learned later that two or three other "rescue messengers" were sent from the Drill Ground to the school to get help. However, they never made it because bridges along the way had been blown down and roads were blocked. We got to Ujina only because we detoured around the back of Hijiyama Hill.

Finally arriving at Second Girls School, we saw that the roof of the wooden building had been blown off. Our large school ground, recently converted to potato fields, was now covered by countless straw mats. Our burnt schoolmates were laid down in rows. The ones with the worst burns, the ones who were about to die, and the ones who were already dead were crammed into the music room and the discipline room. All in all, the girls here were in far worse condition than the friends we had left on the hill.

When we tried to touch the girls we had left behind, their skin peeled off in our hands. These girls in the schoolyard were burned so deep by the heat ray that when you touched them, sticking to your hands was meat as well as skin. One of these girls said, "I have to pee." A teacher brought her a water bowl used for flower arranging and said, "Do it in this." After she was done, pieces of flesh from her bottom were stuck to the edge of the bowl. The indescribable smell of corpses permeated the classrooms. The school was in such chaos we had no slumped people who did not look at all human. It was frightening just to look at them, so we looked away. An overpowering stench filled the air.

About 30 minutes later, I felt nauseous and vomited a large quantity of filth.

Hiroshima Station was smashed. We climbed up on the Ujina Line platform to look over the track in the opposite direction. The city was engulfed in flames and black smoke. Most wooden bridges over the rivers had fallen. Not so the Enko Bridge, which was shorn of its columns but still standing, a streetcar stranded in the middle.

We decided to flee southward along the tracks of the Ujina Line. In fire cisterns along the way, we saw many corpses that looked like discarded mannequins, with only the head sticking out.

In front of the railroad bridge in Ozu (now, Minami-ku), women wearing aprons called out to us. "What school do you go to? Stay strong, you can make it home!" They handed out rice balls from a large rice tub, but we could eat nothing.

The rice balls were covered with ash, and I, fighting nausea, could not put one in my mouth. Gastric juices and vomit continually drooled from the sides of my mouth.

We crawled over the Ozu bridge. By that time, our burns were so painful that walking was difficult. In the river below, corpses floated by —adults, children, horses. Many got caught on bridge girders. Was it a bad dream? Was it hell? How could we believe that this was really happening? All we could think was: get back to school and find people to rescue our friends back at Toshogu Shrine. Supported only by a strong sense of mission and responsibility, we kept going.

Whenever someone passed us up, we pled, "Please tell Second Girls School that students are waiting for rescue at Toshogu Shrine!" But

haul in their hanging skin.

Some girls were trying to hold in their intestines, which had burst out near their hips. Some whose eyeballs had popped out were trying to push them in with the palms of their hands. We tried to grab the hands of prostrate girls and pull them up, but the skin of their palms came off in our hands.

Though the teacher in charge was burned from her face to her waist, she shouted, "Hurry, everyone, come here!" She led us to the shrine on the nearby hill, Toshogu Shrine. Before students began our weeding job, we had left our bags there for safekeeping. Unable to think at all, we desperately climbed the hill. About the time we reached the shrine, I felt, *I'm hot! It hurts!*

I took my canteen out of my bag to pour cool water on my burns, but I couldn't even tell where I was burned. We splashed water on each other to cool our burns. Some of the girls couldn't even screw off their canteen tops because the skin of their hands was sloughing off.

The left sleeve of my jacket was nearly gone. When I pulled it off, I saw the skin had slipped off from the top of my arm to my fingertips, just like long sleeve gloves. Blood was seeping down from my elbow. My right hand was swollen up. From the thigh of my left leg half way up my bottom were deep burns under my burnt monpe workpants.

The teacher asked, "Who can walk?" She told the able ones to walk to our school three kilometers away in Ujina (now, Minami-ku) to get help. Four or five of us started off in a group. Enduring the pain and urging each other on, we walked for our lives.

Starting off down the stairs from Toshogu Shrine seeking help, we encountered lots of people climbing them, fleeing in the opposite direction.

Some had bright red peeled flesh. We passed sooty, charred,

with their combat caps and cry, "You smell! It's catching!" (They meant my keloids). Infuriated, I'd glare and insult them back, but when I got home, I despaired for my future. I tried to kill myself by taking sleeping pills. I tried to end it all by jumping into the night sea.

Over and over, I lamented, "If only I didn't have these keloids!"

## We "rescue messengers" made ourselves go on

At the time of the bombing, I was 12 and a first-year student at Second Hiroshima Prefectural Girls High School. Soon after I entered the school in April, the upperclassmen were heading off for labor service, so my first semester began in a mostly empty school. By June, the worsening war situation put an end to classes, and all students did nothing but labor service.

That day, at 8:00 am, my group began to weed the Eastern Drill Ground on the north side of Hiroshima Station, about 1.7 kilometers from the hypocenter. Everywhere on the drill ground grew new rows of sweet potato vines planted to increase food production.

Suddenly a shout. "Look! A parachute!"

Just as I lifted my face, my body was swallowed in a hot flash. Then a powerful blast threw me. I lost consciousness. I came back to consciousness smelling a strange smell. Ignited weeds were burning. One by one, my friends staggered to their feet, looking like ghosts. Their clothes were charred, hanging like rags, smoking. The girl who had been weeding right next to me had been blown four or five meters away.

Some girls had been looking straight up at the sky. Their faces were already swelling with burns, their eyelids sagged and concealed their eyes. Those whose faces had been sideways to the flash were burned and peeling, the skin hanging—on that side. They walked trying to that became increasingly burdensome. In the end, I filled hot water in the kitchen sink and did a quick scrub down. It was miserable. My ugly keloids continued to cause me great suffering.

After the war ended, though I had graduated from Second Hiroshima Prefectural Girls High School (now, Hiroshima Minami High School), I entered Kokutaiji High School, a school formed under the new coeducation system. Because Second Girls School was attached to Women's Technical School, it would have been easy to go there. However, since the two schools shared a building, and since I knew many of the girls my age and older, I wanted some distance between myself and that world.

It was hard for me to look at my fellow students with burn scars on face and head. They were young women, so they suffered in ways that they could not voice. And I—scarred as I was—had to hear people say, "You're lucky. You didn't get burned on the face."

Soon after the Atomic Bomb Casualty Commission (ABCC) was completed on Hijiyama Hill, American soldiers and their Japanese interpreters pulled up at my school in jeeps and called me—only me—out of my class. Sandwiched between two soldiers, I rode to the ABCC for what turned out to be cursory blood testing and strength testing, followed by countless photos of the keloids on my naked body.

As a self-conscious girl of 17, I wanted to weep with embarrassment and chagrin. When it was over, sent back to school with no diagnosis or treatment, I was left with nothing but the humiliation of being a guinea pig. Ever afterwards, I refused all calls from the ABCC for testing.

Sometimes the bullies were schoolmates who'd escaped the bombing and had whole, strong bodies. Boys would cover their faces

# I speak to children who don't know war

**Setsuko Morita**
Born November 1932. At 12, exposed on the Eastern Drill Ground, about 1.7 kilometers from the hypocenter; sustained deep burns on both arms. Married and moved to Osaka. Moved back to Hiroshima at 56; began telling her story as a member of the Hiroshima Eyewitness Association and the Hiroshima Prefecture Hibakusha Association. In 2010, began telling her story as Atomic Bomb Witness for Hiroshima Peace Culture Foundation in New York, Paris, China, and elsewhere. Eighty-four years old; living in Higashi-ku, Hiroshima City.

## "You smell!" "Get away, it's catching!"

When I walked into the bathing room of the public bathhouse, sharp stares cut into me. Some pointedly walked away from me; those at a distance stared with frank curiosity. Faces registered astonishment and fear.

Ugly, reddish, rubbery keloid scars rose from my arms and my left thigh.

Telling myself to ignore the stares, I continued to wash my body. But then the owner came and really shocked me. "Customers are uncomfortable—they think what you have might be catching. This will hurt business, so won't you come when no one's here, just before we close?" This was not Hiroshima, but Osaka. When my husband was transferred to Osaka, I had gone with a faint hope that my life would be more peaceful in a city where no one knew that I was an A-bomb survivor.

I began going to the bathhouse late at night, just before closing, but the US several times to attend conferences. Some have asked, "Why are you involved in a volunteer organization based in the US? You must have suffered a lot because of the atomic bomb the US dropped."

But I believe we can only create peace if we can transcend hatred. People around the world want peace to prevail. To respect all life equally, to see ourselves as human, transcending race and nationality—isn't this the path to peace?

Seven years later, I returned to Hiroshima to marry. My husband was the son of a teacher I had studied with at First Girls High. My father-in-law had a very good reputation, and my mother was enthusiastic, saying, "It's easy to find a perfect husband, but very hard to find a perfect father-in-law."

My husband was exposed to the atomic bombing at a school in Senda-machi, about two kilometers from the hypocenter. I was exposed at an airplane factory in Koi, about 2.5 kilometers. We knew about each other's exposure, but the effects of radiation were not well understood, so we didn't even think about what might happen. Our two children have been healthy, free of effects of their parents' exposure. We haven't told them we are survivors, but my father-in-law was an A-bomb storyteller, so we often ended up talking about the situation after the bombing. I have a feeling they know, at some level. But I have always deliberately avoided talking about it.

I picked up the phrase "value life" as my motto because of my experience. The nongovernmental volunteer group Pilot International was established in 1921 in the United States. In 1951 the Tokyo Pilot Club was established in Japan.

I established the Hiroshima Pilot Club in 1992. These clubs support mentally disabled people. We support people with various natural disabilities, such as Down's syndrome or developmental problems, and those with brain injuries due to accident or illness.

Specialists offer direct care to these people, of course. We organize social activities and do what we can to get society to accept them. Our volunteer activities are designed to enable disabled people to live in their communities. We raise funds by holding lecture meetings and other events.

The headquarters of the Pilot Club is in the US, so I have gone to

day" would get me next. That fear stayed in my heart a long time.

All the classmates who survived had the same fear. As a result, we have still never talked about "that day." Each of us escaped on our own and had our own experiences, and we were all afraid to talk about it.

When asked, "What happened that day?" some still tremble and remain silent. This profound fear of the future seems peculiar to atomic bomb survivors. We still have never digested our experience thoroughly. We all carry intense feelings of grief, having so abruptly lost family members, friends, our entire communities and even normal daily lives.

There were thousands of orphans. I don't like to boast, but First Girls High was the best girls school in Hiroshima. We had many students from prestigious families, and most of us studied hard to achieve our dreams for the future. However, when I returned to school I heard countless stories of classmates who lost their whole family. Some were left with just a sibling or were taken by a relative to live far away. Thinking about their grief at having lost access to our school and to their dreams, I feel terrible pain in my heart.

Later, I went on to Hiroshima Women's Technical School. I had a weak constitution and was very skinny. My mother was quite worried about me. Saying, "You mustn't do any hard exercise," she never allowed me to do much physically.

It was a time of severe shortages, but she did her best to prepare meals that were good for my health. I didn't have much appetite, so I could eat very little, but I received a lot of tender care. I graduated from Technical School and moved to Hamamatsu to work as a teacher. I lived in a dormitory and ate meals provided by the school with the other students. I worked hard on club activities and got steadily stronger.

grandparents' house in Jigozen. I was isolated in the storage room, not allowed to go out. We kept my "legally diagnosed infectious disease" secret from our neighborhood. My mother went to the bamboo grove in back of the house and buried my vomit and excreta late at night. Soon rumors arose in the neighborhood about "a female ghost haunting the bamboo grove."

I don't know where she heard about it, but Mother said, "Dokudami (a herb) is good for your disease." She picked the dokudami leaves growing in a nearby field every day, roasting them in an earthenware pan, then extracting the essence by boiling them in a kettle.

She made dokudami tea for me to drink. I was forced to drink that smelly dokudami tea instead of water. She was so thorough she used dokudami extract to boil rice gruel for me.

Then, mysteriously, I recovered enough in three months to go back to school. I was rescued by my mother's absolute determination to save her daughter. I believe I was miraculously able to recover thanks to dokudami tea and my mother's love. Even now, when I see the white flowers of dokudami, I feel I am looking at life itself.

Our house in Ote-machi was burnt out, so my mother and I moved to my uncle's hut in Miyukibashi.

When we gathered at school for the first time after the bombing, I learned that many of my friends had perished. A total of 280 upper class students and teachers who had remained at school, along with first-year students mobilized to building demolition in the Dobashi (now, Naka-ku, Hiroshima City) area, were all exposed directly and died.

Later, I heard that schoolmates were still dying one after another. This came as a big shock. Fear pressed on me heavily. I was afraid "that bodies burst open with a strange hissing sound. Pink internal organs popped out, swelling larger and larger.

My mother and I watched all this in a daze.

About one month after the bombing, the big Makurazaki Typhoon hit Hiroshima. Rivers flooded. The entire city was covered in water. We had dug up the soil all through the ruins around our house but failed to find any remains. After the flood, two bodies appeared above ground near a paving stone at the entrance of our house. They were my father and uncle, so we had a funeral and cremated them. My aunt is still missing.

This came more than a month after the bombing, and I still had no emotion. But that night, with their ashes in front of our eyes, my mother and I held each other and cried for the first time.

We cried a long time, and somehow those tears melted my frozen heart. Human feelings revived in me the next day.

## Regained health and, supported by my mother, became a teacher

About the time I recovered my emotions, my body went out of order. I had a continual high fever, bleeding from the gums, then bleeding from the throat. My mouth was continually filled with bloody foam. Blood was also in my stools, and my hair fell out. I was later diagnosed with A-bomb disease but at the time, the cause of my symptoms was unknown. Some doctors said I had an infectious disease. Bleeding from gums and throat were designated by law a sign of diphtheria; bloody stools meant typhoid fever.

With no facility to isolate me, and no doctor or medicine to treat me, I had to fight the disease alone lying in a storage room in my

## I cried for the first time in front of my father's ashes

My father was at home that day. He ran a business with his two brothers. The three of them got along well. They held their property jointly and trusted each other completely.

On August 6, my father was exposed to the bomb with his older brother and his brother's wife, who lived in the same house. In our area, less than two kilometers from the hypocenter, only a few ferroconcrete buildings were left standing. Nearly every structure was burned to the ground. Ujina Port now, Hiroshima Port, south of town, could be seen all the way from Hiroshima Station in the north. My house was 500 meters from the hypocenter. It was impossible to think my father could have survived.

The next morning, my mother and I, along with some relatives, left early to search the ruins of our house in Ote-machi, which were still smoldering. We dug through the rubble then walked around the town looking for my father, uncle and aunt who we assumed were dead.

An incredible number of dead bodies were scattered through the area. There was no space to step. Burnt corpses looked like logs, unrecognizable even as male or female. I looked at their faces one by one, turning bodies over, which caused a terrible stench to fill my nose. Yet I had no sense of fear or disgust. The half-raw half-burnt remains were not all human beings. During the war, our military city Hiroshima temporarily housed the Imperial Headquarters, and a large number of war horses were killed.

After much searching, we failed to find the remains of my father, uncle or aunt. Three days after the bombing when the fires had died down, soldiers gathered corpses, dug holes, placed the bodies on piles of logs and cremated them. They ignited the logs and the fire gradually grew into a huge flame. As the fire gained power, the bellies of the

emergency.

I still can't forget the scenes I saw on the way. Crowds of sufferers looking completely inhuman. Their faces, backs or hands or feet were hideously burned a blackish-red. Their skin peeled off and dangled down to cover their eyes. People wandered here and there like the living dead. I joined this procession and headed for Jigozen.

"Water! Please give me water!" "Help me! Help me!" The final pleas of the dying remain in my ears.

A mother carrying her badly burned baby on her back followed behind the procession. Her child was obviously dead, but the mother seemed not to believe it. She kept walking, constantly turning back to look at her baby. Soon, she ran out of strength. She crouched by the side of the road side, and the procession left her behind. Everybody was stunned, out of energy. Nobody tried to help her keep walking.

As we walked toward the evacuation site, some people living along the road came out of their houses and offered us some tomatoes in a colander, but none of us had the power to stretch out a hand. We simply kept walking in darkness with no reaction.

My mother happened to be at our evacuation site in Jigozen that day. She had gone to get some belongings she had left at my grandfather's house. A yellow alert kept her from going back to Hiroshima, so she escaped death.

Arriving in Jigozen, I was reunited with my mother at last, but I was neither relieved nor happy. I had no feelings at all. It's amazing how human beings can lose all emotion as a result of shock. It was as if something in my mind was broken. I was insensitive. No feelings of any kind sprang up in me.

cloudless blue sky. I could hear a low roar and see a white contrail. I had graduated from Fukuro-machi Elementary School and was going to First Hiroshima Prefectural Girls High School (now, Minami High School.) I was 13, just starting my second year. I was mobilized to Aviation Factory, which was 2.5 kilometers from the hypocenter. I remember polishing duralumin plane parts.

Everybody thought it strange when we heard a plane approaching since the air-raid warning had just been cleared. We went to the windows to take a look. A sudden, intense, orange flash. Then, the building shook violently, as if in powerful earthquake. I heard no boom or explosion. I threw myself on the floor, then got up fled toward the mountain with the others, none of us having any idea what was going on.

After a while, something dripped down on my cheek—black, sticky rain. People were saying, "It seems a gas tank exploded." I thought the black rain was fuel.

I sat in that black rain on that mountain desperately wishing somebody would come and save me. My friend's family came and took her home. Another friend's family came and took her home, then another. These were families who lived far from the hypocenter.

My house was 500 meters from the hypocenter in Ote-machi (now, Naka-ku, Hiroshima City). No one came to get me. I crouched, trembling, watching downtown Hiroshima burn.

The fire spread like a belt across the whole city. Eventually, when another friend's father came to take her home, I went down the mountain with them. We left Hiroshima burning behind us and walked all through the night, heading for our evacuation site in Jigozen (now, Hatsukaichi City.) My father's parents' house was in Jigozen. My father and his brothers had agreed to go to Jigozen in case of an were survivors. She stayed in the hospital for a month. I stayed with her as much as I could every day, and my husband stopped by on his way home from work. We provided the hospital data, like the results of blood tests. We were continually tense, but I trusted my teacher completely. She and the doctor who took charge after the birth were obviously doing their best, so I never lost hope.

After a month, I left the hospital happy, holding my daughter in my arms. We were seen off by many doctors and staff.

The next time I got pregnant, I was compelled to have an abortion, as I described above. I gave birth to our first son in 1961. I was sick all through the pregnancy, but not as severely as I had been the two previous times. Still, the bleeding after delivery was so bad my life was in danger.

Two big woodchips, like wooden clappers, were placed on my back and front. I was sandwiched in between. Using holes at the corners, the boards were laced together with strings. Was this a treatment? Could this stop the bleeding? Feeling nothing but desire to protect my new son and myself, I endured this suffering as well, continually covered in greasy sweat.

I don't know for sure that my excessive bleeding is related to my exposure to the atomic bombing, but both times I delivered children, I bled so much I almost died. After the bombing, I was terrorized by bleeding from the gums. I also had excessive bleeding when a tooth was pulled.

## Loss of human feeling due to shock

That day, the morning came in hot.

I saw an enemy plane, a B-29 bomber, coming through the

heart. I regret my "cruelty."

A year and six months earlier, I had given birth to my first daughter. It had been a difficult delivery. I was sick all through my pregnancy, unable to eat, as if I were seasick. My womb bloated up. If I lay down on my side, on my back in any posture at all, I was in pain.

I endured this situation at home until four months before the due date. I was pulling weeds in the yard when I suddenly started bleeding. I was rushed to Hiroshima University Hospital and stayed there a month. I got sick and was hospitalized again three days before delivery.

The physical pain was severe, but I faced the birth with a calm mind because the doctor in charge was my teacher, a professor at Hiroshima Women's Technical School (now, Prefectural University of Hiroshima).

I gave birth to my first daughter in 1958. I suffered massive bleeding, but the doctor immediately said, "You have a healthy baby!"

At that time, rumor had it that A-bomb survivors usually had deformed babies. Babies were being born with microcephaly and other problems. This was the talk around town. Because both my husband and I were survivors, we were terribly worried about our baby.

We discussed the situation and concluded, "It's useless to fear the unknown. The baby given to us will be our child. No matter what it's like, we'll cherish it." We decided never to worry again, and we haven't.

Still, I remember being relieved to hear our baby was healthy.

On the other hand, my outrageously intense sickness and massive bleeding during the delivery tormented me with fear for my daughter. "She's fine now, but what if something shows up later?" The doctor said, "We need to watch her for a while." After all, both her parents

Hiroshima August 6, 1945

# Trapped in fear as I birthed new life

**Kazuko Kawada**
Born September 1931. Exposed to the bombing at an airplane factory 2.5 kilometers from the hypocenter as a second-year student at First Hiroshima Prefectural Girls High School(now, Minami High School.) Her father was killed at home. Lived with her mother, struggled to survive but health was poor. Married and birthed two children despite risk to her own life. Avoided talking about her A-bomb experience for decades. Asked to give her testimony in 2011, she shared it for the first time. Became a member of Hiroshima District Pilot Club in 1993. Continues working on volunteer activities based on her motto: "Value life." Lives in Minami-ku, Hiroshima City; eighty-five years old.

### Bleeding wouldn't stop when I gave birth. Because of radiation?

"Your life will be in danger if this condition continues! I urge you to give up the child." When the doctor said this, I felt all the strength drain from my body.

It was 1960. I had conceived my second child, and my pregnancy was entering the fourth month. I can't deny I was terribly sad confronting the need for an abortion. On the other hand, to be honest, I was relieved.

Day after day I was suffering overwhelming nausea. Nothing would go down my throat. I couldn't even take water. I was losing strength. I could barely get out of bed. I was extremely thin. It was as if I had a critical illness. My days were full of hardship and suffering. Although it was medically advised and unavoidable, I still feel the pain in my

# CONTENTS

Introduction ········································· 4

Kazuko Kawada ································· 8

Setsuko Morita ·································· 19

Emiko Yamanaka ······························· 31

Ritsuko Seidai ···································· 42

Kazuko Kamidoi ································ 51

Nobuko Suzuki ·································· 58

Emiko Okada ····································· 65

Miyoko Matsubara ····························· 74

Yoshie Oka ········································· 82

Sachiko Yamaguchi ···························· 91

Chisako Takeoka ································ 98

Yukie Tsuchimoto ······························ 108

Hiroe Sato ·········································· 117

Keiko Ogura ······································· 128

In Closing ··········································· 137

The testimonies are presented in Japanese and English. Our most cherished desire is to help bring the world together in solidarity.

Toshiko Shinagawa
General Chairwoman

Hiroko Watanabe
Chairwoman

Soka Gakkai Hiroshima Women's Peace Committee

October 2016

half-underground bunker at Chugoku Military District Headquarters. That bunker has been preserved in the ruins of Hiroshima Castle.

Though our hearts were sometimes crushed listening to such grotesque horror and cruelty, as we were deciding the title, we knew we wanted to express the desire they feel so strongly that "it must never happen again." Finally, incorporating their universal desire that mothers and children be allowed to live in peace, we decided on *Hiroshima August 6, 1945, For a Brilliant, Smiling Future*.

Next year will be the 60th year since our second president Josei Toda started the Soka Gakkai Peace Movement with his Call for the Banning of Atomic and Hydrogen Bombs. President Toda declared that atomic and hydrogen bombs are "weapons of the devil that rob humans of existence and are the work of a fiendishness that lies deep in human life." Successive interpretations of this statement by current President Daisaku Ikeda (of Soka Gakkai International) have contributed greatly to clearing a path to world peace.

Women bear, protect and nurture life itself. That bomb stole the dream of marriage from so many and filled the process of birth with fear. That bomb was a work of evil. We hope you will learn from these women of Hiroshima just how inhumane and destructive any use of nuclear weapons would be. Once you understand, you can speak and act.

We take seriously the commitment "never to build happiness on the misfortune of others." We build friendship and trust to take the baton of peace and give Mother Earth a brilliant, smiling future free from nuclear weapons.

# Introduction

To a survivor whose testimony is in this book, I asked, "Would you like to be in a hibakusha fashion show? There'll be some bridal gowns involved." "Really? I'd love to. I want to wear a white wedding dress!"

Her response struck me right in the heart. I found myself near tears.

Her face disfigured by burns, her one chance to marry was vetoed. But determined to "live for others," she traveled the world supporting the movement to abolish nuclear weapons. When I met her she was 84. "If not for that bomb…" I wonder how many times that thought has come to her.

Another survivor, a year after the bombing, married a man who agreed to live together with her mother, who lost her right eye to the bomb. They had a baby. For people who had lost everything, the birth of new life was a great source of hope and life force. But 18 days after its birth, the baby, who had been nursing happily two hours earlier, suddenly began writhing in pain, then died. That baby had the purple spots of death (purpura) from its chest to its abdomen, just like the spots its mother had seen on her own body. The diagnosis: A-bomb disease.

This book presents the stories that 14 hibakusha women told members of the Soka Gakkai Hiroshima Women's Peace Committee, stories about the prejudice, discrimination, and fear of aftereffects they suffered as women.

One, sitting on her hospital bed fighting with her hearing aid, had her interviewer crying with her as she recalled the painful past in a

# Hiroshima
## August 6, 1945
### For a Brilliant, Smiling Future

> I want to pass it on,
> The baton of life.
> I want to pass it on.
> The scream in my heart:
> *Never let it happen again*

DAISANBUNMEI-SHA
TOKYO

Copyright © Soka Gakkai 2016

Published in Japan in 2016
by Daisanbunmei-sha,Inc.
1-23-5 Shinjuku Shinjuku-ku,Tokyo Japan
http://www.daisanbunmei.co.jp

## 女性たちのヒロシマ
――笑顔かがやく未来へ

2016年11月18日　初版第1刷発行
2017年 1 月 2 日　初版第2刷発行

| | |
|---|---|
| 編　者 | 創価学会広島女性平和委員会 |
| 発行者 | 大島光明 |
| 発行所 | 株式会社　第三文明社<br>東京都新宿区新宿1-23-5<br>郵便番号：160-0022<br>電話番号：03（5269）7144（営業代表）<br>　　　　　03（5269）7145（注文専用）<br>　　　　　03（5269）7154（編集代表）<br>振替口座　00150-3-117823<br>URL http://www.daisanbunmei.co.jp |
| 英語翻訳 | 澤田美和子／エリザベス・ボールドウィン |
| 英文監修 | スティーブ・リーパー |
| 装幀・本文DTP | 木村祐一（株式会社ゼロメガ） |
| 印刷・製本 | 藤原印刷株式会社 |

©Soka Gakkai 2016　　　　　　　　　　　　　　Printed in Japan
ISBN978-4-476-06232-8

乱丁・落丁本はお取り換えいたします。ご面倒ですが、小社営業部宛にお送りください。
送料は当方で負担いたします。
法律で認められた場合を除き、本書の無断複写・複製・転載を禁じます。